# LAW REFORM *NOW*

# LAW REFORM *NOW*

edited by

GERALD GARDINER, Q.C.

and

ANDREW MARTIN, PH.D.

LONDON

VICTOR GOLLANCZ LTD

1964

First published July 1963
Second impression May 1964

PRINTED IN GREAT BRITAIN
BY EBENEZER BAYLIS AND SON, LIMITED
THE TRINITY PRESS, WORCESTER, AND LONDON

# CONTENTS

PREFACE                                                          ix

I    THE MACHINERY OF LAW REFORM                                  1
       Gerald Gardiner
       Andrew Martin

II   THE ADMINISTRATION OF JUSTICE                               15
       Gerald Gardiner
       F. Elwyn Jones

III  CONSTITUTIONAL AND ADMINISTRATIVE LAW                       24
       John A. G. Griffith

IV   THE LAW OF CONTRACT AND TORT                                57
       Aubrey L. Diamond

V    LAND LAW               Gerald Dworkin                       79

VI   FAMILY LAW             Olive M. Stone                      122
                            Antonia Gerard

VII  COMMERCIAL LAW AND COMPANY LAW                             150
                            Lord Chorley
                            Eric Wolff

VIII INDUSTRIAL LAW         Olga L. Aikin                       199
                            (in association with
                            Otto Kahn-Freund)

IX   CRIMINAL LAW           C. H. Rolph                         227

X    REVENUE LAW            Mark Hacker                         270
                            Frederick Honig

XI   LEGAL EDUCATION        Gerald Gardiner                     279
                            Andrew Martin

     INDEX                                                      289

# NOTES ON CONTRIBUTORS

OLGA L. AIKIN — is Lecturer in Law at the London School of Economics (University of London).

LORD CHORLEY, Q.C. — is General Editor of the Modern Law Review and was formerly Cassel Professor of Commercial and Industrial Law in the University of London.

AUBREY L. DIAMOND — is Lecturer in Law at the London School of Economics (University of London).

GERALD DWORKIN — is Lecturer in Law at the London School of Economics (University of London).

GERALD GARDINER, Q.C. — was a member of the Lord Chancellor's Law Reform Committee from its inception until May 1963 and Chairman of the General Council of the Bar (1958–60); he is a Vice-President of the Society of Labour Lawyers.

ANTONIA GERARD — is a barrister.

JOHN A. G. GRIFFITH — is Professor of English Law in the University of London and the Editor of Public Law.

MARK HACKER — is an accountant.

FREDERICK HONIG — is a barrister.

F. ELWYN JONES, Q.C. — is Member of Parliament for West Ham South, Recorder of Cardiff and a former Chairman of the Society of Labour Lawyers.

OTTO KAHN-FREUND — is Professor of Law in the University of London and President of the International Society for Labour Law and Social Legislation.

ANDREW MARTIN         is a barrister; he is a member of the Executive Committee of the Society of Labour Lawyers.

C. H. ROLPH          is an author and journalist specialising in criminal law and sociology. He is a member of the Executive Committee of the Howard League for Penal Reform and was formerly a Chief Inspector of the City of London Police.

OLIVE M. STONE       is Lecturer in Law at the London School of Economics (University of London).

ERIC WOLFF           is a solicitor.

# PREFACE

THIS BOOK is a successor to "The Reform of the Law", edited by Dr. Glanville Williams and published in 1951. "The Reform of the Law" was prepared by members of the Haldane Society and others before the formation of the Society of Labour Lawyers. Contributions were made by, among others, Isadore Caplan, Lord Chorley of Kendal, G. W. Clare, Dr. E. J. Cohn, Dudley Collard, Edgar Duchin, Eric Falk, Bernard Finlay, Wilfrid Fordham, Gerald Gardiner, C. L. Hodgkinson, B. A. Hytner, D. P. Kerrigan, Professor Harold Laski, Dr. Hermann Mannheim, Richard Medley, Stephen Murray, Robert Pollard, Harry Rose, R. W. Somerville, R. H. Whitty and J. L. Williams.

Twelve years have since passed. A number of the changes advocated in "The Reform of the Law" have been carried out and the book is both out of date and out of print. The Society of Labour Lawyers decided to sponsor a new book on the same lines. They ascertained to their regret that Dr. Glanville Williams was unable through pressure of work to undertake the burden of editing and therefore asked us to do so. In our turn, we invited a small number of like-minded people (all but two of them practising or academic lawyers) to join in the writing of the book. All of them have brought to the task much more than their specialised knowledge and experience: they have written with a passionate belief in the need for improving the law and its administration, and for getting on with the job *now* and not tomorrow or the day after.

Limitations of space have made it impossible for us to aim at completeness. We have endeavoured to cover most of those branches of the law where reforms are needed; but there are no separate chapters on Equity, Succession or Private International Law, and only some of the urgent reforms needed in these fields could be given attention in the context of Land Law and Family Law. Indeed, even in those branches of the law on which separate chapters have been written the exigencies of space did not allow the authors to cover all the reforms which are necessary if the law is to meet the needs of this country in a world of changed and changing social and economic conditions.

ix

1*

The reader will find that the chapters vary considerably in length; the main reason for that is that certain branches of the law are not sufficiently familiar to the non-lawyer (and this book is addressed to him just as much as to lawyers), and in these more technical fields it seemed appropriate to summarise the law as it stands before setting forth proposals for reform. With an eye to the non-lawyer it also seemed helpful not to make the chapters strictly self-contained. It will be found, for example, that suggestions for the reform of our revenue laws are not confined to Chapter X; some are contained, in their appropriate context, in Chapters VI and VII.

The authors are nearly all members of the Labour Party and while it must not be thought that the Society of Labour Lawyers or the Editors or any individual contributor is necessarily in agreement with all the views expressed in this book, we hope that it may serve at least to illustrate those reforms in our law which we would like to see carried out by the next Labour Government.

The generosity with which the authors have espoused this project and the patience with which they tolerated editorial harassments were boundless; we are deeply in their debt. Our grateful thanks are due also to Dr. Glanville Williams and to the contributors to "The Reform of the Law", none of whom has raised any objection to use being made in this volume of his original contribution. Such use has been extensive in the chapter on Criminal Law.

Inner Temple                                      G.G.
January 1963                                      A.M.

# I

## THE MACHINERY OF LAW REFORM

WE THINK we are justified in treating as axiomatic the proposition that much of our English law is out of date, and some
of it shockingly so. The fact that this view is shared by the overwhelming part of the legal profession is significant; for, taken
as a whole, no profession could be more conservative. We
attach little or no significance to the fact that the public at large
takes the law for granted, and that the need for reforming the
law on a large scale has never become the subject of one of those
great public debates which have been such a remarkable and
encouraging feature of the British political scene in this century.
This lack of a general public interest in the legal system as a
whole is understandable. People do not campaign for changing
that which to them is unknown; and the complexity of English
law has, by now, reached a degree where the system is not only
unknown to the community at large, but unknowable, save to
the extent of a few of its departments, even to the professionals.
And yet the unsatisfactory state of the law is clearly reflected in
those fragmentary, but almost constant and ubiquitous
demands for changes in this or that branch of the law which
are voiced in the leading articles and correspondence columns
of the daily press, in practically all the trade, trade union, and
professional journals and—an almost daily occurrence—in the
arguments submitted to and the judgments handed down by
our courts.

The problem of bringing the law up to date and keeping it up
to date is largely one of machinery; and if the machinery is to
work efficiently at a time, such as ours, which is a time of
thorough and rapid technological, economic and social change,
it must be kept in continuous operation and minded by full-
time personnel. Neither of these requirements has ever been
met in this country, and it is high time that a fresh look should
be given to certain questions: how to keep under review the
whole field of English law? how to enquire into those sections of
it which do not seem to fulfil the present needs of the community? and how to make sure that whenever a case for

reform is made out, Parliament (which alone has the power and the responsibility of making alterations in the law) should be presented, and be given adequate time to deal, with concrete proposals.

The machinery at present available for the purpose of reviewing the law consists partly of units specially constructed for that purpose, and partly of units which, though constructed for a different purpose, have in practice proved themselves capable of operating efficiently in certain specialised fields.

## Government Departments

It will be convenient to begin our survey with the units in this second category. They are, in fact, the government departments which carry out certain relatively modern functions of the State—the Board of Trade, the Ministry of Labour, the Ministry of Health, the Ministry of Housing and Local Government, and so on. The Ministers in charge of these departments have no direct responsibility for seeing that those portions of the law which they administer are brought and kept up to date : in practice, however, they discharge that responsibility. We have come to take it for granted that whenever the Companies Department of the Board of Trade is satisfied that an overhaul of company law is desirable, the Minister will appoint an expert committee to investigate the position and make a report suggesting such amendments as may be required to bring the law abreast of the changing needs of the business community and the investing public. Equally, we have come to take it for granted that in due course each such report will be followed by a Government bill designed to give effect to the committee's recommendations and that once this bill has become law, it will be consolidated with the earlier law into one great consolidating Act of Parliament, so that the whole of company law can be found within the four corners of one statute. Thus the Report of the Greene Committee in 1927 was followed by the Companies Act, 1928, and soon thereafter by the Companies (Consolidation) Act, 1929; similarly, the Report of the Cohen Committee in 1945 gave rise to the Companies Act, 1947, which itself was soon thereafter included in a consolidating statute, the Companies Act, 1948. Arising from the Report of the Jenkins Committee, published in June 1962, further amending and consolidating legislation is even now in contemplation. No massive statute can ever be up to date; but it can be fairly said that in the case of company law the past 35 years have seen a constant process of revision; and we would lay some stress on the point that while this has been due partly to the constant pressure of the business community and the investing public, the readiness and, indeed, eagerness of officials to admit the case for reform and press the need for amending legislation upon successive Presidents of the Board of Trade has had an important part to play. One could tell a somewhat similar story (without such a strong element of consolidation, though) of the handling of factory legislation by the Ministry of Labour; of sanitation, housing, and health generally by the Ministry of Health; of the law of landlord and tenant, and town and country planning by the Ministry of Housing (and its predecessors, the Ministry of Health and the Ministry of Town and Country Planning respectively). As for the Home Office, although until quite recently it had taken no major initiatives in the direction of modernising the criminal law, it has been instrumental in promoting a series of statutes which have put the old common law on certain subjects (offences against the person; sexual offences; offences against property) into a form which is accessible, though by no means easily understandable, to all.

## Ad hoc Committees

Now, for a closer look at those units of the machinery of law reform which have been created specifically for that purpose. All these units are committees—some of them permanent and others (the majority) *ad hoc*. Here again, it appears convenient to begin with the second variety.

By the phrase "*ad hoc* committees" we mean committees to which specific topics have been referred either by the Lord Chancellor or a departmental Minister; and the phrase also covers Royal Commissions.

Since the end of the Second World War, ten Royal Commissions have reported on subjects potentially calling for legislative reform. In seven cases the reports led to legislation; in two more cases they may yet do so; in one case no legislation proved to be necessary. This is a very satisfactory ratio between the number of reports and the number of instances in which legislative action was taken; but the ground covered by the ten reports, rendered over a period of 15 years, was infinitesimally small in relation to the vast area in which there is a crying need for reform. Much the same applies to the 40 *ad hoc* committees which reported between 1945 and 1960; in 27 cases the reports gave rise to legislation, and in four cases to new or amended Rules of Court, or administrative action by the Lord Chancellor.[1] Statistically, the record is satisfactory; but the resulting legislation (important though it has been in some cases) followed no definite pattern or plan. In the last analysis the Royal Commissions and *ad hoc* committees which have reported since the end of the Second World War have effected not one single fundamental change in the system of substantive law. Such fundamental changes as have resulted from their work (and there were only two: the Legal Aid and Advice Act, 1949, and the Tribunals and Inquiries Act, 1958) were exclusively within the area of the administration of justice.

*Permanent Committees*

Those units of the machinery of reform which were constructed specifically for that purpose are three in number. Two of these operate in a highly specialised field; the third has wide terms of reference.

The older of the two specialised bodies is the Lord Chancellor's Private International Law Committee, set up in 1952. Since then it has produced seven reports. The Committee's recommendations have resulted, in 1958 and 1959, in the introduction of two Domicile Bills, neither of which has become law; another bill, on Wills, is now before Parliament.

The more recent of the specialised bodies, the Home Secretary's Criminal Law Revision Committee, has a more encouraging record. Since its creation in 1959, this Committee has made two reports; these have given rise to legislation in the form of the Indecency with Children Act, 1960, and the Suicide Act, 1961.

The third unit is, in effect, the most important part of the existing machinery. This is the Lord Chancellor's Law Reform Committee, appointed in 1952 to resume those functions which, between 1934 and 1939, were entrusted to the Law Revision Committee appointed by Lord Sankey. The present Committee

---

[1] For details, see Appendix to E. C. S. Wade: "The Machinery of Law Reform", (1961) 24 Mod.L.Rev., p. 3, at pp. 10 and ff.

consists of five Supreme Court judges and law lords, five practising barristers, two solicitors and three academic lawyers; the Deputy Permanent Secretary to the Lord Chancellor and another member of the Lord Chancellor's staff serve as secretaries. The Committee's terms of reference are, at first sight, somewhat narrow:

"to consider, having regard especially to judicial decisions, what changes are desirable in such legal doctrines as the Lord Chancellor may from time to time refer to the Committee"

but these terms have been interpreted liberally, so as to allow the Committee to consider also changes in the statute law. The dominant feature of the Committee's procedure is the reference of each subject approved by the Lord Chancellor for examination to a sub-committee of five or six members under the chairmanship of a judge; occasionally a lawyer with special experience in the particular field (an academic lawyer, as a rule) is co-opted. It is this sub-committee which receives whatever evidence may be forthcoming from outside sources. It is noteworthy in this context that public announcements of actual references to the Committee, accompanied by invitations to the public to give written or oral evidence, have not on the whole provoked encouraging responses. Evidence from external sources has seldom been forthcoming in favour of reform; in support of the *status quo* more copious evidence has been offered by vested interests.[1]

It is not surprising that in this situation, which is characterised by the absence of a clear general demand for a change in the law, the work of the Committee has not so far resulted in any impressive amount of legislative action. In fact, during the first decade of the Committee's existence only one statute of general interest (the Occupiers' Liability Act, 1957) has sprung from its labours; this was a Government bill. The Committee reported on nine more subjects and to five of these reports effect was given by legislation; but all of these five measures have reached the statute book through the initiative of private Members of Parliament. In this context it is worthy of note that the work of the Law Reform Committee has received valuable

[1] E. C. S. Wade, *op. cit.*, at p. 5.

support not only from individual members of the one or the other House of Parliament, but also from non-governmental bodies—in particular, the Council of the Law Society, the General Council of the Bar, and "Justice", the British section of the International Commission of Jurists. All three of these professional bodies have given the Committee the benefit of their own investigations into the need for law reform. The political associations within the Inns of Court (the Inns of Court Conservative and Unionist Association, the Association of Liberal Lawyers, the Society of Labour Lawyers and the Haldane Society) have also played a useful part by sponsoring various proposals for reform.

### THE CASE FOR AN OVERHAUL

The overall picture which emerges from this short survey of the machinery at work is not reassuring. From within the legal profession there comes a fairly steady flow (by no means a stream) of proposals; but there is no articulate public demand for major changes in the law. The governmental machinery for law reform is not geared to steady, planned and co-ordinated operation. Whenever there is need for urgency or for the services of persons specially skilled in a particular branch of the law, the preparation of reforming measures is entrusted to *ad hoc* committees which operate in isolation and with their attention focused on one particular anomaly or group of anomalies. The central unit of the machinery, the Law Reform Committee, relies exclusively on the part-time services of a number of distinguished lawyers and of two senior officials of the Lord Chancellor's Department; and its work is not, nor is it meant to be, continuous. As a result, the Committee's output, although it is high in quality, cannot do justice to the very large number of problems which call for reforming legislation. And yet, there is no assurance that even the relatively small number of proposals emanating from the Committee will in due course be sponsored by the Government or that the Government will make parliamentary time available for the consideration of the Committee's recommendations. Finally, even where the Committee's proposals find their way into the statute book, the resulting Acts of Parliament will be interpreted judicially without reference to the relevant reports of the Committee.

*A Ministry of Justice?*

For well over a century it has been suggested, time and again, that in order to keep the general law under constant review and bring it up to date whenever necessary, this country needs a Ministry of Justice. The setting up of such a Ministry was eloquently urged by Jeremy Bentham; it is almost the only one of the major legal reforms supported by him which has not been secured. In 1918, the Report of Lord Haldane's Committee on the Machinery of Government gave its full approval to the idea that such a new department of State should be created. In 1951 the establishment of a Ministry of Justice, designed to exercise a constant surveillance over the substance and machinery of the law, was the central proposal of "The Reform of the Law". There is a Ministry of Justice in most foreign countries, not excluding the British Dominions and the United States of America. In fact, among countries having a comparably advanced system of political organisation, Great Britain is the only one without a great department of State known as the Ministry of Justice. That does not mean to say that this country has no department discharging the essential functions of a Ministry of Justice; the difference from other countries lies in terminology (which matters very little) and size (which matters a great deal).

It is difficult to think of a rational argument against re-naming and re-organising the Lord Chancellor's Office as a Ministry of Justice; the argument based on tradition is purely emotional, and the further argument that the independence of the judiciary is imperilled in countries which have a Ministry of Justice is ill founded. Nevertheless, we are disinclined to press the case for a change of name; there is no magic in the name of a government department, and the effort, energy and time that would be required to defeat strong traditionalist opposition could be put to better use in pressing the case for strengthening and re-organising the Lord Chancellor's Office. Under recent Lords Chancellors, especially those who were members of Labour Cabinets (Lords Haldane, Sankey and Jowitt), the Office which barely fifty years ago was little more than a private secretariat has been converted into a small but efficient government department. But the time is overripe for strengthening this department so that it should be properly equipped for its functions in the field of law reform.

These functions cannot be discharged efficiently by devoting to them a mere fraction of the Lord Chancellor's time (he is invariably one of the most heavily overworked Ministers in the Cabinet) and of one or two of his principal assistants. Nothing less will do than the setting up within the Lord Chancellor's Office of a strong unit concerned exclusively with law reform in that wide sense which also includes codification, so far as in the peculiar system of English law codification may be desirable and feasible.

## Vice-Chancellor and Law Commissioners

The head of the proposed unit should carry the rank of a Minister of State; it would be logical and convenient to call him Vice-Chancellor. He would be concerned exclusively with law reform, and he would sit in the House of Commons.

The Vice-Chancellor should preside over a committee of not less than five highly qualified lawyers; in the following we will call them Law Commissioners although, here again, we attach no particular importance to this title being used instead of some other. The office and status of the Law Commissioners will have to be established by statute and we think that the following essential requirements should be met:

(1) The appointments should be full-time; they should be made for periods to be agreed at the time of the appointment, but for not less than three years; and each Commissioner should be eligible for re-appointment.

(2) We think that no attempt should be made to predetermine by statute the salaries and pensions payable to the Law Commissioners. They would have to be recruited from among practising and academic lawyers of exceptional merit. The factors of age, previous earnings and duration of appointment will vary from case to case. Having regard to this, the statute ought to leave it to the Lord Chancellor to agree, with Treasury consent, the emoluments payable to any individual Commissioner.[1] However we think that in no event should or could the emoluments be less than those attached to a chair of law in a British university.

---

[1] There is statutory precedent for this kind of flexible procedure; see s. 1(5) of the Foreign Compensation Commission Act, 1950, and s. 4(4) of the Restrictive Trade Practices Act, 1956.

(3) Although the emoluments will be paid out of public funds, it is vitally important that the Law Commissioners should not be ordinary civil servants, but enjoy a high degree of independence. We have in mind a status similar to that of the chairman and members of a statutory tribunal exercising quasi-judicial functions.

The chief responsibility of the Law Commissioners would be to review, bring up to date and keep up to date what may be called "the general law": the common law and equity, and also that part of the statute law which does not fall within the province of any particular government department.

To deal with the exception first: the "administrators' law", i.e. that part of the statute law which is wholly or chiefly administered by one particular department, should continue to remain primarily that department's own concern. We mean by that that whenever any part of the "administrators' law" is in need of reform by amendment, repeal or new legislation, the initiative should come, as at present, from the department concerned. But we would wish to see a link-up with the Law Commissioners in two ways. Firstly, they should always be consulted; this would reduce the risk of departmental initiatives running against the trend of reforms in the general law. Secondly, the Law Commissioners should not be debarred from taking the initiative themselves whenever they think that any part of the "administrators' law" is in need of reform and no initiative is forthcoming from the department which is primarily responsible.

Now for the general law. It should be the Law Commissioners' responsibility to work out and carry out a plan (by its nature it would have to be a long-term plan) for its systematic review. They should also be required to give due and, if necessary, urgent consideration to judicial comments on the state of the law and to concrete proposals for reform coming from the representative organisations of industry (including the trade unions), commerce and the professions. Naturally, we should like the Commissioners to be free to take up proposals originating from non-official and non-representative sources: voluntary organisations and learned societies of all kinds, the universities, learned authors and the Press in general.

Since the amount of work to be done by the Commissioners must depend largely on the scope and phasing of their overall plan for reviewing the general law, it would, we feel, be of little utility if we attempted here and now to specify the resources that ought to be placed at their disposal. But a few general observations may not be out of place. We think that not only the planning but also most of the research and drafting required for the reform of the general law should be concentrated in the Lord Chancellor's Office. It follows that the Law Commissioners should have an appropriate staff of legal assistants, at least some of whom should have had appropriate training in comparative research. Included in or attached to this staff should be a certain number of skilled parliamentary draftsmen; we see considerable merit in the concept of constant co-operation between planners, research workers and those who formulate the law.

If a set-up of this kind were adopted, there would be no need to maintain the Law Reform Committee, the Private International Law Committee and the Home Secretary's Criminal Law Revision Committee as permanent institutions. They could, whenever the need arose, be re-established *ad hoc* for the consideration of any major project that the Law Commissioners might decide to refer to them. The Government's present powers to appoint Royal Commissions and other *ad hoc* committees should continue; but in principle those powers should always be exercised in consultation with the Law Commissioners.

## Codification

This brief survey of the tasks facing the Law Commissioners is perhaps the right context in which to say a word about codification. The unwieldiness of English law has reached a degree which raises one of the more agonising problems of democracy: the question whether the citizen is placed in a position to ascertain the law by which he lives without incurring unreasonable trouble and disproportionate expense. The answer, we fear, is in the negative. There are well over 300,000 reported cases in common law and equity; the statute law, in its most compact edition, fills 42 large volumes; and delegated legislation, over the past 50 years only, runs into a series of 99 tomes. The number of legal problems which can be answered by reference to one single source of law is infinitesimally small; in the vast majority of cases it is necessary to refer to judicial pronouncements *and* statute law (both parliamentary and delegated). Even in that relatively less troublesome category of cases which can be answered by reference only to statute law the answer is hardly ever easy to find; for this country has a time-honoured practice of passing a great many statutes, each dealing with only a small part of a subject and making no reference to previous statutes on that subject unless these are amended or repealed.

There is an extremely strong case for the progressive codification of English law in the sense of reducing to one statute, or a small collection of statutes, the whole of the law on any particular subject. The relatively few codes we have: the Bills of Exchange Act, the Partnership Act, the Sale of Goods Act, the Larceny Act and more recently the Income Tax Act, 1952, have all proved their worth; they have saved much time and trouble to clients and their legal advisers, and in all probability they have reduced appreciably the number of cases which have had to be brought before the courts on points of law. These results have been all the more remarkable as our codifying statutes have tended to preserve the common law and with it many topics of doubt and difficulty; they did not follow the technique adopted, with great success, in many foreign countries where the codifying statutes have expressly provided that no prior statute and no decision of any court made before the effective date of the codifying act must be cited or relied on in any court or for any purpose.

Although the progressive codification of English law is much overdue, we are not suggesting that this should be given a high priority in the programme of law reform. Our reasons can be simply stated. We are not impressed with any of the fashionable arguments against codification. The contention that English law, by its nature, is uncodifiable has been disproved by the experience gained with our own codifying statutes and, on a much wider scale, by the experience of the British Dominions. Nor do we see much merit in the argument that codification would destroy the flexibility of our system. Not even the French codes (relatively the most rigid of all) have proved inflexible, and the German and Swiss codes, which granted wide discretion to the judiciary to decide *ex aequo et bono* or according to the judge's conscience, have created systems which are far less rigid than ours. Finally, we see no merit in the claim that only that kind of law which has been developed through judicial pronouncements and made binding with the help of a doctrine of precedents has the attribute of certainty. It would be facetious to rely, in rebuttal, merely on the well worn (and much cherished) phrase about "the glorious uncertainty" of English law. Instead, we rely on what has already been said about the immense difficulty of ascertaining the law relating to any particular subject, the unresolved conflicts between judicial decisions, and the many doubtful points which are not covered by any binding decisions at all.

These considerations leave us with one single argument against the high priority of codification; but this one argument we regard as valid and decisive. The condition of English law being what it is, codification, if it is to be helpful, must of necessity be preceded by reform; there would be no point in including in any code that Parliament could be persuaded to enact great masses of obsolete or unjust law; it would only have to be taken out again. To reform the law sufficiently (and the suggestions for reform included in the chapters which follow represent minimum requirements rather than the optimum one could envisage) will take many years, and very likely more than one decade. Even with the improved machinery that we suggest, the surveying of the ground and the formulation of legislative proposals will be a slow process. Moreover, so long as Parliament will continue to spend about half of its time controlling the Executive, with only the remaining half being available for legislation, the process of giving effect to these legislative proposals is bound to be even slower. In marginal cases, where reform can be confined to corrections and minor improvements, parliamentary proceedings can be greatly simplified and, indeed, reduced to a somewhat nominal function; the Consolidation of Enactments (Procedure) Act, 1949 (an imaginative measure—unhappily, much neglected in practice—of the first post-war Labour Government) has pointed the way by adopting the bold principle that if, with the concurrence of the Lord Chancellor and the Speaker, a joint committee of both Houses adopts a bill containing corrections of, and minor improvements to, the existing law, these will be deemed to have become law in the same manner as if they had been made by an Act of Parliament. However, the possible range of simplifying measures of this kind is necessarily limited, and major reforms of the law will have to pass through the slow moving waters which fill the normal channels of parliamentary procedure.

*Immediate Reforms*

For these reasons it would be unrealistic to assign to codification anything higher than second place on the agenda of law reform. This may involve a long wait; but while waiting we can take a few steps which would significantly improve the present situation. The first such step would be to make it a rule that no parliamentary year must pass without the enactment of at least one Law Reform Act. We have had, annually and for a long time, an Expiring Laws Continuance Act; it is imperative that to this annual exercise in preserving that which exists we should add an annual exercise in improving that which is deficient. Next, we should make it a rule that whenever a major reform of statute law is carried out, the reforming act should be quickly followed (as in the case of the Companies Acts) by the enactment of a consolidating statute.

Thirdly, we should make it a rule that the reasons for, and the objectives pursued by, any bill laid before Parliament (including, of course, the annual Law Reform Bills) should be fully stated in a Ministerial Memorandum or (where the bill is introduced by a Private Member) a Memorandum issued by the sponsor or sponsors. In addition, whenever a statute of major importance is passed by Parliament, the Government should arrange for the publication of a White Paper. This should set out the changes that the original bill had undergone during its parliamentary passage, and also the Government's interpretation of the statute as finally passed. In this context we would suggest that it should be enacted as a matter of high priority that whenever a court of law or quasi-judicial tribunal has occasion to pronounce on the proper interpretation of a statute, it shall be at liberty to refer to the relevant Ministerial Memorandum and White Paper. We see little merit in the present system which allows the courts to substitute their own idea of the policy of a statute for that policy which Parliament actually had. Finally, the present practice which leaves the Government entirely free to act or not to act on the recommendations of any permanent or *ad hoc* committee dealing with law reform should be abandoned. The least the Government should be required to do is to find parliamentary time for the consideration of any report which recommends a change in the law. Once the new machinery we advocate has been set up in the Lord Chancellor's Office, the Government should be required, by the Act establishing the offices of Vice-Chancellor and Law

Commissioners, to find parliamentary time for the consideration of any legislation proposed by the Law Commissioners or by a Royal Commission or *ad hoc* committee appointed after consultation with them.

In our opinion *all* of the immediate reforms urged in this section are necessary if the law is to fulfil its function in contemporary Britain.

# II

## THE ADMINISTRATION OF JUSTICE

THE ADMINISTRATION of justice in England, taken as a whole, is of a high standard, able to stand comparison with that of any other country. Nevertheless it is not incapable of improvement in certain respects.

### THE ORGANISATION OF THE COURTS

*The Probate, Divorce and Admiralty Division*

It is not necessary to be a lawyer to be struck by the obvious incongruity of the three constituents of this Division. The sole reason for their existence in one Division is the fact that when the Supreme Court of Judicature was established in 1873 these three classes of work were in the hands of the civil lawyers, a body of practitioners separate from the English common lawyers and dealing with totally different systems of law. It was therefore natural at the time to group them into one Division. The Hanworth Committee[1] recommended the abolition of the Division, the assignment of probate work to the Chancery Division and of the remainder to the Queen's Bench Division. The Peel Commission[2] and the Evershed Committee[3] took a different view.

The question is not one of great importance. But if (as is suggested in a later chapter of this book[4]) a "Family Division" is set up within the framework of the High Court, the probate work should be transferred to the Chancery Division, which already deals with the administration of estates, and the Admiralty and Commercial Court should form part of the Queen's Bench Division. In any case, undefended divorce cases should be transferred to the County Courts instead of, as now, being tried by County Court judges acting as High Court judges for the day.

[1] Committee on the Business of the Courts, 1932–33.
[2] Royal Commission on the Despatch of Business at Common Law, 1934–36.
[3] Committee on Supreme Court Practice and Procedure, 1947–53.
[4] See p. 123 *infra.*

### The Privy Council

The plan, discussed on the occasion of the Commonwealth Prime Ministers' Conference held in September 1962, for the reinforcement of the Judicial Committee by the appointment of Commonwealth judges from certain countries should be carried to its logical conclusion, so that all those Commonwealth countries from which an appeal still lies to the Judicial Committee should be represented on it. Consideration should also be given to introducing the "circuit" principle into the work of the Committee, so that it should be able to sit in the Commonwealth country from which the appeal comes.

### The Court of Appeal

Under the Judicature Act, 1873, the Court of Appeal was to be the final Court of Appeal. So few cases reach the House of Lords that it has always been more important that the Court of Appeal should be strong than that possibilities of a further appeal to the House of Lords should exist. Nor, with respect, can it be said that the reputation of that House has been increased by such decisions as *D.P.P.* v. *Smith*[1] and *Shaw* v. *D.P.P.*[2]

At the Annual Meeting of "Justice", held in 1961, Lord Evershed, with his experience of both tribunals, suggested that consideration should be given to abolishing the appellate jurisdiction of the House of Lords and giving jurisdiction to a Court of Appeal of five Lords Justices to reconsider any previous decision of the Court of Appeal.

The cost of appeals to the House of Lords with its £1,000 security for costs has become prohibitive save to the few or to the recipient of legal aid. One appeal is enough if the appellate court is sufficiently strong, as the Court of Appeal would be if it had the present combined strength of both tribunals. The balance of advantage and disadvantage lies in favour of a strong and final Court of Appeal, able to reconsider any previous decision.

### The Court of Criminal Appeal

Few practising lawyers would not agree that of all our courts the Court of Criminal Appeal, which has vital functions, e.g. in correcting judicial errors that may have wrongly deprived a

---

[1] [1961] A.C. 290.
[2] [1961] 2 All E.R. 446.

man of his liberty, has always given rise to most criticism. There are many reasons for this, but the primary cause is that it is not a real court of appeal: its members are not Lords Justices, nor, apart from the Lord Chief Justice, have they any status superior to that of the judges on whose work they have to sit in judgment. It is said by those who support the present system that the Court is a valuable training ground for the few newly appointed Queen's Bench judges who may not have had prior experience of criminal work. No one, however, suggests that when a barrister, whose work has been confined solely to criminal cases, is appointed a High Court judge, he should sit in the Court of Appeal to learn the civil work. The Court of Criminal Appeal should be composed of Lords Justices and be one of the Divisions of the Court of Appeal, the Lord Chief Justice presiding when he wishes to do so. No doubt he and the Master of the Rolls would see that the Lords Justices sitting in that division were primarily those with long experience of criminal work. The Divisional Court's work of hearing cases stated by inferior courts in criminal cases should also be transferred to the Court of Appeal as so reconstituted.

The powers of the Court itself require enlarging. It is a common criticism of the work of the Court that one who is on any footing a criminal stands a good chance on appeal if he has some highly technical point in his favour, while a man whose only complaint is that he is wholly innocent—usually (like Adolf Beck whose case led to the establishment of the Court) because he has been wrongly identified—has little prospect of obtaining leave to appeal. It is important both that the guilty should be convicted and that the innocent should not be; and a power to order a new trial where the Court thought it right to do so would contribute to both ends.

There should also be a right of appeal on a verdict of insanity, and against a verdict on a plea of guilty where that plea has been based on a misunderstanding of the charge, particularly where the accused was not represented.

The present addition of six weeks to the sentence as a penalty for having unsuccessfully appealed[1] should be reconsidered, as also should the circumstances in which sentences can be increased on appeal.

There is a grave defect in the provision of legal aid in criminal

[1] Since the coming into force of s. 38 of the Criminal Justice Act, 1948, this penalty has ceased to be automatic.

appeals. Not only is there no provision for such aid on applications for leave to appeal, but it is doubtful whether s. 23(4) of
the Legal Aid and Advice Act, 1949, covers advice on whether
to appeal or the drafting of a notice of appeal. Even if it does,
an accused who is not represented at all or represented only by
counsel is not eligible for legal aid.

Moreover, the time in which an appellant has to obtain
advice, make up his mind and serve his notice of appeal (ten
days) is far too short, particularly as it will have been impossible
to obtain a transcript within that time. Proper facilities for legal
advice at this stage would reduce the number of appeals and
also ensure that the grounds of appeal are properly set out in
the notice of appeal.

### County Courts

One feature of these—"the poor man's courts"—which
needs urgent attention is the frequently appalling situation
which arises when a long case comes up for trial. There are
sometimes three or four partial hearings of the case, which may
extend over several months. All this is costly and highly
unsatisfactory to the frustrated and inconvenienced litigant.
No shorthand note is normally taken of the proceedings, and an
excessively difficult burden is placed on the judge and on the
lawyers in the case.

### Coroners' Courts

The working of the coroners' courts has given rise to much
criticism. The police make their own enquiries into suspected
homicides, and the work of the coroners in this respect seems to
be supererogatory. The publicity given to their proceedings is
also a disadvantage in so far as it tends to prejudice the jury at
a subsequent trial.

The results of verdicts (e.g. a verdict of suicide) by coroners'
juries may sometimes be grave and not only because of the
distress they may cause to relatives and friends of the deceased.
Life insurance policies normally contain a "no suicide clause",
and a verdict of suicide may well result in depriving dependents
of the deceased of their sole means of support. It is thoroughly
unjust that in so grave a matter the parties affected have no
right to call witnesses, no right to cross-examine the witnesses
who are called, and no right to address the jury. Interventions
made on behalf of relatives have to be made semi-apologetically.

It is true that coroners do normally allow cross-examination of witnesses, but some of them put excessive curbs on the cross-examiner. The denial of the right to address the jury on behalf of the relatives becomes the more galling if a coroner's summing up displays gross partiality. Only in the most flagrant cases can injustices perpetrated in a coroner's court be remedied.

There are no coroners' inquests in Scotland and they should now be abolished in England and Wales.

## The Circuit System

The Evershed Committee expressed the view that it was in the public interest that there should be strong and lively local Bars. However, in addition to suggesting certain minor reforms and a review of their working in two years' time, the Committee recommended unanimously that the special fee payable to a barrister not a member of the circuit should not be more than 50 guineas. A decade has passed since the Committee reported in 1953; but the special fees have not been reduced, nor have all the minor reforms been carried out.

## PROCEDURE

Since the end of the war the procedure in most of our courts has received patient and careful consideration from the Committee on Procedure in Matrimonial Causes, 1946–47 (the "Denning Committee"[1]), the Committee on County Court Procedure, 1947–49 (the "Austin Jones Committee"[2]), the Committee on Supreme Court Practice and Procedure, 1947–53 (the "Evershed Committee"[3]), the Committee on Procedure before Examining Justices, 1957–58 (the "Tucker Committee"[4]), and the "Justice" Committee on Matrimonial Proceedings in Magistrates' Courts, 1963.

Unhappily a number of the reforms recommended have still not been carried out. Many of the proposals of the Denning Committee were not acted upon at the time solely because of the strong opposition of the then President of the Probate, Divorce and Admiralty Division. Effect should be given to them now. Some of the important recommendations of the

[1] Final Report (1947) Cmd. 7024.
[2] Final Report (1949) Cmd. 7668.
[3] Final Report (1953) Cmd. 8878.
[4] Report (1958) Cmnd. 479.

Evershed Committee, including those on evidence and on litigation at the public expense, have not been implemented. The complete revision of the Rules of the Supreme Court, first recommended as a matter of urgency by the Hanworth Committee 30 years ago, and repeated with still more emphasis by the Evershed Committee in its first report[1] 14 years ago, has still not been completed.

Again, the Evershed Committee unanimously recommended that dates should be fixed for *all* witness actions in the jury and non-jury lists of the Queen's Bench Division in London; but this is still not done, although the Committee said that so far as it had been able to ascertain

"England is the only civilized country in the world where litigants are not told, as a matter of course, the date on which their actions will be heard. We find it difficult to believe that it is only in England that it is not in practice possible to do it".

As for the unanimous report of the Tucker Committee, its main recommendations have never been implemented.

It is useless to appoint capable and industrious men and women to serve on these committees if their unanimous recommendations to improve the procedure of our courts are left to moulder in the files of the Lord Chancellor's Office or the Home Office without even being brought before Parliament for discussion.

### THE LAW OF EVIDENCE

Our law of evidence is old-fashioned. It was worked out by the judges long ago for the purpose of preventing juries (which were often illiterate) from giving unjust verdicts because they were unable to appreciate the weakness or strength of the evidence put before them. The system so evolved was excellent in its day, but its continued use involves much unnecessary expense and delay, in addition to increasing the possibility that a good case will break down for technical reasons. At the present time the technicalities of the law are, up to a point, often evaded by lawyers using sheer common sense; and in one court, the Commercial Court, a very much simplified system

---

[1] (1949) Cmd. 7764.

has been in use for many years to everybody's satisfaction. With the abolition of the jury in most civil cases the main reason for the rules of evidence in civil litigation has disappeared. Following the report of the Peel Commission,[1] the Evidence Act, 1938, did something to alleviate the position; but the reforms did not go very far. Among the particularly inconvenient rules are the rule excluding secondary evidence of documents (except in particular cases), and the hearsay rule (which again is not maintained in its entirety, but involves difficult exceptions). It is true that hearsay evidence is generally inferior to direct evidence; yet in some cases its probative value is as great or even greater. For example, owing to the shortness of human memory, a statement is more likely to be true the nearer it is, in point of time, to the event in question. Now, of two statements, it is possible that the one nearer the event can only be proved by hearsay. Suppose that the witness of an accident makes a statement soon thereafter to X, who writes it down. In court the witness may not be able to remember with precision either what he saw or what he said about it at the time. In these circumstances X's evidence may well be of greater value than that of the eye-witness in the box; yet in law it is hearsay. Again, the only available evidence on a particular point may be hearsay, the witness himself having died before trial; yet the death of the witness is, under the present law, not a sufficient reason for admitting the hearsay evidence. However, there is some provision in criminal cases to allow the deposition of a witness who is dangerously ill to be taken and read at the trial.[2] Under R.S.C. Order 37, rule 5, the taking of depositions may also be ordered by the court in civil cases. Various other lesser rules of the law of evidence need reconsideration, such as the privilege against self-crimination for adultery. The law relating to the presumption of death is in an imperfect state, particularly because it fails to provide a single proceeding in which death could be presumed for all purposes, or to establish a rule fixing the notional date of death.

The special rules of evidence for criminal cases are also unsatisfactory, though in reforming these more caution must be used because the triers of fact are still usually either the jury or the lay magistracy. One example of the rules that require reconsideration in criminal cases is the rule forbidding a

[1] (1933) Comd. 5065.
[2] Magistrates' Courts Act, 1952, s. 41.

prisoner in general to attack the character of witnesses for the prosecution, except on pain of having his own character attacked in cross-examination. Also, whatever rule may be thought to be best for civil cases, it is repugnant to our sense of justice that the rules of evidence should operate to exclude relevant evidence tendered on behalf of the prisoner. Even if the hearsay rule is thought right as a fetter upon the prosecution, it should not be allowed to hinder the defence. Attention should also be given to the general question of expert evidence, which under our present system is most unsatisfactory. The American Law Institute has proposed a new Code of Evidence which will sweep away the old absurdities, and these proposals should be looked at when our own system comes up for reconsideration.

New methods of proof made available by scientific discovery should be introduced where practicable. One illustration is the use of blood tests in bastardy cases. By such tests it is possible, in a substantial proportion of cases, conclusively to disprove paternity; yet although these tests have been available for many years, relatively little use has been made of them.

In the field of evidence the recommendations of the Evershed Committee were certainly conservative. Nevertheless they have not been implemented. They should be implemented now, together with the Committee's unanimous recommendation that all the statute law relating to evidence should be consolidated.

## LEGAL AID

There can be no doubt that the Legal Aid and Advice scheme has been a great success. In this country the field in which it can still be said that a legal right that a man cannot enforce is a nugatory right, has become very narrow indeed.

The latest extension of legal aid, to matrimonial cases in Magistrates' Courts, is working very well; and it is interesting to observe from the "Justice" report referred to above[1] that one of the consequences, reported by clerks to Magistrates' Courts, has been a noticeable increase in the number of reconciliations between spouses.

There are, however, four matters which still require consideration.

First, the position of a party (particularly a defendant) who is not legally aided but faces a legally aided opponent is

[1] See under Procedure, on p. 19, *supra*.

not a happy one. There is no reason in principle why the same fund which enabled the plaintiff to bring an action which has failed and would not have been brought without such assistance, should not be responsible for the other party's costs.[1]

Secondly, at present a man charged with an indictable offence cannot be granted legal aid to employ counsel before the magistrates unless the charge is that of murder. Experience has shown that in addition to murder there are other cases in which facilities should be available for the employment of counsel. Magistrates' Courts should therefore be empowered to grant certificates for counsel in all cases where they think it right to do so.

Thirdly, the scope of legal aid in criminal appeals should be widened in the manner which has been suggested earlier in this chapter.[2]

Fourthly, as is suggested in the next chapter, legal aid should be extended to proceedings before all administrative tribunals before which representation is allowed.

---

[1] A bill giving effect to the substance of this proposal was introduced by the Lord Chancellor in the House of Lords while this book was going to press.
[2] See p. 17, *supra*.

# III

# CONSTITUTIONAL AND
# ADMINISTRATIVE LAW

## INTRODUCTORY

THE SUBJECT MATTER of this chapter embraces all that part of central and local government which can be called legal. And this adjective must be widely interpreted or formal distinctions will follow to impede discussion at the vital meeting places of law and politics. It would, however, be manifestly impossible to cover all matters which would fall within the wider definition and so a selection must be made.

Discussion of reforms can be limited at once to those which are political possibilities. And it is assumed that the general pattern of legal and political affairs will continue unchanged for the foreseeable future. It is not, therefore, proposed to consider such matters as proportional representation or the electoral system at large or to make suggestions for the radical re-organisation of central or local administration.

The crucial principles on which the British constitution rests are three. First, the selection, by one and the same act of voting at a General Election, of the Prime Minister (and, through him, of Her Majesty's Government) and of a representative chamber divided between those, of the majority party, supporting the Government, and others in opposition. Secondly, Ministers' membership of one or other of the Houses of Parliament and their accountability to Parliament. Thirdly, the statutory limitation on the life of a Parliament to a maximum period of five years. Other principles of great importance include the independence of the judiciary, and the extent and limitations of free speech and association. Thus, the existence of a critical Press which, though often committed, is sufficiently independent and in that sense unreliable, rests on the tradition of free speech; and the existence of a powerful trade union movement similarly often committed and similarly independent and unreliable rests on the more recently defined tradition of free association.

24

For these and other reasons, a characteristic of the constitution is the considerable power it gives to Governments. Their command of the House of Commons is absolute if they are prepared not to flout outrageously the expressed views of large numbers of their supporters. The Government cannot in practice whip these supporters into the proper lobbies, but it possesses many powerful, and more subtle, methods of persuasion. The withdrawal of a whip is more effective than its laying on. But this must not be exaggerated. The Government has the means at its disposal to round up the wayward sheep and persuade them to enter the pen. But the flock goes there of its own wish because it is of the same mind as the Government. Government supporters support the Government because, being educated in the same political tradition, they agree with the Government. Opposition supporters similarly agree with their leaders. And all talk about party splits and disagreements must be seen against the background of this solidarity.

Governments, then, have great strength as well as great responsibility. Their function is to act, in order to solve within the terms of their political philosophy the multitudinous problems of a complex, industrialised, over-populated society. They must be able to isolate the problems, to legislate to meet them, and to conduct a process of administrative action. In the course of these operations they must make detailed rules, provide for the adjudication of disputes and see that their plans are put into effective action. And all this they must do in the context of powerful interests representing employers and employees and innumerable other organisations seeking their own ends. They must do so not only in a world of uneasy peace, but also with the mechanism of a financial structure built on the provision of privately owned capital which must be persuaded to invest in the affairs of this country rather than, or as well as, in those of others. It is indeed difficult to argue today that the power of Governments ought to be diminished and in recent years the idea that Governments should take increasing responsibility for the ordering of the national economy has come to be accepted as commonplace.

Traditionally, constitutional and administrative law has been regarded as a defender of personal rights and freedoms against invasion by public authorities. The great arguments about delegated legislation and administrative tribunals, about the new despotism and a power-seeking civil service, were the fields of conflict between 1918 and 1939. Today these joustings are primarily of historical interest only. The campaigns which led to the establishment of the Committee on Ministers' Powers (1929–32) and of the Committee on Administrative Tribunals and Enquiries (1955–57) were largely defeated by public exposure. This is not to say that the problem of public power and private rights has been either solved or pushed into the background. But the particular aspects, so popular some years ago, of delegated legislation and administrative tribunals, are now of little significance. They are considered below.

### GOVERNMENT AND PARLIAMENT

The decline of the House of Commons as an important part of the political ordering of the country is relative rather than absolute. As in the past, the House is still the forum for debate of the major issues affecting the life, health and happiness of subjects. It is as an institution to which Ministers are responsible for the day-to-day affairs of their departments that it has, in relation to the great growth of those affairs, failed to develop.

Ministerial responsibility is not a myth. Ministers and civil servants still blunder and Ministers still resign. The accountability of Ministers to Parliament for actions of civil servants, of which the Minister cannot be aware until the damage is done, does much to limit the likelihood that mistakes will be made. The civil servant has his place in the hierarchy, wishes for the ordinary human and personal reasons to do well and to be well thought of, but is, unlike his opposite number in private industry or in business, always liable to see his actions displayed in public for the world to see. And the fact that the world may not know that the action is his does not affect the consequences to his career. This does not mean that there is no case for less secrecy, but it does mean that his anonymity is not a blanket under which he can hide his errors from those whose influence on his future is greatest.

Nevertheless, the machinery for exposure of errors becomes increasingly defective as the area of administrative activity expands and the counter-balancing techniques, through Parliament, remain static. Some of this field must be left for other critics, partly because (as for the debates of parliamentary procedure) it is highly technical and can be properly commented on only by those who till it, and partly because it is, by even the most generous interpretation, extra-legal. These matters are important and include the pay and expenses of Members, their overwhelming need for better accommodation at Westminster and especially for proper secretarial assistance.[1]

There is, however, one group of proposals for parliamentary reform which was first associated with Fred Jowett, M.P., in 1907 and which still seems to offer the best radical solution. This is the extension of the committee system as a means of parliamentary control.[2]

The extension of the powers of control by the House of Commons in particular has, in much discussion, been baulked by an unfortunate coincidence. For it was just at the time when the need for this extension was becoming apparent—before and after the First World War—that a quite separate argument was beginning to establish itself. This was the argument which sought to expose the "liberal fallacy" as expounded by Bagehot and others. The fallacy was to urge that the representative body was the true centre of governmental power and that the Cabinet was an executive arm—or "committee" as Bagehot said—of that body from which it received its instructions. This is not the place to enter upon a detailed criticism of this fallacy, though its immediate origins can be found in the untypical relationship between the House of Commons and Governments in the middle years of the nineteenth century. We are here concerned to note that the opposite thesis of the duty and power of Governments to govern, albeit within a parliamentary structure, made difficult the exposition of the need for an increase in the controlling function of the House of Commons. "Control" itself is ambiguous. Banks control a river; a driver controls his car. When we speak of control by the House, we are nearer to the former image than to the latter. Control here assumes that the force is exercised by another body. Its notion is critical containment, not mandatory direction.

Jowett himself wanted to see the centre of governmental power vested in the House of Commons. One quotation will suffice: "If it is agreed that all members of the House of Commons must be allowed to share in the work of administration, and to have a voice in selecting subjects for legislation; if it is also agreed that all members must be allowed freedom to

---

[1] See B. Crick: *Reform of the Commons* (Fabian Tract 319), 1959.

[2] *Ibid;* and see A. H. Hanson and H. V. Wiseman, "The Use of Committees by the House of Commons" in (1959) Public Law 277.

vote as public representatives, and not be expected to vote merely as supporters or opponents of the Government, *two things must go*. The first is the control (not so complete as it seems) of public departments by individual Ministers. The second is the collective responsibility of Ministers, as it at present exists and is exercised through the Cabinet of Chief Ministers."

If individual Ministers are not to control departments, how are the departments to be controlled? The House of Commons cannot do so directly, but it can do so through committees. And he proceeds to elaborate this idea.[1]

There is, however, no necessary connection between Jowett's view and the development of the committee system for other, quite different, purposes. Laski's proposals had no room for committees of the Commons having any executive powers[2] nor, from a different political view, had those of Lord Salter and G. M. Young.[3] There are many variations of the general idea that the committee system could be enlarged to strengthen the critical function of the Commons.[4] What follows here draws freely on these and is an attempt to suggest reforms which seem at this time of writing to be workable.

Two of the most valuable committees at present operating are the Select Committee on Estimates (with its sub-committees) and the Select Committee on Nationalised Industries. Both these committees follow the procedure usual to parliamentary committees of their type. Their fields of reference are limited and barely overlap. The Estimates Committee decides what particular items of estimated departmental expenditure it will examine. The Nationalised Industries Committee chooses one (or more) of the public corporations within its field and investigates certain aspects of its working, particularly its relationships with Ministers and the way in which it manages its financial affairs. These committees are investigatory, seeking to discover how a section of administrative activity actually operates and they proceed primarily by questioning witnesses drawn both from within the governmental machine and from outside it. Their reports are critical and constructive and their

---

[1] Report drafted (for I.L.P.) on the Reform of Parliament.

[2] H. J. Laski: *A Grammar of Politics* at 349–50; *Parliamentary Government in England* at 211–12; *Reflections on the Constitution* at 52–3.

[3] Campion and others: *Parliament, a Survey*.

[4] A most useful summary is contained in Hansard Society, *Parliamentary Reform 1933–1960* at 43–55.

recommendations draw replies from the bodies concerned which may promise particular adminstrative action to remedy defects. Inevitably these reports from the committees vary in value and insight. Inevitably also the response to them may be helpful or obstructive. But an investigation has been made, administrators have been required to defend their actions and the House of Commons (or at least the members of the committee and those who read its reports) is better informed.

How far and in what ways can this device be extended? The purposes of this reform would be to enable Members to question those responsible for administration; to produce (where necessary) reports drawing attention to particular matters of importance; and to provide Members and others outside Parliament with more information about the policy of departments in relation to specific matters.

From these purposes, something of the pattern emerges. Each committee must be knowledgeable and able to look at special parts of the administrative process. It must, therefore, be concerned with a related group of functions and so it must be limited either to particular subjects or to particular departments. As one of the problems of modern government is the inter-relation of the work of different departments, a case could be made for an allocation based on subject-matter. But there would be considerable difficulty in delimiting subjects; in many cases the whole would in fact fall almost entirely within the scope of a single department; and, most importantly, as the work of each committee would be to scrutinise governmental activity as it operates in practice, the logical answer would seem to be for its investigation to be directed in the first place, to a particular department or a group of departments. In this investigation it should, however, be empowered to pursue its departmental subject into the activities of other departments, where necessary.

It follows also that each committee would need to be relatively small. If, as will be proposed, it should conduct its inquiries principally by the traditional method of questioning witnesses, it could not conveniently exceed 20 in number (which would in practice mean about 15 members present at any one time). There is a further advantage in keeping the number small. About 200 Members "fairly regularly" attend meetings of Standing Committees held in the mornings.[1] It

[1] B. Crick *op. cit.* at 15.

would be optimistic to expect that many more would be willing
to undertake the work of these proposed committees. They
would be appointed sessionally.

The simplest method of exposition is to consider how such a
committee would go about its business. Its first question would
be to decide what precisely it wished to investigate. And its
difficulty would be to choose among an embarrassment of
riches. It would naturally wish to concentrate on a contemporary problem and in the whole range of government activity
there is no shortage of problems. If it were the committee
concerned with the Ministry of Education, it might choose to
look at overcrowding in primary schools, or secondary school
selection, or teachers' training, or the working of the grant
structure. If it were the committee concerned with the Ministry
of Transport, it might choose to look at the way in which
responsibility for roads is divided between central and local
authorities, or at traffic accidents, or at the construction of
motorways, or at the national distribution of capital investment
in highways generally. The list is almost inexhaustible.

In its choice of subject it would normally seek to avoid
duplicating the work of other investigating bodies. And here
we should make clear that these committees are, under this
proposal, seen as additional to existing committees and other
bodies. It has been suggested that each such committee should
become the Standing Committee on bills affecting its sphere of
interest, or that it should take over, within that sphere, the
work of the Estimates Committee and other such bodies. The
present proposal does not suggest this extension of functions.
It follows therefore that the proposed committees would not
concern themselves with matters falling within the jurisdiction
of the Select Committees on Nationalised Industries or on
Statutory Instruments nor would they be likely to choose a
subject which had recently been or was proposed to be examined
by the Select Committees on Estimates or Public Accounts.

Each committee would pursue its investigations by sending
for "persons and papers". It would invite or require memoranda
from Government departments and other public bodies concerned, from any other organisations or associations and from
private persons. It would call to give oral evidence representatives of these groups and individuals as it thought fit.

Much of the evidence would be given by senior civil servants.
But if these committees are to have real value, both policy and

administration must be dealt with. They would therefore wish to call Ministers or junior Ministers also, and require them to defend their policy decisions. But it is fundamental to our system of government and to the function of Parliament itself that these committees should not become the makers of policy. The Cabinet and the departments must remain the decision-makers so that responsibility clearly attaches to them. The proposed committees could of course make reports to the House; these reports would no doubt often be critical; this criticism would inevitably, on many occasions, be concerned with policy; and if the criticism were to be more than destructive, it would contain proposals for a change in policy. This in itself would not be harmful to the working of the constitution. It would become harmful only if departments weakly, and against their better judgment, acquiesced in the change; for this would begin to shift the burden of decision-making to the parliamentary body, and enable departments to escape responsibility, if the change proved to be for the worse, by pleading that they had only acted as the committee suggested.

Here however the party system would reassert itself. Once any important policy came under attack, the committee would almost certainly split on party lines and as each committee would be composed of party members in proportion to the party strength in the House, the Government would carry the day in committee. Indeed this is itself a safeguard. For the committees would obviously be less persuasive on those very questions of policy where they disagreed amongst themselves. And so it would be unlikely that such questions would be much pursued. This may be thought to be unrealistic and it is clearly possible that the Opposition would seek to use these committees primarily to embarrass the Government. Yet the tradition of existing committees is to avoid such situations and there seems to be no reason why the proposed committees should not accept a measure of self-discipline by agreeing that where policy issues on party lines emerged they should not be pursued in committee but left to their proper place, which is the floor of the House.

Without seeking to evade the difficulties which such committees would give rise to, further detailed examination of their working is best left to those with inside knowledge, as Members, of the House of Commons. If the idea were accepted, it could, it is thought, be made to work.

There are, however, two extensions of this proposal which should also be considered. First, existing committees often call to give evidence representatives of outside bodies and other private persons. Members of local authority associations frequently give evidence; so do those of professional bodies. This could be taken much further. If a committee were, for example, concerned with the redevelopment of Central London—a matter which might easily arise because of the functions of the Ministry of Housing and Local Government or the Ministry of Transport, or the Board of Trade—it should be ready to call before it not only the public authorities concerned, but also the owners, the property developers, and the financial organisations behind them. Secondly, a committee should be ready to investigate matters not clearly falling within the immediate control of any Government department. If, to pursue the last example, the committee should decide that the relationship between insurance companies and property developers was itself of sufficient public interest to justify investigation, then it should be willing to make the appropriate inquiries and to call witnesses from these organisations to give an account of their activities. Suggestions of this kind would no doubt give rise to arguments in the committee on its agenda and only by voting would it be possible, in many cases, to decide whether a particular investigation should be carried out. The conflict with private and public companies might become acute. But for those who believe that there are many areas of anonymous or irresponsible power which should be subjected to public scrutiny, this would be a new extension of the parliamentary function of the greatest importance. Safeguards would be necessary to ensure that no committee was able to investigate a particular subject without proper authority. It might therefore be wise to require a resolution of the whole House empowering a committee to make this kind of investigation.

### DELEGATED LEGISLATION

The discussion about delegated legislation—the power given by Acts of Parliament to the Queen in Council or to Ministers to make orders and regulations—derived from a mythical interpretation of the constitution. Delegated legislation was expressed as an invasion by the Executive of the rights and functions of the Legislature. Montesquieu casts a long shadow.

The argument was that the power of making laws was the province of Parliament while that of executing them was the province of the Government. So put this was both constitutionally inaccurate and historically untrue. It is no lawyer's quibble to insist that the legislative power resides in the Queen in Parliament and no out-of-date antiquarianism that Acts of Parliament begin with the words "Be it enacted by the Queen's most Excellent Majesty, by and with the advice and consent of the Lords Spiritual and Temporal, and Commons, in this present Parliament assembled, and by the authority of the same."

The constitutional position can be both accurately and historically expressed by saying that it is the function of the Queen, acting on the advice of her Ministers, to make laws, but that such laws must, unless there is statutory authority to another effect, be submitted to both Houses of Parliament for their consideration and approval. The initiative in law-making, in the great majority of cases, rests with the Government. Any Minister faced with the need to take a particular action involving the rights of subjects must first consider whether he has the statutory power to do so. If he has not, he must either take the most appropriate action for which he has power, or obtain new power, or abandon the project. Where an Act of Parliament has authorised a Minister to make delegated legislation in the form of rules or regulations or orders, the Act will in almost all cases have required him to submit this legislation to Parliament for its approval or disapproval.

Whether a Minister is forced to proceed by bill, therefore, or, because of pre-existing statutory powers, may proceed to make new law by delegated legislation, the initiative in both cases is his. Also, in both cases, much of the pre-parliamentary legislative process—particularly the consultation of affected interests —will be similar. Also, in both cases, the new law will have to be submitted, in differing forms, to Parliament. Also, in both cases, the Government's parliamentary majority will be used to enforce the Government's will.

Once indeed it is accepted that legislation is the Government's function in this sense, the constitutional case against delegated legislation falls to the ground. There are indeed other matters to be considered. The most important of these is the determination, when a new bill is being drafted, of what should be included as substantive proposals in the bill and what can or must be left to the powers of Ministers to make delegated legislation. A second important matter is the need to scrutinise the regulations made as delegated legislation and to ensure that they appear to be the sort of regulations which the empowering Act envisaged and that they do not appear to be giving extra-ordinary powers—such as a power to impose taxation. The Select Committee on Statutory Instruments of the House of Commons has performed this function with a considerable degree of success for nearly twenty years. In addition, if the regulations are not authorised to be made under the empower-ing statute, the courts may declare them to be invalid.

Given the assumption that Ministers, in order to carry out their present-day duties, need the power to make subordinate regulations, the only remaining question is whether the safe-guards against the abuse of this power are adequate. It is suggested that they are.

### ADMINISTRATIVE TRIBUNALS

The other problem traditionally associated by constitutional lawyers with the powers of Governments and the rights of the subject is that of administrative tribunals. Here we are speaking of those statutory bodies consisting of members appointed by Ministers with the function of deciding disputes arising out of the administration of a particular social service. Claims to national insurance or industrial injury payments, or to payment of compensation on the compulsory purchase of land; disagree-ments about the proper value of property for rating purposes; disciplinary charges against practitioners in the National Health Service: these and many other disputes are determined by specially appointed statutory bodies. Most of them concern a public authority on the one side and a private person on the other.

In the main, what decision emerges in any particular case is not of great concern to the department responsible for the administration of the service itself. The standards to be applied (in relation to land valuation, for example), the regulations which shape the service (as in national insurance) are made by the department. Their application to individuals is a matter of assessment or interpretation. No doubt, if decisions show that these standards or regulations operate unfairly or inefficiently, the department does take notice and consider whether the principles should be modified. But the general running of the service is not directly, immediately, or radically affected by individual decisions which are, in this sense, consequential. It follows that administrative tribunals have little discretion and do not touch policy.

As we have seen, delegated legislation was attacked as being an invasion by the Executive of the functions of the Legislature. Similarly, the traditionalists attacked administrative tribunals as being an invasion by the Executive of the functions of the Judiciary. Their argument is perhaps a little stronger in this case. For administrative tribunals do determine questions often indistinguishable from the questions determined by the Judiciary. An action brought by a private person against a public authority, alleging that the authority has invaded his private rights, is likely to be defended on the ground that the authority has statutory power to do what it has done. And the argument will quickly become an argument about the precise nature and extent of this statutory power. It will become a question of statutory interpretation. And this is precisely the sort of question which the national insurance tribunals decide. Disputes on land valuation require the exercise of a judgment about assessment of loss similar to that exercised by the ordinary courts where damages are claimed. And charges against a practitioner in the National Health Service are obviously paralleled by actions for negligence.

If therefore the courts had a constitutional right to determine all these sorts of questions, the argument that they were being usurped would carry some weight. But no body or institution has any such rights. The determination that has to be made is whether, on balance, the advantages of using the courts as the instrument for decision of a particular kind of dispute are greater or less great than the disadvantages. And, conversely, whether the advantages of using administrative tribunals outweigh their disadvantages. The criteria to be thought of are the relative speed, cheapness, expertness, formality, publicity, comprehensiveness, appealability, coherence and so on, of the two systems. And it is difficult to say, looking over the whole range of administrative tribunals, that there are today any outstanding instances where the courts would, applying these criteria, perform the function better than the tribunals. The tribunals have been accepted into the system of justice and judicial decision-making to a remarkable extent by those affected, whether they be employers, employed persons, professional men and women, or private property owners or tenants. The only tribunals which came under consistent attack were the Rent Tribunals. They were peculiar in that they determined disputes, in the usual case, not between private persons and public authorities but between individual lessors and lessees. Their jurisdiction of fixing reasonable rents for lettings has been much curtailed by more recent legislation. And in their early years after 1945, the justice they administered was undoubtedly marred by procedural defects. The fact that the critical opposition came almost entirely from lessors may suggest, from one point of view, their bias or, from another point of view, their efficiency. Their job was to keep the inflation in rents (particularly of furnished lettings) within some bounds. This they succeeded in doing. They had to be numerous and they had to be speedy. For these reasons the quality of their membership was not always as high as would have been possible had they been fewer in number and more leisurely in approach.

The problems associated with administrative tribunals were extensively investigated by the Committee on Administrative Tribunals and Enquiries (chairman: Sir Oliver Franks) which reported in July 1957. The Committee made a large number of recommendations most of which were adopted by the Government and enacted in the Tribunals and Inquiries Act, 1958, and other legislation, or which were implemented by administrative action. Among the results of this investigation were the establishment of the Council on Tribunals (a general supervisory, not an appellate, body), the tightening-up of the powers of appointment and dismissal of chairmen and members of tribunals, a continuing review of the procedure of tribunals by the Council, provisions to ensure that parties should be fully informed of the issues, and the publication of reasoned decisions.

These reforms were valuable. Both because of the general good record of tribunals in the past and because of the additional safeguards against procedural misbehaviour which the Council is able to prevent or to report on, Dicey's spectre has been challenged, talked to and found not to exist.

The Council on Tribunals began shakily and its first annual report (for 1959) was a timorous and platitudinous document. Since then, however, there are many signs that the Council is beginning to find its feet, to chance its arm and to flex its muscles. Its second and third annual reports and its other public activities have greatly improved its status. So long as it manages to continue to develop its independence, particularly of the departments, and to make itself more widely known and felt, its usefulness will grow. The Council has no executive power and it is difficult to see how it could have. It is a supervisory and advisory body, with the limitations that this implies, but it could not, in any event, presume to do the work which tribunals are appointed to do; and as it gains in experience and expertise it should be more and more welcomed as a further valuable addition to the multitude of bodies standing outside the machinery of Government but charged with the duty of commenting on the way that machinery operates.

There remains however one matter where reform is immediately called for. The Committee on Administrative Tribunals and Enquiries, speaking of the right to legal representation, said: "We have no hesitation in recommending that this right should be curtailed only in the most exceptional circumstances, where it is clear that the interests of applicants generally would be better served by a restriction"[1] and this was on the basis that "many people are quite unable to present their own case coherently".[2] The Government accepted this recommendation. The Committee went on to recommend that legal aid to help meet the costs of legal representation should be extended "at once" to those tribunals which were formal and expensive, and to final appellate tribunals, and that any extension of the scheme to cover a wider range of proceedings in courts should be accompanied by an extension of the scheme to other tribunals.[3] The Government, however, refused to extend legal aid to either category of tribunals, on the ground of expense. For this there can be no justification. Legal representation is indeed, as witnesses told the Committee, "an empty concession for poor people" if not linked with legal aid. The distinction between proceedings in the county courts and in administrative tribunals is barren. In many cases, including the most numerous types of proceedings, it is merely a matter of administrative convenience that certain issues have been entrusted to tribunals, rather than to the ordinary courts. The Legal Aid scheme should be extended immediately to all administrative tribunals where legal representation is allowed.

[1] Report (Cmnd. 218) para. 87.
[2] Ibid., para. 85.
[3] Ibid., para. 89.

### THE ADMINISTRATIVE PROCESS

It is possible to mention only a few matters which fall within this considerable subject.

One aspect which has attracted much recent attention is the process which begins with a decision or proposal made by a local authority affecting the property of a private person; that person then appeals from the decision, or objects to the proposal, by informing the appropriate Minister who causes a public local inquiry to be held by one of his inspectors; the inspector at the inquiry hears the evidence of the local authority and the appellants or objectors, together with that given by other interested members of the public; he visits the site and reports to the Minister giving his summary of the arguments and adding his recommendations; the Minister, in the shape of another civil servant, makes his decision affirming, disaffirming or modifying the decision, or allows or dismisses the appeal wholly or in part.

The Committee on Administrative Tribunals and Enquiries was required to consider such procedures. As a result the law has been changed—in particular by the Compulsory Purchase by Local Authorities (Inquiries Procedure) Rules, 1962,[1] and the Town and Country Planning Appeals (Inquiries Procedure) Rules, 1962.[2] Previous practice has been improved and formalised.

The provisions of the Town and Country Planning Rules are the more elaborate. In particular, they require the local planning authority to serve on the other principal parties a written statement of the submissions which they propose to put forward at the inquiry. They require Government departments to send representatives to the inquiry where a relevant Ministerial direction has been given or the local planning authority is relying on a Ministerial view about the particular matter; and these representatives may be cross-examined, except by questions directed to the merits of Government policy. They require the deciding Minister to notify his decision to the principal parties and to send to them at the same time a summary of the inspector's conclusions and recommendations.

Decisions on compulsory purchase, planning applications and other similar matters, must be taken by the department

[1] S.I. 1962 No. 1424.
[2] S.I. 1962 No. 1425.

concerned, for questions of policy are involved which the Minister not only wishes to take but should be required to take. Proposals for the making of such decisions by independent administrative tribunals are misconceived and would enable the Minister to avoid responsibility. They would also greatly weaken him in his essential task of determining such applications of policy.

A number of particular questions is outstanding. The first relates to the disclosure of the Minister's policy at or before the local inquiry. The Committee on Administrative Tribunals and Enquiries recommended: "The deciding Minister should, wherever possible, make available before the enquiry a statement of policy relevant to the particular case, but should be free to direct that the statement be wholly or partly excluded from discussion at the enquiry".[1] This was one of the relatively few recommendations which the Government refused to accept. Yet it embodies a desirable reform for a number of reasons. Such a statement would ensure that the local inquiry was directed to the relevant issues. At the moment the appellant knows, from the statement of the local planning authority, what are its adverse views on his application. But he does not know what the Minister regards as the essential matters nor what view, if any, the Minister takes of this type of application. The application may concern the green belt, or petrol stations, or road access, or in-filling, or "white" land in a particular area, or design, or layout or any other of a number of matters. It may affect transport, or education, or location of industry, or open spaces, or a proposed new highway. All or many of these issues may be dealt with by the statement of the local planning authority. But the Minister may, and certainly should, have views which are relevant to this particular type of applicant. And these views may be different from those of the local planning authority. At present the appellant must seek to cover not only the points raised by the local planning authority but also those which he thinks *may* be in the Minister's mind. It follows that much of the proceedings at the inquiry is likely to be wholly or partly irrelevant or, at best, of greatly varying importance. And the appellant has little guide to relevance or importance. If the Minister would direct attention to the issues he thinks are relevant and important, the local inquiry would centre on those issues and much time and energy would be saved.

[1] Cmnd. 218, para. 409 (68).

Moreover, the Ministerial statement would enable the Minister himself to be more explicit about his policy. He would be required to formulate it more precisely in his own mind and it would gain greatly in coherence. Finally, the policy considerations which the inspector must be aware of when considering his recommendations would be opened to the public, so that again the real issues would be clarified.

The second question concerns the rights of the members of the public, other than the appellant and those with a direct property interest in the land. Neighbours are affected by the development of land. So are all those concerned with the preservation of the countryside and of buildings and the avoidance of substandard and ugly development. The view has been expressed that any person with an interest of this kind— or possibly any recognised organisation—should have the right to appeal against an approval given by a local planning authority, and so force a local inquiry. Such a right would, however, greatly prolong the decision-making process and increase the already considerable delays. What is needed is an opportunity for such views to be expressed to the local planning authority. In a few cases, local planning authorities are required under the existing law to publicise the fact that they have received applications and to give the public an opportunity of seeing the related plans and other documents.[1] This requirement should be made general, so that the public has the right to inspect applications in detail and make its representations to the local planning authority before the decision is made.

The third question also relates to the rights of persons other than the principal parties. The Town and Country Planning Rules have made statutory the previous practice under which the inspector exercised his discretion in deciding how far members of the public should be allowed to appear, to call evidence, and to cross-examine at the inquiry. The Rules deliberately stop short of giving any rights to such persons.[2] Such rights should be given for this purpose. There is no reason to suppose that, as a result, the number of such persons appearing at the inquiry would increase, nor that those without a proper interest would claim their right to intervene.

[1] Town and Country Planning Act, 1962, s. 15.
[2] See Report of the Council on Tribunals on the position of "third parties" at Planning Appeal Inquiries (Cmnd. 1787); and correspondence between the chairman of the Council and the Lord Chancellor, reported in (1962) Public Law at 392–4.

The Rules also empower, and in certain circumstances require, the Minister to re-open the local inquiry when he receives new evidence or takes into consideration any new issue of fact (not being a matter of Government policy) *and* is therefore disposed to disagree with a recommendation made by his inspector. Only the principal parties may require the Minister to re-open the inquiry. Should other members of the public who appeared at the inquiry also have this power? If they are denied the *right* of appearance at the inquiry, it could not be expected that they should have the power to require the Minister to re-open it. But if they were given the right of appearance, it does not follow that they should have this further power and on balance it would seem reasonable that they should not enjoy it. Nevertheless, they should be informed by the Minister of his disagreement with his inspector and given an opportunity of making written representations.

Under the present law, only the principal parties have the status of "persons aggrieved" for the purpose of challenging a Ministerial decision or order in the High Court.[1] If other persons were given the right of appearance at the inquiry, it does not necessarily follow that they should be able to invoke the aid of the courts at a later stage. The grounds of challenge are limited to substantive or procedural *ultra vires*.[2] It is suggested that such persons should be regarded as persons aggrieved for the purpose of being able to challenge the Minister on the procedural ground only, in which case it would be necessary to show "that the interests of the applicant have been substantially prejudiced by a failure to comply with any of the relevant requirements".[3]

Finally, the Committee on Administrative Tribunals and Enquiries recommended that the Minister should delegate to inspectors the power of decision "in cases in which departmental policy was non-existent or of little importance".[4] The Government did not accept this recommendation. Yet with one further safeguard it seems both feasible and sensible. The inspector is aware of departmental policy so far as it has been made explicit. In the smaller cases he is the person best qualified to decide. In only about two per cent. of all the cases, large and

---

[1] *Buxton* v. *Minister of Housing and Local Government* [1960] 3 W.L.R. 866.
[2] Town and Country Planning Act, 1962, s. 179.
[3] Section 179 (4) (b).
[4] Cmnd. 218, para. 393.

small, does the Minister in practice disagree with his inspector's recommendation. The delegation should be made whenever it is thought by the department that no policy issues on which the inspector is not briefed are likely to arise. And the additional safeguard should be that the inspector be required to ask the Minister to revoke the delegation whenever, in the course of the inquiry, it appears to the inspector that issues are raised which involve policy questions substantially wider than those anticipated.

### FREEDOM OF SPEECH

Freedom of speech in the context of constitutional and administrative law means above all freedom to criticise the proposals and activities of public authorities whether they be legislative, executive or judicial. And there is reason to be alarmed at the growth of the restraints on this freedom.

On 4 June, 1962, Mr. Cecil H. King made his annual statement as chairman of the Sunday Pictorial Newspapers.[1] He said of the freedom of the Press: "In the last century this was a real freedom and a prized possession of the British people. Even to this day it is common for speakers to dilate on the freedom of our Press compared to the censorship in other lands. These claims are entirely unfounded. The British Press is as censored as most censored presses, though in an arbitrary and indeterminate way." He referred to libel, breaches of parliamentary privilege, breaches of the Official Secrets Acts and contempt of court. "The actual operation of the rules against contempt of court," said Mr. King, "has meant that of recent years no serious criticism of judicial proceedings above the level of magistrates' courts has been thought to be possible. In fact there has been little or no such criticism, though a good deal from time to time would have been in the public interest. As judicial proceedings are not criticized in the House of Commons, this means that there is no criticism of proceedings in the higher courts."

"Contempt of court" covers many offences,[2] but discussion is limited here to criticism of judges and other comment on their decisions. The Report by Justice referred to below said:

"In our view, for an act to amount to contempt of court it

---

[1] See also the annual report of the General Council of the Press (pub. Dec. 1962).
[2] See the Report by Justice: *Contempt of Court* (1959).

should not be sufficient only to establish that it has some tendency to prejudice justice. To allow conduct which might possibly prejudice the administration of justice may be desirable in the public interest from other points of view. A common example is where the subject-matter of litigation has been pronounced upon by the Court of Appeal and is on its way to the House of Lords, but is likely to be the subject of legislation meanwhile. In such cases, newspaper editors, we are informed, have refrained from publishing letters on the subject on the ground that it is *sub judice*. If, indeed, it is a contempt of court publicly to discuss such a matter, we consider that an unwarrantable shackle on that freedom of public discussion which is essential to the legislative process of a democratic country. It appears to us desirable, in considering whether such an act is contempt, to balance, on the one hand, the effect it might have on the litigation and, on the other, the interest of the nation in free discussion. Similarly, in the case of criticism of a judge, the element of scandalising justice should, in our view, be weighed against the benefits of free discussion and comment."[1]

Once a court has reached a decision, comment and criticism should be free and without fear of proceedings for contempt, whether or not the decision is appealable. The criticism might be directed against the substance of the decision, the social or political assumptions of the law or the decision, the competence of the judge or other like matters. The Report by Justice would deny the right of the Press to allege partiality or corruption on the part of a judge.[2] Further it proposes that if a private person wishes to make this allegation, he should write to the Lord Chancellor or his Member of Parliament and the charge could then be considered either administratively or in the House of Commons or the House of Lords. This limitation on the freedom of the Press is difficult to justify. At the same time, judges must be protected against the possibility of unfounded allegations in the Press that they are corrupt or partial. A remedy could be devised by a specific statutory extension of the law of criminal libel on a complaint being made by a judge to the Lord Chancellor, who could then ensure, if he thought fit, that proceedings were instituted.

There is no reason to suppose that the status of judges would be adversely affected if decisions were open to criticism. Their

[1] p. 6.
[2] p. 15.

power is great and should not be diminished. But because their power is great, it should not be immune from comment and criticism in the Press or elsewhere.

Mr. King also attacked the administration of the Official Secrets Acts which he said were "now used quite cynically, to protect the reputation of Ministers and, above all, of civil servants". And of D Notices he said : "the system comforts only those, it seems to me, who require secrecy as a cloak for their blunders". Here the overstatement for effect is somewhat self-defeating. There is a security problem of real and large dimensions. And the publication of certain information obviously cannot be tolerated by any Government which has, as one of its traditional functions, the safety of the realm to protect. It may be true that the Official Secrets Acts are used not only for purposes beyond their original intention but also for petty purposes. But the problem of reform, so as to restrict those purposes to what is necessary for security, is not capable of solution by the use of different statutory language. The power must be there and must be wide. Wide powers may always be more easily abused in their exercise. But to narrow the powers would also result in preventing action which, by common accord, is necessary. This is the central difficulty of discretionary power and it cannot be removed.

The same argument applies to D Notices which are formal letters of request, issued on the authority of the Services Press and Broadcasting Committee at the Ministry of Defence and circulated confidentially to newspaper editors and others. They advise editors that an item of news, which may be protected under the Official Secrets Acts, is regarded as a secret of importance, the publication of which is contrary to the national interest.[1] D Notices have no legal force and rest on the willingness of editors to co-operate, backed by the possibility of prosecution. They are sometimes criticised for their generality and where they are less precise than is really necessary for their purpose, this is clearly an important fault. But again, proposals for particular reform are difficult to formulate because no form of words will exclude what should be excluded without the certainty of also excluding what should not, in other circumstances, be excluded. The Radcliffe Committee made certain suggestions for the improvement of the *system*, but no new legal

---

[1] See *Security Procedures in the Public Service* (Cmnd. 1681) ch. 9 (Report of the Radcliffe Committee) ; and Comment by G.M., [1961] Public Law 225.

or statutory provisions could operate satisfactorily to control the content of D Notices.

There can be no doubt that much of the law relating to security ought to be reviewed and it is suggested that the question should be referred to an *ad hoc* committee, including both lawyers and persons with extensive administrative experience. The Official Secrets Act, 1911, is an unsatisfactory piece of legislation.[1] The needs of security must be met. But some check must be devised to make it more difficult for departments to use these needs to prevent the publication of information which might be embarrassing or inconvenient on other grounds. Surely Her Majesty's judges may be entrusted to exercise a proper controlling discretion. If new legislation were to make clear that security is the only basis for this type of case, judges (if necessary, a specially nominated group) could with safety be empowered to decide, on papers produced to them *in camera*, whether a *prima facie* case, on security grounds, had been made out by the public authorities concerned. Such a limited amount of controlling discretion might not satisfy Mr. King. And it would no doubt be relatively easy for the Crown, in the great majority of cases, to prove its *prima facie* case. But at least some safeguard would be introduced, the very existence of which might deter the public authorities from making more extreme claims.

A similar problem arises when the Crown refuses to disclose documents in the course of litigation. Here the basis of the Crown's claim is that publication would be injurious to the public interest. And it is suggested that the remedy for the control of this at present unfettered discretion (except in Scotland) is to require the Crown to persuade the judge hearing the case that there is evidence on which a *prima facie* case could be made out.

It is improbable that judges would be found to be so blind to the needs of security or of protecting the public interest that the Queen's government could not be carried on if they exercised these powers.

Finally, Mr. Cecil King said: "The operation of the libel laws is even more serious. Judges and juries are increasingly inclined to regard any criticism as defamation and to award damages out of all relation to any harm done. The trouble here is not that newspapers do commit libels and do pay heavy

[1] See, for example, *Chandler* v. *D.P.P.* [1962] 3 All E.R. 142.

damages, though that happens on occasion. The damage is done by the omission of reports or the watering down of reports that should have been printed. We have now reached a point where strictures on a provincial police force will produce a libel action from the chief constable, which he will probably win. Criticism of a hospital's management will bring a libel action from the matron or the medical staff or both. The paper may be in possession of plenty of evidence to support its claims, but too often in this kind of case witnesses are unwilling to go into the box, or, if they are subpoenaed, suffer from lapses of memory. Criticism in such spheres is gradually being confined to comment on circumstances that have been revealed in Parliament or in court, which enjoy privilege."

It will not do to dismiss these comments by the chairman of a group of newspapers on the ground of self-interest. Nor can they be disposed of as being overstatements. Perhaps he does protest too much. Perhaps also he weakens his case by not putting the other side—which is that the individual members of the public need protection against Press mis-statements or falsehoods which can do great damage and the retraction of which does not wipe clean the impression already created. Nevertheless his criticisms remain valid to this extent: that the suspicion of incompetence, of negligence, sometimes of corruption itself is increased, often without cause, because of the stifling of criticism.

The present state of the law of libel and of contempt of court demands reform much more in the public than in the private sphere of life. Freer criticism of public affairs, of persons in public life for their public acts, of public institutions, is the need. The parliamentary forum is, once again, not wide enough for this purpose. Any person or body in positions of public authority or public power, whether a Minister of the Crown or a local authority or a public company or a trade union, should expect to receive outspoken criticism as the price of its authority and power. And the bodies controlling mass media—broadcasting and the Press—must themselves not be too sensitive to the sort of attack which they wish to administer.

We need a double standard: one, which the present law is adequate to uphold, for the protection of private persons against damaging and unfounded criticism of their private lives; and another, much less rigorous, for the protection of public institutions and of persons in their official capacities. For defamation of the latter it should be necessary for the plaintiff to show that the defendant had knowledge of the untruth of his allegations or was reckless whether they were true or false or was actuated by personal malice (spite or illwill).

## JUDICIAL REVIEW

The courts exert political power for which they are not accountable to any outside body. And, within ill-defined limits, they determine the scope of this power. We speak of the courts extending their remedies, abdicating their responsibilities, creating their own standards or effectively nullifying statutory provisions. Any reform of the area of the courts' jurisdiction must be based on opinion of the role they are fitted for and ought to perform.

The question we are seeking to isolate and to answer is: on what grounds and for what purposes should the courts be able to control the decisions or actions of public authorities?

The powers we are considering are almost wholly statutory in origin and we will disregard those based on the prerogative. Statutory powers are special, bestowed on public authorities to enable them to act in ways which would be beyond the competence of legal persons exercising their ordinary common law rights. They include powers to tax, to acquire land compulsorily, to decide disputes, to licence, to inspect, to grant and withhold permissions, and to do much else besides. The powers are limited and some body must be able to declare what those limits are. If a public authority goes beyond those limits its action is *ultra vires* and, generally, invalid. An authority may act *ultra vires* in a narrow sense, if it deals with a subject matter outside its competence—as, for example, a furnished houses rent tribunal fixing the rent of an unfurnished house, or a local authority acting as a bank or as a retailer of goods.

Adjectival limitations are often made on the power of public authorities. A local authority has power to fix "reasonable rents" or to pay "reasonable wages". In such cases some body other than the authority must exist to determine whether the standard—however imprecise—has been conformed to. Similarly, specific procedural requirements are often stated in Acts of Parliament: publicity in the local Press, the service of notices, the holding of an inquiry. Again it is necessary that some body should decide whether these requirements have been fulfilled and what is the consequence, if this is not spelled out, of the failure to fulfil.

The rule of law, in the precise and legal sense, must operate in these circumstances. Discretionary powers are necessary and desirable. But public authorities must be restrained to the limits of their given powers. This is most certainly the proper function of the courts. Here their independence and their political irresponsibility are positive advantages. No doubt the courts will, from time to time, hand down decisions which appear foolish or even politically or socially biased. But although, as we have argued above, criticism of such decisions should be much more free than at present, it is idle to ask for perfection from human judgment and impossible to attain universal recognition of what that perfection is. In this matter each of us, Her Majesty's judges no less, has different views of the way in which particular powers should be interpreted in the personal conflict between social justice and the rights of the individual. And the "proper" answer to the question whether the Housing Act, 1936, did or did not empower a local authority to make a closing order on a whole house is not discoverable.[1]

It is when we leave this more limited area of *ultra vires* that the real difficulties arise. We do not expect the courts to decide on the basis of their political, economic or social wisdom. This, we say, is for Parliament to decide. And only rarely do the courts openly show that they have been influenced by such considerations. Nor do judges consciously permit their personal political, economic, social, religious or other views to determine the way they exercise their judgment.

But where the grounds for judicial intervention are imprecise, judges are forced to make choices and to attempt to demarcate both the nature and the extent of their own powers.

We have already noted that where a statute expressly imports a standard, the courts must make what they can of it. But where there is no express provision, the courts nevertheless, on occasion, import their own standards which they then interpret. The most familiar of such importations in administrative law are the rules of natural justice that the courts have applied to all procedures which, in their opinion (a second importation), are judicial or quasi-judicial, and not administrative, in character. This latter classification, as is well-known, has led them into anomalies. The definition of judicial or quasi-

[1] See *Birch* v. *Wigan Corporation* [1953] 1 Q.B. 136.

judicial has been extended to the issuing of a certificate by a medical practitioner,[1] the proceedings of a Legal Aid Committee,[2] the consideration of a scheme for the re-organisation of electricity supply,[3] the giving of licences for the Sunday opening of cinemas,[4] the hearing of a town planning application.[5] But the definition has not been extended to a textile controller revoking a dealer's licence,[6] a police commissioner revoking a cab driver's licence,[7] nor to a chief fire officer exercising disciplinary authority over a fireman.[8] So also the courts do not regard any part of the negotiations or discussions between local authorities and central departments which precede the making of a statutory objection to a proposed order as quasi-judicial and so subject to the rules.[9]

Again the courts are willing, in certain circumstances, to insist that powers should be exercised "reasonably" although this word does not appear in the statute. If what is challenged is a local authority bye-law, the statement of reasonableness may always be invoked. But if, at the other extreme, what is challenged is the exercise of a wide discretionary power by a public authority, the courts will be more reluctant to intervene.[10] Between these two types of case lies a large and ill-defined area.

Abuse of discretion is also vague as a ground of challenge. Allegations of corruption are generally listened to by the courts with traditional sympathy. And it had been thought, until recently, that the courts would also do all they could to extend their jurisdiction if the allegation was of bad faith. But in *Smith* v. *East Elloe Rural District Council*,[11] the House of Lords (or some of its members) bowed down with unprecedented servility before a statutory provision which they chose to interpret as excluding judicial intervention. Improper purpose is another ground on which the courts may be persuaded to quash the

---

[1] *R.* v. *Postmaster-General* [1928] 1 K.B. 291.

[2] *R.* v. *Manchester Legal Aid Committee* [1952] 2. Q.B. 413.

[3] *R.* v. *Electricity Commissioners* [1924] 1 K.B. 171.

[4] *R.* v. *L.C.C.* [1931] 2 K.B. 215.

[5] *R.* v. *Hendon R.D.C.* [1933] 2 K.B. 696.

[6] *Nakkuda Ali* v. *Jayaratne* [1951] A.C. 66.

[7] *R.* v. *Metropolitan Police Commissioner* [1953] 1 W.L.R. 1150.

[8] *Ex parte Fry* (Lord Goddard C.J.); upheld on different grounds by Court of Appeal [1954] 1 W.L.R. 730.

[9] *Frost* v. *Minister of Health* [1935] 1 K.B. 286 and other cases.

[10] *Associated Provincial Picture Theatres Ltd.* v. *Wednesbury Corporation* [1948] 1 K.B. 223.

[11] [1956] A.C. 736.

decision or action of a public authority. It may overlap bad
faith, but it also covers innocent though mistaken belief that
what was done was part of what Parliament intended should be
done. Recently, in *Prescott* v. *Birmingham Corporation*,[1] the Court
of Appeal, at the instance of a ratepayer, declared invalid and
*ultra vires* a scheme proposed by the City Council of Birmingham
to provide free travel on the corporation's omnibuses for certain
classes of old people, although the licensing authorities had
approved it as being reasonable and although the statutory
provisions empowered the corporation to charge such fares as
it thought fit. The Court held that the corporation owed a
fiduciary duty to its ratepayers analogous to that owed by a
trustee. "Local authorities," said the Court, "running an
omnibus undertaking at the risk of the ratepayers, in the sense
that any deficiencies must be met by an addition to the rates,
are not, in our view, entitled, merely on the strength of a
general power, to charge different fares to different passengers,
or classes of passengers, to make a gift to a particular class of
persons of rights of free travel on their vehicles, simply because
the local authority concerned are of opinion that the favoured
class of persons ought, on benevolent or philanthropic grounds,
to be accorded that benefit."

This decision is a striking example of the willingness of the
courts to set aside the exercise of a discretionary power of a
local authority on relatively novel grounds. And it contrasts
markedly with the reluctance of the House of Lords to intervene
in *Smith* v. *East Elloe* (above).

Very rarely have the courts been willing to review a discretionary power said to be exercisable "if the Minister is
satisfied". What the Minister has to be satisfied about is either
the existence of a factual situation (e.g. "land shown to his
satisfaction to have sustained war damage"[2]) or the wisdom of
a course of action (e.g. "if the Minister is satisfied that it is
expedient in the national interest that any area of land should
be developed"[3]). The expression of the Minister's satisfaction
is regarded by the courts as conclusive and they will not allow
evidence to be called to show that he could not have been
satisfied.

One other example is the relationship of the courts to

[1] [1955] Ch. 210.
[2] Town and Country Planning Act, 1944, s. 1.
[3] New Towns Act, 1946, s. 1.

administrative tribunals. Until the passing of the Tribunals and Inquires Act, 1958, the control of the courts was largely by means of the prerogative orders of *certiorari*, prohibition or *mandamus*. This meant that the courts would quash for excess of jurisdiction, for breach of the rules of natural justice or for errors of law appearing on the face of the record (which in practice meant reasoned interpretations of statutory provisions). Under the Act of 1958, the courts may now, in addition, quash for errors of law (interpretations) not appearing on the face of the record, and for gross inadequacy of evidence.[1]

These are the principal areas of conflict between the Courts and public authorities. What reforms are called for? In the first place, where a public authority is given an unfettered discretion, the courts should not review on the ground that the exercise is unreasonable. In such a case, to say that a public authority has acted "unreasonably" is to discard one criterion and to use another. Even the remote possibility envisaged in the *Wednesbury Case* should be denied. Similarly, the *Prescott* v. *Birmingham Corporation* type of case should be excluded from the courts. The courts are right in refusing to question the expression of the Minister's satisfaction in those cases where the wisdom of a course of action would have to be debated. It is also very doubtful whether there should be a right of appeal from an administrative tribunal to the courts on the ground that the tribunal has misinterpreted a statutory provision not going to jurisdiction. It would be better if the tribunal structure were so designed that such questions were determined, within that structure, by a legally qualified person or tribunal.

On the other hand, statutory provisions should never be allowed to exclude judicial review on the ground of corruption or bad faith or wherever it is suggested that the public authority was deliberately using its powers with an ulterior motive. One reason why in practice the courts have sometimes leant against intervention has been that to quash would be to upset extensive schemes of public authorities, to delay desirable reforms, and to throw those authorities into a state of the greatest uncertainty. But the remedy is to hand. If to quash an order, or a decision, or to nullify an action, would cause such

[1] Under s. 11(3) of the Act of 1958 the powers of the Secretary of State under s. 26 of the British Nationality Act, 1948, and the determinations of the Foreign Compensation Commission are excluded from the operation of *certiorari* and *mandamus*. There seems to be no justification for these exceptions to the general principle and this subsection should to this extent be repealed.

chaos (or, indeed, even if it would cause only much administrative inconvenience) then the remedy should be in damages, leaving the administrative activity, in this legal sense, unimpaired. Again, where the Minister must be "satisfied" of the existence of a state of facts before he can act, he should be required to produce evidence on which, in the court's view, he could have been so satisfied. Such evidence would not need to be substantial but it would need to be significant.

Finally, the courts should curb their present enthusiasm for exercising a discretion whether or not to give a remedy when they have found which side is supported by the facts and the law. Their emphasis today on the discretionary nature of the remedies of the prerogative orders and the declaratory judgment is introducing a further element of uncertainty into a part of the law already uncertain. Some discretions they must retain—it cannot always be clear, for example, whether damages will suffice or whether a declaration is necessary—and it is difficult to lay down any firm rules. But more judicial self-discipline and self-limitation are necessary so that the rights of individuals are not obscured further by the introduction of an ambiguity and uncertainty on the bench. *Ubi ius, ibi remedium.*

### ALIENS AND COMMONWEALTH IMMIGRANTS

The control exercised over aliens under the Aliens Order, 1953,[1] is twofold. The first control forbids an alien from landing, except with the leave[2] of an immigration officer (who must normally withhold leave if the alien cannot support himself, has been sentenced abroad for an extradition crime, is of unsound mind or mentally defective or if a medical inspector certifies that it is undesirable for medical reasons that he should land). Under the second control, the Secretary of State may make deportation orders either after a court certificate and recommendation or where he "deems it to be conducive to the public good to make a deportation order against the alien".

Refusal of leave to land and the power to deport are,

---

[1] S.I. 1953 No. 1671, as amended by S.I. 1957 No. 597.

[2] For a consideration of the phrase "leave to land" see *R.* v. *Secretary of State for Home Affairs ex parte Soblen* [1962] 3 All E.R. 373; the facts show how the very wide discretionary powers of immigration officers can be used, in certain circumstances, to "deport" an alien convicted of a political crime which is not an extradition crime, not only *from* this country but *to* the country where he had been convicted.

similarly, the basic controls introduced by the Commonwealth Immigrants Act, 1962.

Part I of the Act of 1962 specifies two groups of persons who are not subject to the restrictions on entry. They are those born in the United Kingdom, and citizens of the U.K. and Colonies holding U.K. passports issued by Her Majesty's Government in the U.K. All other Commonwealth citizens, British-protected persons and citizens of the Republic of Ireland are affected by this Part of the Act. Returning residents, their wives and children are admitted without question provided they are not subject to a deportation order. Immigrants seeking employment in the United Kingdom must be in possession of a voucher from the Ministry of Labour. Students prepared to devote the whole or a substantial part of their time to their courses may enter. So may those who can support themselves and their dependants without taking work in the U.K. Except for returning residents, an immigration officer may refuse admission on medical grounds or because he has reason to believe a person has been convicted of an extradition crime or because, in the opinion of the Secretary of State, there are security grounds for refusal.

Under Part II of the Act of 1962, certain Commonwealth citizens may be deported if they are "convicted of offences punishable with imprisonment and recommended by the court for deportation". Ministers in Parliament gave assurances that the power to deport would be used only where the offence was serious and other circumstances of the offender made deportation "absolutely necessary".[1]

To the constitutional or administrative lawyer the outstanding characteristic of these provisions affecting aliens and Commonwealth immigrants is the wide discretionary power vested in Ministers and civil servants (including immigration officers), the way in which this power is exercised, the extent to which it reduces personal freedom and, therefore, its justification. Where leave to land is refused or a deportation order is made, opportunities for challenging the legal validity of the action are very limited.

There are three principal types of discretionary power exercised by immigration officers under the Act of 1962. Under the first, the onus is placed on the entrant to "satisfy" the

---

[1] See on this, and generally, C. Thornberry: "Law, Opinion and the Immigrant" in (1962) 25 Mod.L.R. 654.

officer that he or his wife or children are returning residents of the U.K.; that he wishes to enter the U.K. for employment (and is the person described in the Ministry of Labour voucher); or that he is a student or a self-supporting visitor. Under the second, permission to enter may be refused "if it appears to the immigration officer" on medical advice that the entrant is undesirable on medical grounds. Under the third, permission to enter may be refused "if the immigration officer has reason to believe" that the entrant has been convicted of an extradition crime.

The existing case law on phrases like those used in the first two of these types of power consistently shows the extreme reluctance of the courts to question whether the person exercising the power was or could have been "satisfied"; or whether some thing appeared or could have appeared to him. The courts will not review the decision of a Secretary of State who deemed it to be conducive to the public good to make a deportation order against an alien.[1] If an immigration officer refuses admission to a Commonwealth immigrant on the ground that he has "reason to believe" the immigrant has been convicted of an extradition crime, would a court listen to evidence to show that the immigrant had not been so convicted? In *Liversidge* v. *Anderson*,[2] the House of Lords declined to require the Secretary of State to show what was his "reasonable cause to believe", and although that decision has been much doubted by subsequent judicial and other comment, "reason to believe" may prove to be a weaker basis on which to construct a challenge.

Through this complicated group of provisions there run two dissimilar criteria for action: those of fact and of policy. The policy today on the giving of leave to aliens to enter seems to be that permission should be given unless a particular alien looks like being a bad economic, security or health risk, or has been convicted of an extradition crime. The policy has to be administered according to the facts of each case. The position for Commonwealth immigrants is the same, with one important exception: the fear of the consequences of mass entry. Whether this fear is well-based is much argued, but, accepting the purpose of the Act of 1962, the limitation on gross numbers to

---

[1] *Ex parte Venicoff* [1920] 3 K.B. 78; and *Ex parte Duke of Chateau Thierry* [1917] 1 K.B. 922.

[2] [1942] A.C. 206.

be annually admitted (if this proved to be necessary) could be effected only by some sort of quota system. With this we are not here concerned. We are concerned with the powers of Ministers and civil servants to refuse individuals leave to land when they present themselves.

The individual factual problems under the Act of 1962 are of two kinds. The first is technically, perhaps, a mixed question of fact and law. Into what category falls a person presenting himself for admission? For example, is he a native of the U.K., or a returning resident, or one seeking employment, or a student, or a self-supporting visitor? The second is whether he is medically undesirable, has been convicted of an extradition crime, is a bad security risk. Comparable questions arise when aliens seek admission.

If we except the security risk, it is suggested that none of these questions should be decided finally by the determination of civil servants or Ministers; and that some review of decisions is essential. These are the sort of questions most obviously suited for appeal to administrative tribunals, as they do not involve, in the individual case, any element of policy. The Act provides the rules, sets the policy. The implementation of the policy is made by the interpretation of those rules and their application to individual cases. Mr. Thornberry has drawn attention to the immigration boards under the Aliens Act, 1905,[1] and to the contemporary criticism of their working. But we have learnt a little about such bodies in the last fifty years. The problem is sufficiently important in principle to apply the pattern of the national insurance tribunals, with a local appellate body having a legal chairman and two lay members, and above these bodies, a final tribunal of the status of the National Insurance Commissioner. The proposal should be referred forthwith to the Council on Tribunals for their consideration.

Security risks remain. It should be made necessary for the Secretary of State to persuade a nominated judge of the High Court, *in camera*, that there are *prima facie* grounds for concluding that the risk exists in the individual case.

The power to deport aliens is in the hands of the Secretary of State although there is normally a right to a hearing before the Chief Metropolitan Magistrate, who advises the Minister. This procedure is not applicable where a deportation order has been made on the grounds of national security or where the alien

---

[1] *Op. cit.* at 607, note 74.

landed in the U.K. without permission, or, having been in the U.K. less than two years, has failed to observe conditions attaching to his stay. The Secretary of State may, as we have seen, deport aliens either on the recommendation of a court or because he believes to do so would be conducive to the public good. He may deport Commonwealth immigrants under the Act of 1962 only on the recommendation of a court. In both cases the court may recommend deportation only after conviction of an offence punishable with imprisonment. The number of recommendations for aliens has been about 100 every year; but for Commonwealth immigrants, during the first three months of the operation of the Act of 1962, the number was 125[1] and there was much parliamentary protest at the proposal to deport Miss Carmen Bryan convicted of a first offence of shoplifting.[2] Deportation is so serious a punishment, and may so easily punish the innocent members of a family as well as the guilty, that it should be reserved only for the most exceptional case. It is suggested that the power to recommend should be reserved to judges of the High Court and that any inferior court, believing deportation to be the proper course, should be obliged to remit that aspect of the case to a nominated judge of the High Court. It is further suggested that this should apply to aliens as well as to Commonwealth immigrants and should cover all cases. Finally it is suggested that before the Secretary of State makes a deportation order on an alien, otherwise than on the recommendation of a court, he should be obliged to make out a *prima facie* case, if necessary *in camera*, to a High Court judge.

---

[1] Thornberry *op. cit.* at 669.
[2] 663 H.C. Deb. 1018–44 (23 July 1962).

# IV

# THE LAW OF CONTRACT AND TORT

## CONTRACTS

THE LAW OF CONTRACT is concerned with promises and agreements—can they be enforced in the courts and, if so, how? Like much of English law, it has grown up over the centuries as a result of decisions in the courts. As a particular dispute arises between two individuals, a judge has to decide the dispute: he is concerned more with doing justice between the parties to the case in accordance with established ideas than with developing a coherent body of principles. The result is that there is no underlying philosophy of the law of contract. We have a mass of rules, but lawyers are not at all sure just what the fundamental objects of this branch of the law are.

Nineteenth century lawyers had fewer doubts. A great judge, Sir George Jessel, could say in 1875:

> "If there is one thing which more than another public policy requires, it is that men of full age and competent understanding shall have the utmost liberty of contracting, and that their contracts when entered into freely and voluntarily shall be held sacred and shall be enforced by courts of justice."[1]

We cannot, today, accept this strident declaration of *laissez-faire*. We do not believe that because two parties agree on a form of words the law has no alternative but to enforce those words literally. For centuries the courts have refused to enforce contracts on the ground that they involve some illegality, or immorality, or are for some other reason "against public policy" or against the policy of the law. For over a century the courts have intervened to relieve a person of liability when something unforeseen has left the contract without purpose or function. For several centuries the law, in the guise of "equity", has intervened to restrain the literal enforcement of transactions

[1] *Printing and Numerical Registering Co.* v. *Sampson* (1875) L.R. 19 Eq. 462, at p. 465.

such as mortgages. And under the Restrictive Trade Practices
Act of 1956 a court has been enabled to declare a contract
void for economic considerations, on the ground that it is against
the public interest.

### Standard Forms

There has been growing concern in the legal profession over
what have become known as "standard-form contracts". These
are forms of words prepared by one party—usually the supplier
of goods and services—which the other party—usually the
customer or the consumer—has no option but to accept if he
wants to deal with the supplier at all. Sometimes the contract
is signed, as where an order form is signed for a car, or a hire-
purchase agreement is entered into, or a mortgage to buy a
house is obtained, or arrangements are made to take a supply
of gas or electricity. Sometimes the conditions are contained
in a ticket, such as a railway ticket, or a cloakroom ticket. Sometimes the terms of a contract are simply contained in a notice
exhibited on the wall, like signs in garages or hotels disclaiming
liability for loss or damage to cars or luggage.

All these situations have this in common: the party proposing
the form of words has prepared them in advance, usually at
leisure, often with legal advice, and all too often thinking only
of his own interests. The other party—the consumer—is
presented with them, and there is no question of negotiation
as to the precise form of words or the legal liabilities and
immunities which they represent—indeed, often the consumer
has no idea that a contract affecting his legal rights is being
entered into.

The detailed questions of consumer protection when buying
goods, or taking them on hire purchase, will be considered later,
in the chapter dealing with commercial law.[1] Here we are
concerned with general principles: and we think the law should
recognise as a general principle that where there is no equality
of bargaining power or opportunity of negotiation it is idle to
talk of "freedom of contract". The policy of the law should not
be to enforce a detailed form of words contained in a printed
document, such as a ticket, but to see that the reasonable
expectations of both parties are fulfilled. The law (or, technically, that branch of it known as equity) has managed very well
to control harsh words contained, for example, in mortgages of

[1] See p. 150 and ff., *infra*.

land or houses. A similar spirit should pervade the whole law of contract.

A particularly unsatisfactory feature of the present law is the way in which detailed conditions can be incorporated into a contract by reference, when no reasonable layman—or, indeed, very few reasonable lawyers—could discover the conditions. The principle is said to be that reasonable steps must be taken to draw the conditions to the other party's attention. But this requirement has been satisfied where a passenger bought a railway ticket which referred to the timetable, which cost 6d. to buy. Included in the timetable were the conditions of carriage covering many pages, and it was held that the passenger was bound by all these conditions. There is much to be said for the precedent established by the Hire-Purchase Act of 1938, which stipulated that certain conditions in hire-purchase agreements would only be effective if the consumer's attention was drawn to them before he signed the agreement, and their effect made clear to him. Since "The Reform of the Law" was published, the railway passenger has received considerable protection by the establishment of the Passenger Charges Scheme of the British Transport Commission, which had been approved by the Transport Tribunal and which had eliminated some of the worst features of standard-form contracts. The Transport Act, 1962, continues this policy. This example could be followed in many different fields, steps being taken to ensure that standard-form contracts have been vetted as reasonable in the consumer's interests.

Under the general law, a person who enters into a contract must carry it out and in many circumstances a person who is negligent—that is, who fails to take reasonable care in what he is doing—is liable to compensate the other party for all loss caused by his negligence. The law does not regard it as unreasonable to attempt to contract out of liability for negligence. We think that as a general principle it should not be possible to contract out of liability for negligence, and that only in exceptional circumstances should this be permitted.

### Consideration

Another field where the lack of any underlying philosophy has led to technicality and, often, injustice, is the need for what is known as "consideration". Briefly, this means that one-sided or gratuitous promises—a promise to give a present, or a donation to a charitable fund, for example—will not be enforced in the courts. Sir Frederick Pollock described consideration as the price paid for a promise: it may literally be a price, as in a shop where the consideration for the purchase of goods is the price paid by the customer, or it may itself be an act, or even a promise (e.g. "in consideration of your promise to make me a suit, I promise to paint your house").

The doctrine of consideration has been defended as the embodiment in the English law of contract of the idea of "bargain". The basis of the law, it is said, is not the enforcement of promises but the enforcement of bargains. Gratuitous promises can be made enforceable by incorporating them in documents under seal, which for historical reasons do not require consideration. We are not concerned here to argue the virtues of a concept of contract based on bargain as opposed to one based on promise. Suffice it to say that insistence on consideration has led to results which, we think, tend to bring the law into disrepute.

Situations where the need for consideration works injustice, or defeats reasonable expectations, are not difficult to find. For example, a creditor's agreement to take a smaller amount than is owed from a debtor in settlement is an agreement not supported by consideration. In 1602 it was clearly established in *Pinnel's Case*[1] that payment of a lesser sum cannot be satisfaction for a greater sum owed, but that if anything, however trivial, is given in addition to or instead of the lesser sum, it can be good satisfaction. In 1881 Sir George Jessel said of this rule, in the case of *Couldery* v. *Bartrum*:[2] "According to English common law a creditor might accept anything in satisfaction of his debt except a less amount of money. He might take a horse, or a canary, or a tomtit if he chose, and that was accord and satisfaction; but, by a most extraordinary peculiarity of the English common law, he could not take 19s. 6d. in the pound."

There are a number of ways round this technical rule. For example, it seems to be well established that a composition with creditors is binding. As Sir George Jessel put it in the same case: "As every debtor had not a stock of canary-birds or tomtits, or rubbish of that kind, to add to his dividend, it was felt to be desirable to bind the creditors in a sensible way." Nevertheless, it is clear that the law does not reflect the practice of

[1] (1602) 5 Co. Rep. 117a.
[2] (1881) 19 Ch. D. 394.

businessmen, who regard an agreement to accept less as a valuable incentive to payment, nor does it accord with the reasonable expectations of the parties.

Another unsatisfactory aspect of the doctrine of consideration is in relation to options. If $A$ gives $B$ the option on his car for seven days, there is nothing to stop $A$ revoking the option within the seven days. The reason for this is that the option is a mere offer to sell the car, accompanied by a promise not to revoke the offer for seven days. Under the general law an offer may be revoked at any time before it is accepted, and unless the promise to keep the offer open for seven days is itself an enforceable contract, supported by independent consideration, it is unenforceable.

In 1937 the Law Revision Committee under the chairman-ship of Lord Wright presented an authoritative report on the doctrine of consideration.[1] Many members of that committee would have liked to see the doctrine abolished root and branch, but hesitated to recommend this because of the suspicion and hostility which such a proposal would arouse. We believe that our law would benefit tremendously if it fell into line with the law of France and of Germany, and of many other European countries (including Scotland), and did away with the whole notion of consideration. If such a proposal is thought to be too revolutionary, we have no doubt that the positive recommenda-tions of the 1937 Committee should be adopted and that the following types of agreement should all be enforceable without proof of consideration:

(1) Promises made in writing.
(2) Agreements to accept a lesser sum in discharge of an obligation to pay a larger sum.
(3) Agreements to keep an offer open for a definite period of time.
(4) Promises made in consideration of the other party doing or promising to do something which he is already bound to do.
(5) Agreements supported by past consideration.
(6) Promises which the promisor knows, or reasonably should know, will be relied on by the promisee, if the promisee has altered his position to his detriment in reliance on the promise.

[1] Sixth Interim Report of the Law Revision Committee, Cmd. 5449.

The Committee also recommended that a promise made in consideration of the promisee performing an act should constitute a contract as soon as the promisee had entered upon a performance of the act, unless the promise included, expressly or by implication, a term that it could be revoked before the act had been completed. Under the present law a promise given in consideration of the doing of an act does not become binding until the act is completely performed. Thus if *A* promises *B* £50 if he walks from London to York in three days, *A* can probably withdraw his promise at any time before *B* has actually arrived at York.

All these recommendations, if adopted, would go far to mitigate the injustices of the present law.

### Privity of Contract

The Law Revision Committee, in the report above referred to, also considered the doctrine of privity of contract. It stated: "The common law of England stands alone among modern systems of law in its rigid adherence to the view that a contract should not confer any rights on a stranger to the contract, even though the sole object may be to benefit him."

The effect of this principle is that if *A* agrees to do work for *B*, *B* agreeing to pay *C* for *A*'s work, *C* not being a party to the contract between *A* and *B*, cannot sue *B* if *B* fails to pay. For example, in *Green* v. *Russell*[1] an employer took out an insurance policy to benefit his employees in case they were injured or killed while working for him. The employer paid premiums to the insurance company, which agreed to pay sums of money if certain employees were killed or injured. The policy stated that its purpose was to secure payment of benefits to the named employees or their next of kin. One of the named employees was killed, and it was held that as neither he nor his widow were parties to the contract of insurance between the employer and the insurance company, the widow could not sue the insurance company for the money payable on the death of her husband. Although in this particular case the insurance company had not refused to pay, and the question had to be determined in order to decide a subsidiary point, it is clear that the rule is capable of causing great injustice. The Law Revision Committee in 1937 recommended that "where a contract by its express terms purports to confer a benefit directly on a third

[1] [1959] 2 Q.B. 226.

party, it shall be enforceable by the third party in his own name subject to any defences that would have been valid between the contracting parties. Unless the contract otherwise provides it may be cancelled by the mutual consent of the contracting parties at any time before the third party has adopted it either expressly or by conduct".

## Statute of Frauds

In "The Reform of the Law" criticism was levied at those rules, contained in the Statute of Frauds, 1677, and other statutes, which required written evidence of certain contracts before they could be sued upon in the courts. The recommendations were substantially carried out by the Law Reform (Enforcement of Contracts) Act, 1954, a measure introduced into the House of Commons by Mr. Arthur Skeffington, a Labour M.P. However, one anomaly remains: the Statute of Frauds Amendment Act, 1828, s. 6. This provides that a person cannot be sued by reason of a representation made by him relating to the character, conduct, credit, ability, trade, or dealings of another person, intended to enable that other person to obtain credit, money or goods, unless the representation was made in writing and signed by the party to be sued. The effect of this section is that if a reference as to someone's creditworthiness is given, the person giving the reference cannot be sued unless the reference was in writing and was signed. Signature by an agent is not sufficient. However, even if the reference was in writing and signed, in the normal way the giver of the reference could not be sued for negligence unless he owed some contractual or fiduciary relationship to the recipient of the reference. He could only be sued if the reference was given fraudulently. The result is that this statute of 1828, ostensibly passed to prevent fraud, serves to protect fraudulent people unless they had been imprudent enough to put their fraud into writing and to sign it. We recommend the repeal of this section.

We are largely content with the remaining provisions of the Statute of Frauds and other statutes to the like effect. We would, however, be in favour of some lessening of the rigorous rules laid down by the cases as to the nature and contents of the written evidence. For example, in *Hawkins* v. *Price*[1] a verbal agreement was made for the sale of a freehold bungalow. The purchaser

---

[1] [1947] Ch. 645.

paid a deposit of £100, and the vendor signed a receipt which contained all the details of the transaction except the agreed date for the giving of vacant possession. Although the court accepted the verbal evidence as to the date—indeed, it was admitted by both parties—it refused to enforce the agreement on the ground that the receipt for the deposit did not contain a record of all the terms of the contract.

### Intention to Create Legal Relations

Although there may be a clear and unambiguous agreement between two parties, amply supported by consideration, there may yet be no contract if there is no intention on the part of the parties to be legally bound by their agreement. We have no quarrel with this concept in so far as it enables the courts to decline jurisdiction in cases of a domestic nature. The common application of this principle is in agreements between husband and wife, where the courts have adequate means to control the relationship between the parties without the necessity of recourse to the law of contract.

The courts have, however, held that it is open to the parties in any kind of agreement, even of a business or commercial nature, to deny expressly that they intend their agreement to have legal effect. For example, all football pool coupons include a provision stating that the transaction is "binding in honour only" and that it gives rise to no legal relationship or rights. It has been held that, despite the substantial sums involved, the courts cannot adjudicate on any disputes between an entrant and the pool promoter.

This development is particularly surprising since it has long been held that any attempt in a contract to oust the jurisdiction of the courts is against public policy and automatically void. In the striking words of Lord Justice Scrutton, "there must be no Alsatia in England where the King's writ does not run".[1] We recommend that all commercial agreements designed to oust the jurisdiction of the courts, whether expressly or by denying an intention to create legal relations, should be declared illegal and void.

### Inaccurate and Misleading Statements

In the course of negotiations leading to the formation of a contract, each party may make statements to the other. Some-

---

[1] *Czarnikow v. Roth, Schmidt and Co.* [1922] 2 K.B. 478 at p. 488.

times the courts regard these statements as so important that they are taken to form part of the contract itself, and take effect as conditions or warranties of the contract. If not, however, they are relegated to the status of "representations".

This is a vital distinction. If a statement is part of the terms of a contract, its falsity will give the other party the right to claim damages; in some cases it may also give him the right to refuse to continue with the contract. But if the statement is a representation, its falsity gives rise to no claim to damages unless the statement was made fraudulently, that is to say, made with the knowledge that it was untrue, or without belief in its truth, or recklessly, not caring whether it was true or false. If a statement was made honestly, there is no right to claim damages, and the only possible remedy available to the injured party is a limited right to refuse to continue with the contract.

The law relating to conditions and warranties we shall consider shortly. In general, the law relating to fraud works satisfactorily, and we do not propose any changes. But the law relating to innocent misrepresentation is most unsatisfactory in a large number of respects. For example, the distinction between terms of the contract and misrepresentation is difficult and often unpredictable. The criterion is said to be the intention of the parties, but the court has to determine the intention from inadequate evidence and inconclusive words. Again, if the statement is an innocent misrepresentation, the only remedy is rescission of the contract. Once that remedy is lost—as it may be by lapse of time, or by the intervention of innocent third parties, or by some act of the injured party affirming the contract, even if he does not intend to do so—the injured party is left without a remedy; see, for example, *Long* v. *Lloyd*.[1] There is no remedy for a misrepresentation of law as opposed to one of fact. There is no remedy for misrepresentation as to future intentions, save in limited cases tantamount to fraud.

In 1962 the Law Reform Committee[2] recommended important amendments to the law of innocent misrepresentation. Its most important recommendations were as follows:

(a) It should be possible for the court to order a party guilty of innocent misrepresentation to pay damages to compensate the other party in the following circumstances:

---

[1] [1958] 1 W.L.R. 753.
[2] Tenth Report (Innocent Misrepresentation), Cmnd. 1782.

    (i) if he cannot prove that he believed the representa-
tion to be true and had reasonable grounds for his
belief, or

    (ii) where the court could order rescission of the con-
tract but is satisfied the damages would adequately
compensate the plaintiff.

(b) Rescission of all contracts, other than those for the sale
or other disposition of land, should be possible even after
the contract has been completely carried out, unless the
right to rescind has been lost for some other reason.

The Committee was of opinion that clauses in standard-form
contracts attempting to take away liability for misrepresentation could nullify the effect of its recommendations. Accordingly, the Committee recommended that it should no longer be
possible to exclude liability for misrepresentation unless it
could be proved that the person who made the representation
had reasonable grounds for believing it to be true.

We welcome these recommendations and support their
immediate implementation by Act of Parliament. Our only
criticism is that in our view they do not go far enough. We
believe that the law would gain if the subtle distinction between
a mere representation and a term of the contract was abolished,
and all representations were treated as terms of the contract.
This would mean that the courts could grant the remedy of
damages in all cases, and in addition could rescind the contract
if the representation was sufficiently serious.

*Mistake*

The rules which govern the position of the parties where one
(or both) is mistaken are among the most difficult to apply in
the whole of our law. The rules have become absurdly technical,
and the whole topic would profit from a detailed review by the
Law Reform Committee. Indeed, the technicalities are so
abstruse that it would not be helpful to discuss details in a book
of this kind. We have, however, two specific comments to make.

In the first place, many mistakes could be avoided—and the
law relating to misrepresentation would be considerably
strengthened—if the law recognised a general duty of good
faith in contracts, similar to the principle adopted in many
Continental countries. This would impose on each party entering into a contract a positive duty to disclose material facts to

the other, a duty which at present exists only in a few exceptional cases, such as the taking out of an insurance policy. Moreover, the courts should reconsider the present principle that a mistake must be fundamental before it can have an effect on a contract. The law's notion of what is fundamental is extremely narrow, and seems to leave out of account completely what is frequently the main if not the only motive of the parties for entering into the contract, namely, the financial effect of the contract. For example, in *Bell* v. *Lever Brothers Limited*[1] one party paid the other £30,000 for something which, if the true facts had been known, they could have obtained for nothing. It was held that the mistake was not sufficiently fundamental to affect the validity of the contract.

The second suggestion we have to make concerns the effect of a fundamental mistake on the existence of a contract. The position taken by the common law is that if the mistake is sufficiently fundamental to have any effect at all, its effect is to prevent any contract coming into existence. This means that no rights can be acquired by either party under the contract, and the result is that innocent third parties are sometimes seriously prejudiced. For example, in *Ingram* v. *Little*[2] a lady who owned a car sold it to a rogue who fraudulently represented himself to be a person of substance. A few days later the rogue sold the car to an innocent purchaser who paid the full value for it. It was held that the original seller was mistaken as to the identity of the person to whom she sold her car, that therefore this sale had no effect in law, and that she was entitled to recover the car or its value from the innocent purchaser. Thus the fraud, which at first sight was committed against the original seller, was in the final result committed against the innocent purchaser, who suffered the whole loss. We think that in this sort of case the courts should be given a power to apportion the loss between the two innocent parties. We return to this suggestion in more detail in the chapter on Commercial Law and Company Law which deals, among other subjects, with the principle known as *nemo dat quod non habet*.

### Breach of Contract and Remedies

There is a variety of remedies for breach of contract. They

[1] [1932] A.C. 161.
[2] [1960] 3 W.L.R. 504.

include a right to claim money from the other party—either damages (representing compensation for the loss caused by the breach), or the price or other money agreed to be paid under the contract; a right to refuse to continue with the contract— for example, in a contract for the sale of goods the buyer can reject the goods and refuse to pay, or recover the price if he has already paid; and the possibility of obtaining an order for specific performance—that is, an order directing the other party to carry out the contract as agreed, on pain of punishment by the court for failing to obey its order.

Whether the innocent party is entitled to damages, or if he can treat the breach as a repudiation of the contract by the other party and refuse to continue with it, is a difficult question, and the law is in a confused state. Sometimes the effects are said to depend on the seriousness of the breach of contract. In other cases they are said to depend on the nature of the contractual term which has been broken—whether it is (to adopt the terminology of the Sale of Goods Act, 1893) a "condition" or a "warranty", irrespective of how serious the breach is. In our view the proper criteria should always be the nature of the breach and its effect on the other party, and we think that the Sale of Goods Act should be amended to reflect this principle. Another question concerns an order for specific performance. In English law, for historical reasons, this is regarded as an exceptional remedy, only obtainable in special circumstances. in Continental law, on the other hand, such an order is regarded as the primary remedy for breach of contract. We do not think it is necessary or desirable to adopt the Continental rule in its entirety, but we would welcome wider powers for the courts to grant specific performance in appropriate cases.

*Capacity*

There are two classes of contracting parties whose capacity to contract deserves reconsideration. In English law infants, that is to say all persons under the age of 21, are in a special position and can only be sued for breach of contract in certain well-defined circumstances. We have two proposals for the reform of the law. In the first place, we consider that while the age of 21 may be reasonable in relation to property transactions, settlements, inheritances, and similar matters, it is too high for the vast majority of transactions which infants today might reasonably be expected to undertake. We would think that the

age of 18 is one at which young people might be expected to
have sufficient knowledge and experience to enter into contracts relating to everyday life, including the purchase of
furniture and electrical equipment. This is particularly so for
those young people who are already married and setting up a
family by that age.

We also criticise the principle of law whereby, although a
contract of employment entered into by an infant may be binding on him if, as a whole, it is for his benefit, a contract of a
trading nature can never be binding on an infant, not even if
he is in business on his own account. While there may be a case
for discouraging young people from setting up in business on
their own, we do not think that this should be done by protecting infants to the prejudice of other persons with whom they
may deal.

Corporations—a term which includes all limited companies
—are also in a special position so far as their capacity to contract
is concerned. Corporations created by Act of Parliament or
registered under the Companies Acts have the scope of their
activities laid down in a public document. According to the
*ultra vires* rule, any contract entered by a corporation, beyond
the scope of its powers as laid down in the public document, is
ineffective. The main result of this rule has been to prejudice
innocent parties who have dealt with the corporation. In one
case, for example, a coal merchant was unable to claim the
price of coal from a limited company because it ordered the
coal in the course of running a business different from that
specified in its constitution.[1] Whatever the merits of the *ultra
vires* rule may be as between the shareholders in a company and
the management, we think it should be abolished so far as it
affects third parties.

*Illegality*

In certain exceptional cases the courts must refuse to enforce
a contract on the grounds of illegality. These cases include not
only contracts involving the commission of a criminal offence
or other illegal act, but also contracts involving some sort of
moral turpitude or even contracts which are said to be against
public policy, such as contracts in restraint of trade (a common
law principle which preceded the Restrictive Trade Practices
Act of 1956 by over four hundred years). In our view, the major

[1] *Re Jon Beauforte (London) Ltd.* [1953] Ch. 131.

reform needed in this branch of the law is to grant the courts a far wider discretion than they have at the moment. We think that before the courts refuse to enforce a contract they should be entitled to consider not only the kind of illegality concerned, but also the harm done to the community as a whole, the relationship of the parties and the effect on all of them of refusing to enforce the contract. To some extent courts do at present take these factors into account, but we think that they should be given a specific power to enforce a contract despite acknowledged illegality if the justice of the case requires it. There have been a number of unsatisfactory decisions in this branch of the law, of which the case of *Boissevain* v. *Weil*[1] is an outstanding example of injustice.

### Quasi-Contract

Quasi-contract is that branch of the law which provides for the restitution of benefits the retention of which would be unjust. Our law of quasi-contract has much to learn both from the Continent and from the United States of America. Our rules are deficient in knowing no remedy for *negotiorum gestio* (money expended for the benefit of another without his authority), and such rules as we have (for instance, those relating to the recovery back of money paid by mistake) are often over-subtle. In particular, a remedy should be given for money paid under a mistake of law.[2]

### TORTS

The law of tort is the law of civil wrongs (wrongs not arising from a breach of contract or breach of trust) which, quite apart from any possible criminal proceedings, entitle the injured party to claim compensation of some kind. The list of torts is a varied one. It ranges from negligence (the most important of all contemporary torts) to defamation, from nuisance to fraud, from trespass to inducing a breach of contract. It will not be possible in this chapter to survey every technical difficulty in every individual tort, but some questions of fundamental policy, and others of practical importance, will be singled out for attention.

---

[1] [1950] A.C. 327.
[2] Several valuable suggestions for the reform of this branch of the law were made by Robert Goff in "Reform of the Law of Restitution" (1961) 24 Mod.L.R. pp. 85 and ff.

*Negligence*

Most civil litigation, apart from matrimonial disputes, is based on the law of tort. Most tort actions are based on the tort of negligence. And no doubt most negligence cases spring from industrial accidents and road accidents. This tort, and these causes, therefore deserve careful consideration.

It must be emphasised at the start that the mere fact that someone has been injured in an accident does not mean that the victim is entitled to compensation. So that damages may be awarded it must be shown that someone, or some organisation, has committed a tort. The onus is on the plaintiff in a negligence action to prove that the defendant was in such a relationship to him as to owe him a duty to take care; that the defendant failed to take reasonable care; and that the injury or damage was the result of that negligence. Thus as a result of a road accident a pedestrian may sue the driver of the car which struck him. It is well established that all road-users owe a duty of care to all other road-users, so the pedestrian will easily surmount the first hurdle. But he may have great difficulty in surmounting the second—in proving that the driver failed to take reasonable care. If, for example, the accident was caused by the negligence of some other road-user, whether motorist or pedestrian, and the driver had done all that a reasonable driver could have done, he may not be liable; or if the accident was caused by some defect in the car which no reasonable man could have foreseen or prevented, the driver will escape liability. Similar considerations apply to accidents at work and, indeed, to all other kinds of accidents where reasonable care has been taken.

The first question to be considered, then, is whether this emphasis on the defendant's negligence is justified. We are not —or should not be—concerned in the law of tort with punishing carelessness, but with compensating the injured. Should the tort of negligence, with the disputes and litigation which almost inevitably accompany it, be replaced by some universal scheme of insurance which will bring to injured persons irrespective of whether anyone was at fault the sort of compensation they at present receive in successful negligence actions?

It may be that such a scheme would be impracticable or uneconomic. It may be that the premiums required would be so vast that there would be no reasonable possibility even of considering such a scheme as a political reality. Strangely

enough, we do not know. There is a need for a high-level
investigation, using modern techniques of economic and social
enquiry, and taking into account the financial and psychological
benefits of avoiding the wasteful expedient of litigation and reducing the use of highly-trained judges and other lawyers. At
the very least we should investigate the possibility of such a
scheme for road and industrial accidents. Roads and factories
are facilities from which we all benefit, whether we use them
personally or not. We have enough experience of both to know
that, however much care is taken, some accidents are inevitable.
The cost of accidents may be regarded as part of the cost of
maintaining these facilities. It is clearly unjust if the whole risk
of these accidents, which we know are going to occur, is thrown
on to the unfortunate victim. There is little we can do about the
risk of personal suffering, save in so far as money can alleviate it
or compensate for it, but we can try to share the financial risks.
For road accidents we should all contribute, though it would
no doubt be fair to grade the contributions according to the
use made of the roads. For factories, it might be enough if
factory-owners paid the contributions and it was left to them
to recoup the cost either from profits or from the public at large
by the necessary increase in price of the product. It is not
enough to dismiss such a scheme—on the ground, for example,
that it would make it harder for manufacturers to compete in
foreign markets owing to their increased overheads—until we
have some authoritative idea of how much it would cost. After
all, industrialists already find it necessary to insure against the
risk of claims founded on their negligence, and the increase
might not be startling; so, too, all motorists must already insure
against certain third-party claims under the Road Traffic Act,
1960. The system of road accident insurance in force in Saskatchewan merits close study.[1]

Even if such a system of insurance is not adopted, it might be
possible to utilise the concepts and machinery of the existing
law by imposing liability on motorists irrespective of fault. The
idea of "strict liability" is not unknown to the law. For example,
anyone who keeps a pet tiger in his home is liable for all the
damage and injury it may cause if it escapes, even though he
takes every possible precaution. Motor cars may not be wild

---

[1] See T. Green, "Automobile Accident Insurance Legislation in the Province of
Saskatchewan" (1949) 31 Jnl. Soc. Comp. Legsln. 39; D. C. Wright, "The Law of
Torts" (1948) 26 Can. Bar Rev. 73.

animals, but their toll of human life justifies stern measures. Whether or not this suggestion is adopted, the present system of compulsory third-party insurance should continue. However a number of defects in the present scheme must be remedied: notably, insurance to cover injuries to passengers, both of vehicles and motor-cycles, should be compulsory.

## Procedure

A striking difference exists between criminal and civil procedure. If a factory-owner is prosecuted for a breach of the Factories Act, the criminal proceedings will come before the court within a matter of a few months. The facts will be investigated, the court will decide whether there has been a failure to take the precautions required by the Act and, if there is a conviction, the punishment will be determined.

Precisely the same accident will usually entitle the injured worker to claim damages for breach of statutory duty. This will involve civil proceedings in a different court. The same issues of fact will be before the court, the evidence may be the same as in the criminal case, but the civil court must come to its own decision and is not bound by the result of the criminal case. The civil claim will, however, usually take much longer to come before the court than the criminal prosecution: many months, perhaps even a year or two, will pass, and during the whole of this time the injured worker is uncertain whether he will receive any compensation or, if he does, how much. The strain on him during this period is great, and even judges now recognise the existence of "litigation neurosis".

We see no reason why the criminal court, hearing the prosecution prepared and brought by H.M. Inspector of Factories, should not at the same time decide the issue of civil liability. It may be too early in some cases for the total amount of compensation to be finally assessed and this issue might be postponed to a later date; but the main dispute is usually as to liability, and this could be disposed of much more expeditiously than under the existing procedure.

## Damages

If and so far as the tort of negligence remains, there will also remain the problem of remoteness of damage. If damage is caused, directly or indirectly, by the defendant's negligence, to what extent must he compensate the plaintiff? Under the present law the compensation must extend to all damage which could reasonably be foreseen as a result of the negligence. The problem is whether it should also extend to unforeseeable damage which is nevertheless the direct physical consequence of the negligence. In *Re Polemis and Furness, Withy & Co.*[1], the Court of Appeal held that it should. In that case a stevedore negligently dropped a plank into the hold of a ship. The plank struck a spark which ignited petrol vapour in the hold and destroyed the ship. It could be foreseen that a falling plank might cause some damage, but not a spark nor the consequential fire, yet the stevedore's employers were liable to compensate the shipowners for the direct consequence of his negligence. More recently, in *The Wagon Mound*,[2] the Privy Council refused to follow that decision. Oil was carelessly spilled overboard from the defendant's ship in Sydney Harbour. It could not be reasonably foreseen that the oil might ignite, but ignite it did, damaging the plaintiff's wharf. The Judicial Committee held that the defendants need not compensate the plaintiffs.

The conflicting principles in these two cases have caused acute controversy among lawyers. But the issue at stake is not one on which lawyers are likely to be any better informed than other people: it is fundamentally a question of social policy. *A* suffers loss which he would not have suffered but for *B*'s negligence. *B* could not have foreseen *A*'s loss. Who should bear the loss, *A* or *B*? It may well be thought to be unfair to call on *A*, who is not in any way to blame, to bear the whole loss (as in *The Wagon Mound*). On the other hand *B*, who is morally culpable to some extent, is perhaps suffering an unreasonable burden by being made to stand the whole unpredictable loss (as in *Re Polemis*). Here is another instance where the common law fails to do justice between the two parties, and where some system of apportioning the loss between them would be the most equitable solution.

Another limitation is that damages can be recovered in negligence only for injury to the person or to property. There is, it seems, no general duty to avoid causing pecuniary loss. As Professor Street puts it:[3] "The slowness of the judges in developing duties in respect of pecuniary damage can only be attributed to their unawareness of the great shift of economic

---

[1] [1921] 3 K.B. 560.
[2] [1961] A.C. 388.
[3] *Law of Torts*, 2nd ed., p. 111.

emphasis in this century from tangible property to intangible pecuniary assets." This situation merits reform.

A particular example of this limitation is the decision in *Candler* v. *Crane, Christmas & Co.*[1] Accountants prepared a balance sheet of a company so that it might be shown to potential investors. The plaintiff lost £2,000 because the accounts, on which he relied, had been prepared negligently. By a majority, the Court of Appeal dismissed his claim against the accountants on the ground that they owed him no duty to take care. This is an unrealistic decision and the dissenting judgment of Lord Justice Denning should be established as the true legal rule.

We must also refer to the problem of assessing the amount of damages payable for negligence. In claims for personal injury, assessments are particularly difficult, because the elements to be considered in any given case vary infinitely from other cases; there can be no fixed and unalterable standard. True though this is, the wide variation in the amount of damages awarded in different cases is a matter of deep concern. It is difficult for some plaintiffs to avoid the feeling, after judgment has been given, that they were unlucky; it is equally difficult for some defendants to avoid feeling that their plaintiffs have been lucky. Moreover no one can settle such a case out of court with a feeling of certain satisfaction.

The basic principle is that the damages awarded should be sufficient to put the plaintiff, so far as money can do so, into the position he would have been in had he not been injured. He should, therefore, be compensated for all the following expenses and losses, tangible and intangible: (a) medical and nursing treatment and any necessary convalescence; (b) the wages or salary lost while he is in hospital or unable to work; (c) earnings he is likely to lose in the future; (d) pain and suffering; (e) any physical effects of his injuries, such as the loss of a limb or an eye; and (f) loss of social amenities, including the loss of prospective happiness. Of these, (a) and (b) can be calculated fairly accurately up to the date of the trial, and are known as "special damages". The practice has been for the judge to award in addition a sum as "general damages" to represent (c) to (f), without breaking down the award into its component parts. This is the reason for the wide variation in awards. We think that in future the practice should be to calculate (c) on an

[1] [1951] 2 K.B. 164.

actuarial basis, having regard to expert evidence by actuaries and others as to the probable working life of the plaintiff and his earning prospects. In the absence of court soothsayers this can never be more than guesswork in any individual case, but over the whole field of accident litigation the result should be much fairer than the present system, when judges (for un-scientific reasons which would, for example, never be employed by insurance companies in calculating premiums and risks) eschew mathematical calculations in favour of intuition or guesswork. It will not, it is thought, be possible to separate the assessments for (d), (e) and (f), though the evidence adduced on (c) will be useful in estimating (f).

It is to the damages under head (c) that the rule in *British Transport Commission* v. *Gourley*[1] applies: the fact that the plaintiff would have had to pay income tax on future earnings is to be taken into account in deciding the amount of his future loss of earnings. It is highly controversial whether this rule is substantially just. We favour an alternative (which might well command wider assent) whereby the damages would represent the gross loss, but would be taxable in the plaintiff's hands; however, as long as the rule in *Gourley*'s case is applied the plaintiff's investment income on his damages under head (c) should be tax-free—a further reason for distinguishing the amount awarded under this head. Perhaps fewer problems would arise if the plaintiff was entitled to receive, as compensation under head (c) in respect of the loss of future earnings, regular monthly or yearly payments from the defendant (or, in practice, from the defendant's insurance company). Such a system is worthy of closer examination than it has yet received.

We must also draw attention to the decision in *Metropolitan Police* v. *Croydon Corporation*.[2] A motorist negligently injured a policeman, who received full pay from his employers during his incapacity, as required by statute. The damages payable to the policeman did not, therefore, include any amount in respect of loss of earnings. It was held that the police authority could not sue the motorist to recover the wages they had paid to the sick policeman. A simple amendment to the law is required for such cases, to enable the injured person to claim for a notional loss of earnings and to account for the sum recovered to his

[1] [1956] A.C. 185.
[2] [1957] 2 Q.B. 154.

employer: in this way substantial justice would be done and multiplicity of actions avoided.

## Limitation

Some amendments to the law on limitation of actions are urgently called for. The period of limitation in tort is six years for most actions, but damages for personal injury must be sued for within three years. Time starts to run when the tort is committed, but many cases have arisen in recent years where the prospective plaintiff did not know, and could not have known, of the injury until after the period had expired. These include not only diseases contracted at work, like pneumoconiosis, which frequently cannot be diagnosed until after the three years have expired, but also more prosaic cases, like flooding caused by plumbing that was negligently installed over six years before. A Committee under the chairmanship of Mr. Justice Edmund Davies recently recommended a change in the law relating to personal injuries.[1] We ourselves think that a general principle should be introduced into the law of limitation of actions that time should not start to run until the plaintiff has discovered that he has suffered or will suffer injury or damage, or until he ought with reasonable diligence to have discovered that.

## Exclusion of liability

We have referred earlier, in the section on Contracts, to the need to limit a person's right to contract out of liability for negligence. This problem is not only concerned with the question of negligence in carrying out contracts. In principle any liability in tort for negligence can be excluded where the parties are in a relationship in which a contract between them is possible. Thus a manufacturer can, by a contract with a purchaser of his goods contained in a form of "guarantee", exclude his liability for negligence which arises under the rule in *Donoghue* v. *Stevenson*.[2] An occupier of land, liable to his visitors under the Occupiers' Liability Act, 1957, may be able to exclude his liability by a contract. It is therefore important that contracts purporting to contract out of liability for negligence should not be permitted.

## Animals

The law relating to liability for damage caused by animals is

[1] (1962) Cmnd. 1829.
[2] [1932] A.C. 562.

archaic, confused and unjust. Ten years ago, in 1953, a distinguished committee recommended far-reaching changes in the law,[1] but nothing has yet been done. The most urgent need is to replace many of the old rules by a general principle of liability for negligence. It seems clear that the ancient rule, appropriate to an agricultural community, that a landowner is not under any duty to fence his land so as to prevent cattle straying, could now be invoked by a resident in a busy London street who negligently permits his dog to bound out of the front door into the road, injuring a passing motorist.[2]

## Other Torts

The time has come when a right of privacy should be recognised by the law, as it is in many American States.[3] In 1961 the Right of Privacy Bill introduced into the House of Lords was opposed by the Government. This Bill should now become law and a new tort thus established.

In *Smith* v. *Selwyn*[4] the old rule was affirmed that the victim of a tort which is also a felony cannot sue in tort until the defendant has been prosecuted for the felony. This is said to be necessary to ensure the enforcement of the criminal law. As the rule evolved before the establishment of police forces, it no longer has any relevance and should be abolished.

The torts of conversion and detinue, whereby possessory and proprietory interests in chattels are protected, are absurdly difficult and technical, and even the question of how damages are to be calculated is uncertain. The simplification and clarification of this branch of the law are urgently required.

Finally, we regret that there is no general principle recognised by the law that unjustified harm done by one person to another is a tort. Such a principle would enable compensation to be awarded to a person injured by another's malicious conduct where the motive is spite and there is no positive justification. The Scottish doctrine of "abuse of rights" might serve as a model. Such a principle would also clear the way for a more ready development of the law of tort to deal with new wrongs; it might, for example, make it unnecessary to create a right of privacy by statute.

[1] Committee on Law of Civil Liability for Damage done by Animals: Report (1953) Cmd. 8746.
[2] *Cf. Ellis* v. *Johnstone* [1963] 1 All E.R. 286.
[3] See the classic article by Warren and Brandeis in (1890) 4 Harv. Law Rev. 193.
[4] [1914] 3 K.B. 98.

# V

# LAND LAW

THE PRINCIPLES of land law have a long and complex history. Ancient doctrines have been established and modified over the centuries. Legislation has, from time to time, violently attacked these doctrines. In our modern society changes in land law, some of major importance and some relating to technicalities, occur each year. The problems of housing have produced violent political arguments over fundamental social rights. Public law matters, such as town planning and public health, are an integral part of the system.

Because of the complexities of the system and the differences in political attitudes towards land law, it is not possible to deal only with clear-cut major principles of reform. Some matters of detail must share places with matters of principle.

### REAL PROPERTY AND CONVEYANCING

The major reform of land law took place in 1925 when a vast legislative programme set out to modernise, as far as possible, the law of property. It had been described as "a rubbish heap which has been accumulating for hundreds of years"; but only some of it was incinerated in 1925. The aim was to streamline the rules so that the transfer of land could be made simple, even though it could never be as easy as the transfer of stocks and shares.

### Land Registration

Possibly the most far-reaching measure of this 1925 legislation was the Land Registration Act. The object of land registration is to provide a method of creating and transferring interests in land which is simple, speedy and cheap. To this end the Land Registry examines the title of the owner of unregistered land (usually following the first purchase of the land after registration of title in that area becomes compulsory) and creates a register of each proprietor's title. This register defines the property and the estate owned by the proprietor and then specifies all the interests to which a transfer of the registered estate would be subject. Any purchaser for value from the registered proprietor gets exactly what is contained on the Register—the title and its defects and limitations (if any) are open for inspection on a State-guaranteed document. If there are any interests which affect the estate but which are not noted on the Register, then these may be ignored and defeated by the transaction. The owner of such a "minor interest" must ensure that it is noted on the Register if it is to be effective. However, this simple pattern is broken by the existence of the class of rights and liabilities known as "overriding interests" which bind the land whether they are noted on the Register or not. These interests will be discussed presently.

The success of the system of land registration depends upon three fundamental principles: the mirror principle, the curtain principle and the insurance principle. "The mirror principle involves the proposition that the register of title is a mirror which reflects accurately and completely and beyond all argument the current facts that are material to a man's title."[1] The curtain principle embodies the familiar idea of keeping trusts off the title (i.e. the register). The insurance principle provides the State-guaranteed title and the consequent indemnity to any person who suffers loss if any mistakes occur.

Compulsory land registration is becoming widely accepted as providing a more efficient and cheaper method of conveyancing, and fresh areas are being taken over by the system each year. There are several counties and boroughs which have requested compulsory registration and are still waiting for the Land Registry to reach them. At present more than a quarter of all conveyancing transactions in the country concern registered land. It is eminently desirable that the process of land registration should be made compulsory over the whole of England and Wales as soon as practicable.

Many of the branches of the law of real property which require reform and which are mentioned later, must be read within the context of the system of registered land. However, there are some matters of principle concerning land registration itself which require attention and reform.

*Overriding Interests.* A major theoretical criticism that can be levelled at the mirror principle as it operates today concerns the continuing existence of overriding interests. These interests are gathered together mainly in s. 70 of the Land Registration Act,

[1] T. B. F. Ruoff, *The Torrens System*, p. 8.

1925, and the diverse list includes rights of common, legal easements, public rights, the rights of persons in possession of land, rights acquired or in the course of being acquired under the Limitation Acts, local land charges and leases not exceeding twenty-one years granted at a rent without a fine. These are described by the Chief Land Registrar as "certain well-recognised burdens that are matters of common knowledge or are easily discoverable outside the register although they cannot, or cannot conveniently, be entered on it."

The mirror principle can never be complete until everything affecting the title (and the legal use and enjoyment of land) is reflected on the register. This means that the category of over-riding interests should be abolished, or, if this is not possible, drastically reduced. To have a series of interests, both legal and equitable, not on the register, which bind a legal owner of land regardless of notice is inconsistent with the whole concept of registered title. Various reasons have been put forward for the existence of overriding interests. One reason is that there is a danger of making the register too bulky. This is wrong. It is not the fundamental purpose of registration to confine every title to one or two pages: the purpose is to put down in one place as simply as possible everything that is of present and future importance to the title. If a title is complex because there are many rights and liabilities affecting land, that is all the more reason why they should be expressed as clearly as possible in a place which is readily accessible to a purchaser.

Inevitably there would be problems of prescription, limitation and implied grants, but these are problems which are capable of solution, and indeed, as will be mentioned later, some of these concepts themselves require reform.

Surely nothing is more desirable than that a purchaser should be able to look at one Land Certificate, whether small or bulky, and see on it practically everything that can affect his title.

*Leases*. This is one of the most confusing topics in land registration. The relevant provisions are scattered throughout the Act and many lawyers have delighted in stressing the difficulties and doubts of statutory interpretation.

The position is as follows:

(1) A lease originally granted for twenty-one years (or less), or a lease with only twenty-one years (or less) to run at

the time of application *cannot* be registered, whether the land is in a compulsory or non-compulsory area.

Such leases may be protected as overriding interests.

(2) In the case of leases over twenty-one years but less than forty years:

> where the freehold or superior leasehold title is registered, the lease *must* be completed by registration of the new title if the lessee is to obtain the legal estate whether in a compulsory or non-compulsory area; and
> where the freehold or superior leasehold title is not registered, the lease *may* be registered.

(3) A lease for a term of forty years or more or an assignment on sale of leasehold land where the lease has not less than forty years to run *must* always be registered in a compulsory area; in a non-compulsory area registration is not necessary unless the freehold or superior leasehold title is registered.

If a lessee fails to register when he ought to do so, he will not obtain a legal estate in the land; he may be protected as having an overriding interest if he is in actual occupation of the land or in receipt of the rents and profits.

The present writer puts forward the following criticisms and proposals for reform and simplification:

(a) To have different categories of "mays" and "musts" is confusing and pointless, especially when some "mays" mean "musts". No reasons appear to have been given for the distinction between leases of over and under forty years. If the Land Registry is perfectly willing to register a lease of, say, thirty-five years at the option of the lessee, then registration might just as well be made compulsory, and uncertainty avoided. The law should be amended to direct that all leases over twenty-one years *must* be registered.

(b) It is constantly being emphasised that the object of land registration is to simplify and expedite the transfer of land. Most leases for very short terms are not transferred, and so it would be pointless to register a separate title for each short lease if transfer were the purpose. However, land registration should not be concerned exclusively with the transfer of land; it should also pursue the object of providing a true record of legal titles, whether the transfer of that title is likely or not. In any event, to imply that leases under twenty-one years are rarely transferred is wrong. Leases granted for twenty-one years or less should be capable of registration. If this type of lease were to come within the class of registrable interests, then it would help to reduce a very large class of overriding interests and so tie up with the suggestions already made concerning these. All these leases would be the subject of separate titles and would also be noted in the registers of the lessors' titles. But it would not be possible to register all leases without radical amendment of the substantive law of real property. It would be neither necessary nor desirable to register as a separate title every minor legal estate, such as a weekly or monthly tenancy. If one is to draw a line where should it be? Seven years would be a more realistic figure than twenty-one years, for seven-year leases and over are often transferred. To be a little bolder, it should be enacted that the only leases incapable of separate registration are those which may be created informally under s. 54 (2) of the Law of Property Act, 1925 (i.e. leases which take effect in possession for a term not exceeding three years at the best rent reasonably obtainable without taking a fine). Since all other leases must be made by deed in order to create a legal estate, why not extend that rule and require registration as well?

(c) Leases containing an absolute prohibition against all dealings therewith *inter vivos* should be capable of being registered. This follows from the previous discussion.

### Extending the System of Registration

In the coming years Orders in Council will be made extending the compulsory registration of titles to more areas. Generally, the making of each Order in Council will depend upon the competent local authority passing the necessary resolution. Whether or not a resolution is passed may depend upon factors quite irrelevant to the main issue. This may be a truly democratic process, but it can also be quite chaotic. What is wanted is a gradual extension of compulsory registration in a logical and orderly way, without incurring too much cost or involving too great a delay in dealings. It is unlikely that local authorities are the best judges of the time when compulsory registration should reach them. The initiative should be transferred from the local authority to the Land Registry, which is in the best position to know when an extension is desirable and practicable and thus help to reduce the delay in the registration of transactions. Local authorities should certainly be consulted: it is only the emphasis that should be changed. The extension of compulsory registration should begin in built-up areas. In this way the benefits of registration would first be felt by the owners of dwelling-houses and the Land Registry would not become bogged down in the difficulties which beset the registration of open land.

GENERAL IMPROVEMENTS IN LAND LAW

Although the 1925 legislation has proved to be remarkably successful in practice, it is widely felt that the spirit of that reform can now be taken further and that even greater simplification is possible.

*Settlements and Trusts For Sale*

Historically, the strict settlement was the method whereby the nation's aristocracy passed large areas of land on to their descendants. The land was retained in the family and, since tenants for life had very limited powers, it was difficult or impossible to alienate the land or even to deal with it to its best economic advantage.

The trust for sale, on the other hand, was the typical trader's settlement; here trustees were given power to deal with the land with the beneficiaries' best interests as the guiding light.

Through the centuries the courts and the legislature struggled to prevent persons who created strict settlements from imposing too strong a grip upon the land for generations to come. The property legislation of 1882 and 1925 finally gave the tenant for life of settled land adequate powers to deal with land to its best advantage and also to alienate or mortgage it, if necessary. The 1925 legislation provided that the two traditional methods of settlement, the strict settlement and the trust for sale, should be the only methods of settling land. The strict settlement is now governed by the Settled Land Act, 1925; it imposes many formal rules and regulations not applicable to the trust for sale.

Nowadays the express creation of strict settlements of land is rare. The reasons for its unpopularity are economic, income tax and estate duty being the most important deterrents. The trust for sale, and especially the discretionary trust, is by far the most popular method of settling land. Here the legal estate and thus the power of disposition, is vested in the trustees (and not the life tenant, as in a strict settlement) and, paradoxically, for those who wish to keep the land in the family the only effective way is the trust for sale.

Strict settlements are still being created, but, mostly by accident. If a husband by his will leaves a house to his wife for life and after her death to their children, he has (unwittingly, as a rule) created a strict settlement. The technicalities of the Settled Land Act are thus brought to bear upon those small settlements for which they were not designed, whereas the type of settlement contemplated by the Settled Land Act is now being channelled into the concept of the trust for sale.

There seems to be little purpose today in retaining this dual system of settlements, and it would be a relatively simple matter to introduce legislation making all settlements "trusts for sale", and extracting from the two systems a modern, simple, comprehensive code. If this were done, a mass of unnecessary technicalities would be swept away, and the probate practice involving land would also be simpler.

*Perpetuities*

The rules against perpetuities are closely associated with settlements and provide another example of rules which have grown up to prevent ancestral domination. The existing law may conveniently be grouped under three main heads. First, there is a rule against remoteness of vesting; it invalidates any trust or limitation which might possibly fail to become vested within the permitted period of the life or lives of any person or persons alive at the date of the settlement and 21 years thereafter. Secondly, there is the closely allied rule against restrictions on alienation; this invalidates trusts or limitations whereby property is rendered inalienable for longer than the permitted period. Thirdly, there are rules against excessive accumulations; these restrain the accumulation of income for longer than the appropriate statutory periods.

To the outsider, the most striking and foolish aspect of this branch of the law is the treatment of perpetuity problems as an exciting battle of wits; the game is to try to find a point, no matter how remote and improbable, where the limitation under consideration might possibly offend the perpetuity rule. Thus, the courts have successfully defeated the best interests of a settlement by, for example, assuming that the aged and senile might produce children ("fertile octogenarians") and that babies might themselves reproduce in infancy ("precocious toddlers"). The rules of the game are complex and the penalties severe.

The Law Reform Committee, which reported on this branch of the law in 1956[1] felt that, in general, no change in the perpetuity period should be made. The period of lives in being and a further 21 years was still considered to be a convenient period for parents to have a family and for children to attain full age. However, if an instrument creating the limitation specified a period of years only, without mentioning the life of any person, it seemed unreasonable to confine such a period to 21 years; it was recommended that there should be allowed a period not exceeding 80 years, provided such a period was specified in the instrument.

As for the sub-rules, the Committee recommended many important changes which were designed to allow the courts to act more realistically than at present. These changes would include:

(1) a presumption (rebuttable by evidence tendered at the time at which the matter falls for decision, but not subsequently) that no woman of 55 years or more is capable of bearing a child, and that no male or female below the age of 14 years is capable of procreating or bearing a child;

(2) the admissibility of medical or surgical evidence that a male or female of any age is incapable of procreating or bearing a child, the court being empowered to assess the value of such evidence as it thinks proper;

(3) a rule whereby any decision of a court based on the presumption or the kind of evidence mentioned under (1) and (2) above should remain effective, even if a child is subsequently born; but if the child has any property right which is not itself void for perpetuity, that right will not be prejudiced by the decision of the court;

(4) a principle whereby the validity of a limitation under the rule against perpetuities would depend not on the facts which may occur but upon the facts which do actually occur; i.e. a principle of "wait and see";

[1] Cmnd. 18.

(5) a right for trustees or any other persons concerned to apply to the court at any time for a declaration as to the validity of any limitation in regard to perpetuity.

Among other important recommendations of the Committee were the following:

*Class gifts.* Where a person makes a gift to a class of beneficiaries and it is possible that one member of the class might take a vested interest outside the perpetuity period, then, under the present law, the gift will fail as a whole; even those members of the class who would certainly have taken interests within the perpetuity period will get nothing. The Committee recommended that no class gift should be invalidated by the failure of the limitation to some only of the members of the class, and that the limitation should be construed and take effect as a limitation only to those members of the class who comply with the perpetuity rule.

*Options to acquire interests in land.* The present law relating to options may be summed up as follows:

a lease can only be granted if it takes effect within 21 years;

an option to renew a lease for a term exceeding 60 years is void;

a lease which contains a perpetual option for renewal is by statute converted into a term of 2000 years and the benefit of such an option runs with the lease;

subject to the above, options to renew leases are outside the perpetuity period;

an option to purchase land is generally subject to the perpetuity rule.

The Committee recommended that any option contained in a lease and enabling the lessee for the time being to purchase the freehold or other superior interest should be wholly exempt from the rule against perpetuities; and further, that any other option to acquire an interest in land which purports to be exercisable for a period in excess of 21 years from the date of the grant should be valid and exercisable during 21 years, but should thereafter be void even as between the original parties.

Several other important recommendations were made, and the enactment of a new comprehensive code relating to perpetuities is now overdue.

4

*Covenants Affecting Land*

Covenants relating to land can be either positive or negative (restrictive). Positive covenants occur e.g. where a land owner undertakes to build fences, repair buildings, or maintain a road; usually a positive covenant requires the expenditure of money. Restrictive covenants cover, and can prevent, a wide range of activities; they vary from an agreement not to hang out washing on a Sunday to an agreement not to erect more than one house on a plot of land. When the land passes into new hands, problems arise as to how far, if at all, the new owners are bound by or can benefit from such covenants.

The present law is complex, but can be summarised, very generally, as follows:

If the covenants, whether positive or restrictive, are contained in a lease, then, provided that the covenants "touch and concern the land", they can be enforced by and against the successors of both the landlord and the tenant. If the covenants are not contained in a lease, but are imposed, say, between neighbouring landowners, then new owners of the land can enforce all covenants in their favour but are, it is generally believed, only liable for restrictive covenants. To put it differently: if a person acquires freehold land he can acquire with the land the right to enforce an obligation upon a neighbour, but he cannot acquire a liability to a neighbour unless it is to refrain from doing something.

These rules have had a haphazard historical growth, and pose several problems in a modern society.

First, a considerable area of the law of covenants is obscure and it is often difficult to know whether an owner of land has, in fact, acquired the benefit of a covenant. The rules require statutory clarification and precise definition.

Secondly, the obscure and unsatisfactory state of the present law has introduced serious problems in connection with the sale of flats and maisonettes, particularly in recent years. When a person buys a flat or maisonette, important considerations arise, for example, in connection with repairs. If, as often happens, the repairing obligations are shared responsibilities, how easy is it for one owner to force his neighbour to carry out his obligations? What rights are there to enter adjoining premises to carry out repairs? What right is there to compel a contribution from a neighbour in respect of the cost of repairs to the common parts? The difficulties which have arisen here have encouraged property developers to grant long leases of flats and maisonettes at a premium and nominal ground rent, rather than to sell the freehold outright. There are certain ostensible advantages in creating a lease to impose effective community management. The freeholder will reserve a right of re-entry which will be in existence throughout the length of the lease and not only during the perpetuity period; no problem arises over enforcing the burden of positive covenants on the successors of an original purchaser. Also, when there is a lease, the common parts of a building may remain vested in the freeholders, and this does away with the difficulties that might arise if the common parts were conveyed to one or the other of the owners. However, there still remain difficulties because all these rights exist between landlord and tenant and not between different lessees. There is, apparently, no easy way of granting to one tenant the right to enforce repairing covenants against another tenant. Thus, the present law of covenants encourages the grant of long leases instead of the sale of freeholds, and that, as will be shown later, is often socially undesirable. Because the law of covenants is still ineffective in many respects, the thousands of flats and maisonettes which have been sold since the war are likely to cause grave problems within the next few years, when the question of enforcing repairing covenants between neighbours is likely to arise. Further difficulties will present themselves when the problem of re-building such premises becomes topical.

The reform which is vitally important here is to provide that the benefit and burden of all covenants, positive and restrictive, pass with the land, provided they are connected with the land. Where covenants are imposed for the benefit of two or more neighbouring landowners, then each landowner affected should have the right to enforce the covenant, even though there may be no contractual relationship between the parties.

The third major problem concerns restrictive covenants which prevent or hamper building development. It is a common hazard for property developers to find that the land on which they propose to build is subject to restrictive covenants imposed 50 or more years ago. Such restrictive covenants, whether or not they were socially desirable at the time, are often wholly unrealistic today. Thus a restrictive covenant imposed in 1900 which prohibits the building of more than one house per half-acre may be completely alien to modern ideas of housing development, and this will usually be borne out by a planning permission which permits building on a much more densely-populated scale. Often, owing to changes in the character of the neighbourhood over the years, it will be obvious that the restrictive covenants are obsolete. Also, there may be no person in existence who can enforce the covenants. Yet the property developer must tread very warily before he can ignore them.

The existing procedure for overcoming these obstacles is to apply to the Lands Tribunal under s. 84 of the Law of Property Act, 1925, for an order modifying or discharging the restrictive covenants, with or without payment of compensation. The applicants must show *either* that by reason of changes in the character of the property or the neighbourhood or other material circumstances the restriction is obsolete and its continued existence would impede the reasonable use of the land without giving practical benefits to anyone; *or* that all the persons of full age and capacity who are entitled to the benefit of the restrictions have agreed, expressly or by implication, to the discharge or modification sought; *or* that the discharge or modification would not injure the persons entitled to the benefit of the covenant.

Many small property developers find that a Lands Tribunal application involves awkward delays, and often (e.g. when it is fairly certain that there is nobody who could enforce the restrictive covenants in question) it has the appearance of a sledgehammer-nut process. One way to avoid an application to the Lands Tribunal is to purchase an indemnity policy against eventual claims; but this method is not always desirable or practicable.

Two solutions are possible: we must either abandon the system of restrictive covenants completely or provide an additional procedure for avoiding them.

The argument for abolition is that town planning restrictions are now superseding that kind of control over the use of land which used to be exercised by means of restrictive covenants. This sounds attractive when an old restrictive covenant is compared with an up-to-date planning permission granted in respect of the same land. However, restrictive covenants often serve useful purposes, and many landowners would prefer to impose them when selling part of their land rather than rely upon town planning control. Inability to impose restrictive covenants could well operate to deter many people from selling off part of their land for building purposes.

If, as is suggested, restrictive covenants are to be retained, the following reforms would be desirable:

(1) Where an owner of land feels confident that there is no person likely to enforce a given restrictive covenant, and that no full application to the Lands Tribunal is necessary, he should place a notice on the land, indicating the proposed development, and serve it also on all neighbouring landowners who are likely to be affected. If no objection is raised within two months, the developer should be free to ignore the covenant. Should any objection be raised, it will be necessary to make the usual application to the Lands Tribunal, and if it can be shown that the persons objecting do so unreasonably, they may be penalised in costs.

In order to safeguard the developer and preserve his place in the Lands Tribunal queue, the person giving the relevant notice should register this with the Lands Tribunal and obtain directions as to which adjoining owners he need serve. If no objections are made within the period of two months, the matter can be withdrawn from the Lands Tribunal. If objections are raised, there will have to be a full hearing.

(2) A new provision should be added to s. 84 of the Law of Property Act, 1925, giving the Lands Tribunal power to discharge or modify a restrictive covenant (subject to the payment of compensation if necessary) where it is reasonable to do so.

Such a wide power would enable the Lands Tribunal to deal sensibly with those situations where, though an individual might benefit by the continued existence of restrictive covenants, it is on balance reasonable to override the individual interest in favour of the public interest.

## Party Walls and Structures

When property is being developed, difficulties often occur in connection with party walls separating lands or buildings. These difficulties concern the rights of owners of adjoining properties in relation to building, strengthening, maintaining and using walls and structures over or adjoining the boundary line of the two properties. These problems often cause delay and obstruction. In some parts of the country rules and regulations have been laid down by statute. In London, Part VI of the London Building Acts (Amendment) Act, 1939, provides a detailed code of procedure which works efficiently. This statute should be extended to cover the whole country.

### Easements and Profits

The law relating to easements is a confusing morass of ancient rules. Rights over another person's land, such as a right of way, a right of light, a right to cut and take away timber, can be acquired by express grant or by implied grant or by prescription. The period of prescription is based mainly on the badly-drafted, complex and obscure Prescription Act, 1832. The whole of this branch of the law requires to be re-considered and codified.

However, one important problem deserves special mention here. In the system of registered land, easements and profits are within the class of overriding interests. As discussed earlier,[1] such interests must be re-examined so that this dangerous category can be confined as closely as possible. Considerations of land registration thus strengthen the case for reforming radically the law of easements and profits. The most important initial step would be to abolish in stages (in such a way that existing rights are preserved) the process of acquiring easements and profits by prescription. The present system of prescription is haphazard and inappropriate to a modern society with closely planned land tenure. The Rights of Light Act, 1959, has made it much simpler for persons to prevent, by registration, easements of light being acquired over their own land. Reform should go further, so that rights of light can only be acquired by express grant. In most cases the access of light to a house is protected by town planning principles anyway. Several other common law jurisdictions have already curtailed or abolished the acquisition of easements by prescription, and the law is much clearer for that.

If this reform were carried through, it would be possible to make nearly all other easements registrable, and so cut down the category of overriding interests and make more efficient the system of land registration.[2]

---

[1] See p. 81, *supra*.
[2] See Crane, (1962) L.S. Gaz., p. 317.

*Land Charges*

A large number of matters affecting land, especially rights of third parties, are known as land charges, and under the Law of Property Act and the Land Charges Act, 1925, provision has been made for the registration of these rights.

There are two complementary systems of registration. The first system comprises a number of registers, kept centrally by the Land Charges Department in London, affecting un-registered land. These cover such matters as restrictive cove-nants, certain mortgages, contracts for the sale of land, and bankruptcy matters. The second system comprises registers of local land charges, kept by each district or borough council and each county council. These cover a large number of matters of a more public nature, such as charges for the making up of roads, charges for sanitary works, and town planning matters. Registration of any instrument or matter in the appropriate register constitutes actual notice to all persons, and for all purposes connected with the land affected, as from the dates of registration. Thus, all purchasers of land automatically have legal notice of these charges, and must make the necessary searches in the registers when they purchase the land. The most significant distinction between the two systems is that the charges registered under the central system are registered against the name of the owner of the land at the date when the charge was created, whereas local land charges are registered against the land itself, and are therefore much easier for prospective purchasers to discover.

Each system has its difficulties and will be examined separately.

*The central land charge system.* Since 1 January, 1926, when a person contracts to purchase land he is entitled to investigate the title of the vendor, by tracing the vendor's ownership from a root of title at least 30 years old, unless a contrary intention is expressed in the contract. For many years after 1926 there was no problem about discovering the names of the legal owners against whom land charge searches were to be made. However, since 1 January, 1956, it is possible for a purchaser of land to be given a good 30 years' root of title which does not disclose the name of every estate-owner since 1926, and it may thus be possible for a purchaser of land to be deemed to have actual notice of a charge registered against a previous owner whose name he (the purchaser) had no means of finding out. A simple example will illustrate this. In 1926 *A* owns a piece of land and sells it to *B*, imposing a restrictive covenant on the land. The restrictive covenant is duly registered as a land charge and constitutes notice and binds everybody. In 1927, *B* sells the land to *C*, in 1929 *C* sells the land to *D*, and in 1932, *D* sells the land to *E*. After several other transactions, the land is owned by *V*, who, in 1962, contracts to sell to *P*. Under the provisions of the Law of Property Act, *P* is entitled to investigate *V*'s title to a good root of title at least 30 years old, and this root of title will be the sale by *D* to *E* in 1932. Thus *P* may not know anything about the restrictive covenant imposed on the land in 1926 if there is no reference to it in any of the deeds since 1932, and he will therefore be bound by the covenant without having had any opportunity to discover it. This situation is quite unfair.

In 1956, the Roxburgh Committee on Land Charges[1] reported (*inter alia*) on this particular problem. The Committee agreed that the situation could not be defended on any juridical principle but thought that the problem was insoluble until it solved itself upon completion of the registration of all titles to land. All land charges would then be noted on the register against the name of the owner.

Although it was felt that the problem was insoluble it was suggested that restrictive covenants, which comprise half of all registrations under this land charges system, should, after an appointed day, cease to be capable of registration. Most restrictive covenants are referred to in each new conveyance in any event. Thus, there would be a return to the pre-1926 system, whereby all purchasers would be bound by restrictive covenants, unless they could show that they were *bona fide* purchasers of the legal estate for value without notice, actual or constructive, of the covenants. In those areas of England where compulsory registration of title is not likely to come into force for the next 30 years or more, such a measure would be beneficial and would narrow down considerably the existing problem.

However, this is not a complete answer to the problem. It could be solved if the present system of registration against the names of owners were converted into a system of registration against the land affected, within the central registry itself. This solution was rejected by the Committee on the argument that

[1] Cmnd. 9825.

it would be costly and impracticable to re-register about two million existing land charges. This is probably true; but what is there to prevent all future charges being registered against the land and not the name?

Thus the two solutions that would considerably alleviate the possibility of future hardship are, first, to remove restrictive covenants from the system of registration, and secondly, to change over on an appointed day from a "names system" to a "land system". Incidentally, the cost of searching the register would inevitably become cheaper.

Another problem in connection with land charges, particularly under the central land-charge scheme, is that often, when a lease is granted, a lessee is not entitled to investigate the lessor's title. If there are any charges registered against the lessor, whether in the Land Charges Register in the unregistered land system or against the title of the lessor in the registered land system, the lessee and his successors will be bound by these charges, even though they may not know what they are until it is too late. The Roxburgh Committee made certain recommendations in the case of unregistered land, which were not wholly satisfactory, and it seems that the best thing is for lessees to stipulate for the right to investigate the lessor's title.

In the case of registered land an important and positive step was recommended. The Committee proposed that the Land Registration Acts should be amended in order to give a prospective lessee, or assignee of a lease of, registered land a right to inspect the charges register of the freehold and any superior leasehold title. This reform should be introduced immediately. It is interesting to note that many countries which have a system of land registration allow public inspection of land registers. Eventually, this may well be introduced here.

## Local Land Charges

When acting for the purchaser of land, a solicitor automatically makes searches in the register of local land charges; in addition, he will address various enquiries to the local district or borough council and the county council concerning matters which are not registrable.

In 1952 certain recommendations were made by the Committee on Local Land Charges,[1] but no action has so far been

[1] Cmnd. 8440.

4*

taken. There is a strong case for adopting the following recommendations:

All local land charges should be registered in one place locally. County registers should be abolished and all items entered in one local register (except perhaps in London). Alternatively, the county register alone should be retained for the whole or any part of a county and the local authority registers should be abolished.

Certain matters about which additional enquiries are usually made should be contained in the local land charges register, e.g. combined drainage orders or entries in registers under the Furnished Houses (Rent Control) Act, 1946. All definite items of information should be entered on the register of local land charges, to give the answers legal validity. Answers which do not bind local authorities should be confined to matters which involve a mere intention of local authorities or cannot be answered with sufficient certainty to make registration possible.

Complicated rules exist under which some, but not all, matters requiring registration become void if they are not registered. These rules should be amended as recommended by the Committee, so that compensation can be paid for failure to register or disclose an entry.

Legislation should be introduced as soon as possible to amend the Land Registration Acts, so that local land charges (overriding interests) shall be registered against the landowner's title.

In *Re Forsey and Hollebone's Contracts*[1] it was suggested that where a vendor contracted to sell land to a purchaser without disclosing certain charges registered against the land, the purchaser was bound by these (because registration constitutes notice) and had no remedy against the vendor. This difficulty is easily overcome in the case of local land charges, because a purchaser is able to search the registers before contract (these being registrations against the land). But the purchaser cannot usually search in the central land charges registers until after contract, because here registration is against the names of the previous owners.

The Roxburgh Committee recommended that s. 198 of the Law of Property Act, 1925, should be amended to ensure that, while for the protection of the owner of the registered charge registration shall constitute notice to all the world, it shall not,

[1] [1927] 2 Ch. 379.

as between vendor and purchaser, be deemed to give the purchaser knowledge, at the date of the contract, of any matters of which he is in fact ignorant. Parties should be allowed to contract out of this provision in the case of local land charges but not in the case of land charges registered in the central register. This reform should be implemented.

## Mortgages

The 1925 legislation introduced a new method of creating a mortgage, known as "a charge by way of legal mortgage", in addition to the existing method of a mortgage by demise, i.e. a lease for a long term of years. There are no legal disadvantages in the new charge as opposed to the old form of mortgage, and in many cases it has certain advantages.

The new creation has proved successful and popular, and is generally used by most building societies and other bodies whose business it is to lend money on mortgage. Since the legal charge is much simpler and shorter and more easily understood by laymen, it is proposed that for further simplification, the legal charge should be the only method of creating legal mortgage.

There is a well-known insoluble problem in the provisions relating to the priority of mortgages. There is a conflict between s. 97 of the Law of Property Act, 1925, and s. 13 (2) of the Land Charges Act, 1925. Section 97 provides that every mortgage, legal or equitable, affecting a legal estate in land, where the mortgagee does not obtain possession of the title deeds as security, shall rank for priority according to its date of registration as a land charge. However, s. 13 (2) provides that any such mortgage is void against a subsequent mortgagee of the land, unless it is registered as a land charge before the completion of the later mortgage. The problem can be seen by the following illustration:

*A* takes a mortgage of land to secure £2,000 on 1 January, 1963.

*B* takes a mortgage of the same land to secure £2,000 on 2 January, 1963.

*A* registers his mortgage on 10 January, 1963.

*B* registers his mortgage on 11 January, 1963.

If it proves necessary to sell the land to recover the sums advanced, what happens if the land only raises £2,000? Who is entitled to this sum? Section 97 of the Law of Property Act, would give priority to *A*, because *A* registered his mortgage first, whereas s. 13 (2) of the Land Charges Act would give priority to *B*, because *A*'s mortgage was not registered when *B* took his mortgage. There are variations on this theme, and since no court has been called upon to decide this problem, there have been many subtle but unsatisfactory solutions put forward. The conflict between these two sections requires legislative clarification.

## Sales by Survivors of Joint Tenants

Where two or more people own land jointly, they can own their beneficial interests either as joint tenants or tenants in common. If the land is held by joint tenants and one of them dies, the whole interest automatically passes to the survivor; whereas if the land is held by tenants in common, the death of one tenant in common does not extinguish his interest, and such interest forms part of the deceased's estate. Thus, if *A*, *B* and *C* own land as joint tenants, the death of *A* means that *B* and *C* are now entitled to the land. And if *B* dies, then the survivor, *C*, becomes the sole owner of the land. If *A*, *B* and *C* own land as tenants in common, then, on the death of *A*, the land is held for *B* and *C* and the persons entitled under the estate of *A*; and when *B* and *C* die, the same consequences arise.

In order to make conveyancing simple, the 1925 legislation provided that the *legal* estate should always be held by the owners as joint tenants, as trustees for themselves beneficially either as joint tenants or as tenants in common. A purchaser of the land is only concerned with the legal estate, and provided there are two or more trustees or a trust corporation, he obtains a valid receipt for the purchase money and is not concerned with the actual trusts.

A conveyancing problem, which has proved to be extremely inconvenient, often arises when a husband and wife (*H* and *W*) buy a house in their joint names. They decide at the time of the conveyance whether they would like to hold the property beneficially as joint tenants or as tenants in common. If they decide to hold the land as tenants in common, then the technical position is that *H* and *W* hold the *legal* estate as joint tenants, as trustees upon trust for *H* and *W*, as tenants in common beneficially. If *W* dies, then *H* will hold the legal estate upon trust for himself and the beneficiaries of *W*'s estate as tenants in common. Before $H$ can sell the land he must appoint another trustee to act with him, because there must be at least two trustees.

However, if, as very often happens, $H$ and $W$ decide to hold the land as joint tenants, so that on the death of one the survivor takes automatically, the technical position is that $H$ and $W$ hold the legal estate as joint tenants, as trustees, upon trust for $H$ and $W$ as joint tenants beneficially. When one person, say $W$, dies, then $H$ will hold the land for himself beneficially, and the trust will cease automatically. There can be no trust when a person owns land for himself absolutely.

A purchaser of this land, however, may be unwise to accept a conveyance from $H$ alone. The reason for this is that it cannot be proved with complete certainty that $W$ did not, before her death, change her beneficial joint tenancy into a beneficial tenancy in common, since such a change can be effected simply in writing. If this did happen, then $H$ will own the legal estate as trustee for himself and the estate of his wife as tenants in common beneficially. Since $H$ is still a trustee, a purchaser will not receive a valid receipt for the purchase money unless another trustee is appointed to act with $H$.

This problem frequently arises in practice, and it makes the work of the solicitors of the vendor and the purchaser awkward. A purchaser's solicitor, if he is cautious, will insist that whenever a surviving joint tenant of land sells, another trustee must be appointed to act with him. If, as is probable, the purchaser's solicitor advises his client that there is little risk, and the conveyance is taken from a surviving joint tenant only, there is a possibility that if anything goes wrong the solicitor will be liable for negligence.

The simple reform which is urgently required is to enable a surviving joint tenant of land to sell on the basis that he is solely and beneficially interested. This will dispel the doubts which now exist and eliminate an unnecessary conveyancing problem.

*The Sale of New Properties*

When between 200,000 and 300,000 houses are being built each year, it is inevitable that the building standards of some developers should be very low. If there was no housing shortage and purchasers could distinguish clearly between good and bad building, consumer consciousness would operate to drive out of business developers with low standards, or force the standards up. Unfortunately we have not yet reached this stage.

The legal position appears to be as follows:

The overriding principle is *caveat emptor*. The buyer is deemed to take the property as it is. He bears the risk.

If the house has been completed and is then sold or let to a purchaser, the fact that the house is defective will not apparently make the vendor liable unless he gave an express warranty that the house was reasonably sound and fit for habitation.

If the house is to be built for the purchaser after he has entered into a contract to buy or lease the land, there is an implied term that the house is fit for human habitation. But this warranty will always yield to the express terms of the contract, and if a builder completes the house in accordance with the contractual specifications, he may not be liable if it is in fact unfit for human habitation. Thus in *Lynch* v. *Thorne*[1] the defendant builder sold a plot of land to the plaintiff with a partially erected house on it and undertook to complete the building in accordance with the plans and specifications annexed to the agreement. The specification provided for nine-inch brick walls. After the house was completed, in accordance with the specifications and with sound materials and good workmanship, it was discovered that the nine-inch wall on the south side of the house did not keep driving rain out, and one of the bedrooms was consequently unusable. The Court of Appeal held that the builder had carried out his part of the contract, and since the house could only have been made fit for human habitation if additional work had been done (which was inconsistent with the terms of the contract), there was no room for the operation of any implied warranty that the house should be fit for habitation. This was so even though the plaintiff had relied on the builder's plans and specifications.

Neither the vendor nor the lessor of property is under any liability in tort for its dangerous condition once he has parted with possession to the purchaser or lessee. Thus in *Otto* v. *Bolton*[2] a builder negligently built a house which he then sold. Six months later the ceiling of the first floor fell down and injured the purchaser's mother. The purchaser was able to recover

[1] [1956] 1 W.L.R. 303.
[2] [1936] 2 K.B. 46.

compensation for the cost of repairs to the ceiling and for damage to furniture, because the judge found that the builders had expressly warranted that the house was well built. However, the purchaser's mother was not able to recover damages for her injuries. Presumably, had there been no express warranty the purchaser would have had no remedy either. The learned judge remarked that "I can find in no case any suggestion that a builder selling a house after completion is, in his capacity of builder, under any obligation to take care towards a future purchaser, let alone other persons who may come to live in it."

The law appears to be unfairly weighted in favour of property developers. The practice of builders also varies. Great play is made today with "defects undertakings" which builders give to purchasers when the house is erected. These undertakings usually provide that the builder will remedy any defects due to defective materials or workmanship which appear within a certain time. The period specified usually varies between six months and two years. Such undertakings, if they are sufficiently wide and last for a reasonable time, are useful, but often the purchasers' solicitors are not allowed to change the standard "defects undertaking" given by the builders. The law should be reformed so that the balance is redressed in favour of the consumer.

Today's widespread building has its attendant evils and purchasers often find that having put their life savings into a brand new home and entered into heavy long-term financial commitments, they have bought nothing but an expensive disappointment. The law must be altered so that greater responsibilities are placed upon property developers and the following changes are suggested:

(1) When a purchaser or lessee moves into a new property there should always be implied a warranty by the builder and/or vendor or lessor that the house is fit for human habitation, and this term should be defined quite clearly and widely (cf. Housing Act, 1957, s. 4).

(2) When the house has been built in accordance with plans and specifications prepared by builders, and the purchaser has relied on the builders' skill and experience, then, underlying all the plans and specifications there should be an implied warranty that the completed house is fit for human habitation.

(3) There should be an implied term that there is liability for

all defects appearing in the property within a minimum period
of two years from erection. Further, the right of enforcement
should be capable of being assigned to any person who acquires
the house within that time.

(4) Builders should owe the common duty of care, as set out
in the Occupiers Liability Act, 1957, to any person who is
injured on the premises as a result of their negligence.

Recently the Private House Owners (Protection) Bill was
introduced into the House of Commons. This is designed to
protect private house-owners from the consequences of sub-
standard building by making compulsory the registration of
all building firms with local authorities (if complaints of gerry
building and sub-standard building are made, the local
authorities would have power to withdraw the registration)
and providing that such firms shall take out insurance policies
to compensate private house-owners if the building is not
completed owing to the bankruptcy of the builder.

### Speed and Cost of Conveyancing Transactions

To persons buying and selling property, speed and cost are
matters of greater concern than legal technicalities. These two
factors call for a re-examination of the present machinery and
practices.

*The Time Factor in Conveyancing.* The average conveyancing
transaction takes between eight to ten weeks to complete. To
many clients, whose decision has been made early on and who
are anxious to move, such delay is irksome and difficult to
understand. It would be possible to shorten the majority of
conveyancing transactions by several weeks.

The bulk of a solicitor's work today has shifted from post-
contract to pre-contract matters. This is especially so in
registered land conveyancing. In the sale and purchase of the
majority of dwelling houses, the investigation of title and the
preparation of the conveyances, transfers and mortgages
are routine procedures. A delay of some weeks before the contract is signed is inevitable. Searches and inquiries have to be
made, surveyors must examine the house and submit their
reports, and financial arrangements with building societies,
insurance companies and other institutions must be tied up.
Also, where a vendor is simultaneously buying another house
or a purchaser is selling his own, these matters must be syn-
chronised. Once the contract is signed, the usual date inserted

in the contract for completion is four weeks. Frequently, the completion may not take place for five or six weeks.

This post-contract period can be shortened in one of two ways. The first way is for the bulk of the post-contract work to be done prior to the contract. Thus, if the vendor's solicitors forward the abstract of title with the draft contract, the purchaser's solicitors can investigate the title and deal with other matters during the time-lag before the contracts can be exchanged. There are two objections which can be raised to this procedure. First, if the matter falls through, solicitors may object that they are doing unnecessary work. This additional work in a small proportion of abortive cases is a fair price to pay for speeding up conveyancing generally. Secondly, most vendors would consider it undesirable to disclose to the purchaser the price he and his predecessors paid for the property. This problem can be easily met by excluding from the abstract of title the prices paid, and supplying such details after the contract. This is often done today in registered conveyancing.

The second method of reducing time is to accept that there are a large number of small conveyancing transactions where a contract can be safely dispensed with. All the initial work can be directed towards completion, and when all the usual matters, especially the mortgage arrangements, are settled, completion can be arranged speedily.

It should be possible, by the use of these procedures, to reduce the time of the average conveyancing transaction to six to eight weeks.

*Conveyancing Costs.* When a person buys a house, or sells one house and buys another, the legal costs and disbursements appear to be quite high. To many laymen all costs and disbursements are lumped together under the heading of "legal fees" and solicitors acquire an unfair reputation for being expensive. The resentment caused by the high cost of the transfer of houses could be removed or reduced if careful explanations were given to clients, showing how the cost is divided up, and the services which were rendered.

As regards the costs themselves the following matters require particular attention:

Generally, the largest single item in the total cost is the estate agent's commission. The agent's scale commission when the property is sold for, say, £2,500 is £75, whereas the solicitor's scale charge is £45 if the land is unregistered, or £30 if the land is registered. The agent's scale commission on a sale for £5,000 is £137 10s.; the solicitor's scale charge is £67 10s. (unregistered), or £43 15s. (registered).

The rates of the estate agent's commission may be quite low by commercial standards, but they are very high from the point of view of the vendor. This is especially so when the housing position, as at present and for the foreseeable future, gives rise to a seller's market and the agent has to do relatively little to earn his money.

If, as is certain, agents are not prepared to revise their scales, other methods of finding purchasers might well be considered. There is no absolute necessity for a vendor to employ an estate agent. House owners could well be encouraged to sell the property through their own efforts, e.g. by advertisements. Encouragement might also be given to associations and clubs, and possibly trade unions, to set up registers containing particulars of houses offered for sale by members and to employ officials to advise members on prices.

Two further points might also be considered. First, estate agents should be prohibited from purchasing, through nominees, properties which they are instructed to sell, unless the owner is fully aware and approves.

Secondly, the existing practice whereby estate agents often hold the purchaser's deposit as stakeholders until completion should be changed. The principal reason for the present practice is that the estate agent can recover his commission immediately the sale is completed by deducting it from the deposit. In several cases, agents have misappropriated deposits and the purchasers have lost these sums. If the practice were changed and the deposits were held by the vendor's solicitor, as stakeholder, then in the event of any misappropriation, the Law Society's Compensation Fund would compensate the purchaser. The alternative, of course, might be for the estate agents' profession to have a central compensation fund to meet these contingencies. The profession is battling with this problem at present.

There appears to be no major case for reducing solicitors' scale fees generally, although there is no justification for any increase. Inflation in property values has increased solicitors' remuneration. The following points should be considered in bringing down legal charges:

Solicitors' scale fees are lower for registered land transactions.

As suggested earlier, the system of land registration should be extended to the whole country as soon as possible.

When a purchaser of property also obtains a mortgage, he incurs further solicitors' fees in connection with the mortgage. These are based on the same scale as for purchases, the fee being based on the amount of the loan. When the money is advanced by a building society there is an agreed scale of charges, which is usually lower because the work is often stereotyped. This reduced scale should be extended to all cases where a purchaser obtains an institutional mortgage, for example from insurance companies.

Borrowers are usually required to pay the legal costs of the person or institution granting a mortgage. Where the solicitor for the purchaser is also on the panel of building society solicitors, he will also act for the building society in the transaction, and the solicitor's charges for the mortgage are halved. If this can happen in many cases, it should happen in all, so that a purchaser's solicitor will automatically represent the building society.

There is a case for rationalising the scale of solicitors' costs in connection with leases.

The stamp duty on conveyances has been reduced considerably in recent years, and now there is exemption from duty for conveyances of £3,500 or less. With the ever-increasing rise in the value of property this relief should be extended as much as possible.[1]

## LEASES GENERALLY

It is not possible here to deal in detail with all those aspects of the law of landlord and tenant which require overhauling. The following matters require urgent consideration.

### The Rent Acts

Whether or not rent control should be extended or relaxed is purely a political decision. However, as long as the Rent Acts type of legislation exists, there is an urgent need for a consolidating or codifying Act to do away with the present

---

[1] Since this book has gone to press, the Chancellor of the Exchequer has, in fact, proposed that the stamp duty on conveyances (and mortgages) should be halved, and the exemption available for house purchasers raised to £4,500; see *The Times*, 4 April, 1963.

maze. This need is all the greater as the policy behind the various Acts, some designed to impose control, some to allow decontrol, has been inconsistent.

When this reform takes place, certain other matters should be considered:

*Transmission of controlled tenancies on death.* At present, when a statutory tenant dies, the tenancy can pass once, either to the widow of the tenant residing with him at his death, or to a member of the tenant's family who has resided with him for at least six months immediately before the death. A case exists for extending the number of transmissions which can take place, and possibly removing the limit on transmissions completely. In addition, the definition of the "tenant's family" should be widened so that it clearly covers "family residences" even where there is no marriage and the tenant or his partner has a legitimate family elsewhere. Another acceptable modification might be to allow the statutory tenancy to be transmitted to any woman who resided with the statutory tenant for the five years preceding his death.

*Service tenancies and tied cottages.* Where Rent Act premises have been let by an employer to an employee, the landlord can recover possession on the termination of the employment if the premises are required as a residence for another person in the landlord's full-time employment. This is a reasonable provision in itself, and, because of increasing decontrol, of decreasing importance. However, for tenants at present affected and also for the future, if control is to be re-introduced, the rule should be amended in two respects to avoid possible hardship. The first is to modify the decision in *Braithwaite* v. *Elliott*[1] which established that it does not matter whether the tenant knew that an ostensibly "controlled" tenancy was created in consequence of his employment; the only matter that the court ought to consider is the reason which actuated the landlord in letting the house.

The second point is that at present the landlord can recover possession even if another suitable house is available for the employee for whom possession is sought: *Lowcock* v. *Brotherton*.[2] It would be desirable to amend the law so that the landlord should have to prove greater hardship.

Tied cottages (that is to say, dwelling-houses where the

[1] [1947] K.B. 177.
[2] [1952] C.P.L. 408.

person residing is required so to reside by his employer for the better performance of his duties, or is permitted to reside, without there being an intention on either side to create a tenancy) are outside the scope of the Rent Acts. Resolutions advocating the abolition of tied cottages have been passed for many years at T.U.C. and Labour Party congresses. The usual argument against their abolition is that it is essential for agricultural labourers to live on the premises and that, given the shortage of houses in rural areas, tied cottages are a necessity to enable farmers to house their workers. The Rent Act provision relating to service tenancies would give sufficient protection to the farmer, and should further Rent Act control be introduced there will be no justification for the continued existence of tied cottages.

*Local authority housing.* Houses built by local authorities are not subject to the Rent Acts. Even if further control were to be introduced, in view of the number of new houses that are being built by local authorities, the proportion of dwellings not subject to control will increase enormously. This is unsatisfactory from the point of view of security of tenure. It is argued that local authorities only claim possession when the public interest or the interest of other tenants demand it; but that is a matter of inference and assumption. If homes built by local authorities were made subject to control, the authorities could in proper cases get possession (the grounds would have to be set out in the new Act), and the tenant would enjoy security of tenure in the knowledge that the local authority could not get an automatic order for possession on inadequate grounds. At present, reasons need not even be disclosed to the court.

*Furnished dwellings.* The Rent Tribunals, set up under the Furnished Houses (Rent Control) Act, 1946, to investigate and control the rents chargeable for dwelling-houses where the rent includes payment for furniture or services, work fairly well. The Tribunal may approve, reduce or increase the rent; the rent so dealt with must be entered on a register kept by the local authority, and thereafter it is an offence to require or receive a rent in excess of the rent so registered. The Tribunal also has power to grant security of tenure.

However, the present procedure of invoking the jurisdiction of the Tribunal is unsatisfactory. The reference is usually made by aggrieved tenants and this naturally puts the tenant out of favour with his landlord. The security of tenure granted by the Tribunal will not last indefinitely, and landlords usually get rid of their public spirited tenants as soon as they can. For this reason some tenants are deterred from applying to Rent Tribunals even though they may be paying exorbitant rents.

A better procedure would be for the rent of furnished dwellings to be provisionally fixed by the local authority, with a right of appeal to the Rent Tribunal by landlord or tenant. Revision of the rent should be similarly licensed by the local authority, and it should have powers of inspection to ensure that a proper standard of accommodation is maintained.

### Business Tenancies

The security of tenure provisions in Part II of the Landlord and Tenant Act, 1954, also appear to be working reasonably well. Business tenancies continue in force when the lease expires until they are determined in one of the ways (usually written notice) permitted by the Act, and the tenant may apply to the court for the grant of a new tenancy.

Certain matters of detail, however, require change:

*Sub-tenancies.* The most difficult problems under the 1954 Act arise out of sub-tenancies. One difficulty can be illustrated in the following way: $T$ holds a lease of business premises from $L$, and has sub-let part of the premises to $ST$. If $L$ serves a notice under the Act determining $T$'s tenancy subject to his right to a new tenancy, $T$ is awkwardly placed in relation to his sub-tenant $ST$. $T$ cannot serve a notice on $ST$ determining the sub-lease until he acquires a new lease himself. This, of course, takes time, and so $T$ may find that he has to pay the increased rent to $L$ long before he himself can obtain an increased rent from $ST$. The Act should be amended so that in these circumstances the increased rent payable by sub-tenants $(ST)$ would take effect from the same date as the tenant's $(T)$ payment of increased rent to the lessors $(L)$.

*Date of commencement of new leases.* It was decided in *Re No.* 88 *High Road, Kilburn*[1] that where a court grants a new lease, the commencing date is three months from the date on which the application to the court is finally disposed of. Until that time, the old rent continues to be payable. There is often a considerable time-lag between the date of termination of the old lease and the final decision of the court, particularly where

[1] [1959] 1 W.L.R. 279.

the application is not to a County Court but to the High Court. To eliminate injustice to landlords, new leases should be made to run (whenever this is reasonable) from the expiration of the notices to terminate the original lease.

*Repairs*

There is much confusion in the minds of tenants concerning the landlords' responsibility for repairs. In recent years, if the lease or tenancy agreement contained the usual covenant that the tenant would keep the interior of the premises in good and substantial repair, the tenant usually assumed that the landlord would keep the structure and exterior in repair. He did not always realise that, although there was no covenant that the tenant would keep the structure in repair, the landlord was usually under no obligation to do so.

Legislation has more recently effected important and sweeping changes. A tenant may be protected in the following ways:

*Furnished lettings.* Where a house is let furnished, there is an implied condition that it is reasonably fit for occupation at the commencement of the tenancy. This implied condition does not impose any obligation to maintain the house in that state, and it does not extend to unfurnished premises.

*Housing Act,* 1957, *s.* 6. It is provided that where a house is let at a rent not exceeding £80 a year in London or £52 elsewhere (the figures are £40 and £26 respectively if the house was let before 6 July, 1957) there is an implied condition (which cannot be excluded) that the house is reasonably fit for human habitation at the beginning of the tenancy and an implied undertaking by the landlord that he will keep it in that state throughout the tenancy. These provisions are also extended to agricultural tied cottages. However, the condition is not implied where the letting is for at least three years upon terms that it is for the tenant to put the house into a condition reasonably fit for habitation. The standard required of the landlord was changed in 1954 when an attempt was made to put into force the recommendations of the Standards of Fitness Sub-Committee of the Central Housing Advisory Committee (1946). Regard is now to be had to the condition of the house in respect of repair, stability, freedom from damp, natural lighting, ventilation, water supply, drainage and sanitary convenience, and facilities for storage, preparation and cooking of food and the disposal of waste water. A house is deemed to be unfit for human habitation if, and only if, it is defective in one or more of these matters and is not reasonably suitable for occupation in that condition. By confining the standard to these specified matters, there may be certain cases where a house is unfit for human habitation for other reasons (e.g. infestation by vermin) and the landlord will not be responsible. The standard requires amendment so that the court is free to consider other matters in addition to the specified ones. Further, although the rent limit was doubled in 1957, this statutory repairing covenant only applies to small dwelling houses, and operates haphazardly, especially as rent includes rates. The reason why the limit is based on rent is, apparently, historical. The logical change here would be to apply these provisions to houses within certain limits based upon rateable value.

Although the provisions of the 1957 Act were useful they obviously did not cover all leases and tenancies adequately. Hence the most recent reform.

*Housing Act*, 1961, *ss.* 32 *and* 33. It is provided that in any lease or tenancy of a dwelling for less than seven years (except business or agricultural leases) granted after 23 November, 1961, there is an implied covenant by the landlord:

(a) to keep in repair the structure and exterior of the dwelling-house (including drains, gutters and external pipes) and

(b) to keep in repair and proper working order the installations in the dwelling-house—

    i. for the supply of water, gas and electricity, and for sanitation (including basins, sinks, baths and sanitary conveniences but not, except as aforesaid, fixtures, fittings and appliances for making use of water, gas or electricity), and

    ii. for space heating or water heating.

Further, any covenants by the lessee for the repair of the premises is declared to be of no effect in so far as it relates to the above matters. The landlord is not required to repair damage caused by flood or fire, or damage caused by the tenant himself acting in an un-tenantlike manner. Apart from this, however, the covenant is absolute and the parties cannot contract out of it.

These sweeping provisions are welcome, but some time will

be necessary to see how effective they are. However, when the
position is re-examined, a useful reform would be to extend
the lessor's implied covenant to all leases with an option for
the parties to contract out if the lease is for seven years or more.

Also, it would be useful to define by statute the precise
meaning of those technical terms which are relevant to the
standards and types of repair. As yet, the case-law has not
supplied unequivocal definitions.

## "Outgoings"

"Outgoings" and "charges" cover a multitude of expenses
in respect of a house, including paving and drainage charges
raised by local authorities. Strictly, these are capital improvements which should not fall on a tenant. Unless such outgoings
are expressly mentioned and defined in the lease, the words
"outgoings" and "charges" should not include any payment
other than a periodical payment.

## Covenants Against Assignments

It is provided by the Landlord and Tenant Act, 1927, s. 19,
that where there is a covenant by the tenant not to assign
without the landlord's consent it is implied that the consent
will not be unreasonably withheld. This provision can be
easily evaded by the landlord imposing an absolute covenant
upon the tenant not to assign; the landlord then obtains complete discretion. This loophole should be closed by providing
that if the landlord on being requested by the tenant to accept
a surrender of the lease or tenancy refuses to do so, then the
covenant against assignment will be treated as a covenant
within the 1927 Act, and the landlord will be unable unreasonably to withhold his consent.

## Covenants Relating to the Right to Grant Leases and Quiet Enjoyment

Hardship may occur where a tenant who has committed no
breach of covenant suddenly finds himself turned out of his
home because the landlord had no right to grant the lease or
tenancy; if the covenant for quiet enjoyment was in the usual
form, the tenant may have no right even to damages against
anyone. Thus, if a tenant pays rent to a mortgagee creating a
yearly tenancy, the provisions of the mortgagee's own lease are
not automatically included, so that the lessee may lose possession
if the mortgagor has the right to possession against the mortgagee. Again, if a mortgagor grants a lease not under his

statutory power and without the consent of the mortgagee, on
the latter taking possession the tenant will have to vacate. If
an under-lease is granted out of the lease for a longer term than
the lease, the under-lease is determined. Finally, if an under-
lease is granted contrary to the terms of the head-lease, it may
be determined immediately on the expiry of the head-lease.

In each of the above examples, the lowest tenant is liable to
eviction before the end of his term, without any remedy. There
should be implied by law, notwithstanding any agreement to
the contrary, in every grant of a tenancy a warranty that the
grantor is entitled to grant the tenancy which he purports to
grant. An action for damages would then lie by the grantee if
the warranty were broken.

### Insurance, Reinstatement and Abatement of Rent

Under the existing law the tenant is liable for the rent of
premises destroyed by fire or some other unusual event, unless
there are special covenants with the landlord. Even if the landlord is liable for repairs, and therefore rebuilding, the full
rent is payable in the absence of an abatement clause. Further,
if the tenant is liable for repairs and the landlord is insured,
he cannot be compelled to spend the insurance monies without
notice being given to the insurers under the Fires Prevention
(Metropolis) Act, 1744. The problems arising from the destruction of a house by fire are full of anomalies.

It is proposed that a landlord should adequately insure his
houses and buildings against fire, and be liable to reinstate them
when they are damaged (as distinct from destroyed). The
tenant should not have to pay rent when the premises no longer
exist owing to fire, enemy action or inevitable accident, and
he should have the right to determine the lease. Where in
existing leases there are no provisions for insurance, the
insurance premium should be paid by the party liable to repair
under the lease. If the liability is not specified, the landlord
should pay the premium.

### Notices to Quit

There is a mass of case law on notices to quit, and it would
be desirable to remove excessive technicality by codification.

In particular, attention should be paid to the date when the
notice to quit expires. At present, notices to quit have to expire

on the "proper day" which frequently is not known with any certainty. Many notices to quit are invalidated for this reason. It should be provided that, in the absence of a written agreement specifying the proper day, a notice to quit can be validly given to expire at any time after a given period, the length of which will vary with the tenancy. In the case of monthly tenancies or less, the period could be one month, for a quarterly tenancy one quarter, and for a yearly tenancy six months. Agricultural tenancies would require to be treated differently.

Waiver of notices to quit should be only by the consent of both parties, express or implied. Waiver will then be a question of fact, to be decided in each case. In particular, the acceptance of rent should not in itself operate as a waiver. A recent example of the strange rules relating to waivers can be seen in *Windmill Investments (London) Ltd.* v. *Milano Restaurant Ltd.*[1] In that case the tenant broke a covenant in a lease. After the landlord became aware of the breach, the next payment of rent was accepted from the tenant "without prejudice" to the breach of covenant, and the following payment "subject to your breaches of covenant set out in a notice served on [you] so that this receipt of rent can in no way be treated as a waiver of the breaches". In spite of these clear statements, the court held that the qualified acceptance of the two instalments of rent did amount to a waiver.

### Forfeiture and Other Remedies

The remedies available to landlords are fairly numerous and the relevant legal processes even more so. For nearly 200 years from the middle of the seventeenth century most of the new statutes governing this part of the law of landlord and tenant were in favour of the landlords. During the past century legislation was merely a patchwork of consolidation. Consolidation of the law in its present state would be a waste of time. Some remedies must be swept away and the rest reduced to manageable and intelligible terms.

In practice a landlord requires a remedy for three matters only:

(a) non-payment of rent;
(b) breach of covenant by the tenant;

---

[1] [1962] 3 W.L.R. 651.

(c) unlawful retention of the premises by the tenant after the lease has terminated.

Sufficient remedy for these can be given upon application to a County Court as follows:

(a) a judgment order for the rent due, with or without an order for possession at the discretion of the court, having regard to the previous conduct of the parties;

(b) an order to remedy the breach of covenant, or for forfeiture, with the provisions for relief now set out in s. 146 of the Law of Property Act, 1925;

(c) an order for possession in favour of the landlord when the tenant unlawfully holds over or obtains possession, together with appropriate damages.

These proposed remedies should be compared with some of the existing ones which can now be abolished. For instance, distress (which cannot be used anyway without an order of the court) is not so effective as a judgment order for a sum of money which can be enforced by execution. Distress may involve all sorts of irregularities, whereas execution, being carried out under the control of the sheriff, is out of the landlord's hands and is not liable to create further complications. If a landlord cannot obtain the rent from bad tenants, he should either obtain a judgment order followed by execution, or a possession order. He should be forbidden to re-enter without judgment of the court.

Actions for double rent and double value should be abolished. They originated in penal statutes. There is no moral or legal reason why landlords should be entitled to a double value in the nature of damages; it is contrary to all the principles of the common law. When these remedies were created there were no County Courts. It should be ample protection for a landlord to have an order of the County Court for possession, with appropriate damages based on the rent.

The Small Tenants Recovery Act, 1838, which gives landlords the right to take proceedings against certain tenants in the Magistrates' Courts is another obsolete relic. Justices themselves realise that they are not well qualified to decide the difficult questions which sometimes arise in such proceedings. But where justices made a practice of referring these cases to the local County Court, the High Court held that they had no power to do so. The County Court is clearly the proper place for such proceedings, and the 1838 Act should be repealed.

## Streamlining Leases

Many leases are unduly lengthy and sometimes badly drafted. They should be streamlined by using short forms of standard covenants. It is curious to note that the Leases Act, 1845, provided machinery for shortening leases. The Act was too advanced for the times and was opposed by the legal profession. However, several jurisdictions in the Commonwealth have introduced similar statutes and in fact make use of them. The legal profession in this country has recently shown a fresh interest in this problem. New legislation should be introduced to bring the 1845 Act up to date.

## Leasehold Enfranchisement

This is one of the most urgent matters requiring legislative action.

The characteristic mid-nineteenth century technique of housing development was for large areas of land in England and Wales to be let for long terms (usually 99 years) at a ground rent. If the houses were already built, premiums were paid when the lease was granted; more often, the lessees or building contractors built the houses after the leases were granted. In London the practice has nearly always been for the freeholder to lease land to a contractor for the erection of a row of houses. The contractor then either assigned his lease or sub-let. The hardships caused by this property system are nation-wide, but particular publicity has been given to the difficulties (and the bitterness) in South Wales.

Industrial expansion in South Wales dates from about 1870. The mining, steel and tin-plate industries attracted large numbers of men and families from country areas. The choice for these people was either to live in the companies' houses or to build their own homes. If they wanted to build their own homes they had to buy land, usually from one large landlord, and this land was usually available on a 99 year lease only. Often the houses were built by the families who lived in them, and in many cases the descendants of the original lessees still live there. These leases are running out, and the remote and unreal problems created 99 years ago have become urgent realities. The house which had been an item of security for so long suddenly appears to be confiscated and reverts to the ground landlord and, in addition, the tenant may be presented with a dilapidations claim.

Partial relief was given by Part I of the Landlord and Tenant Act, 1954, which gave security of tenure at the end of the long lease (as if the tenant was a protected tenant under the Rent Acts), but provision was made for the rent to be increased, often to the market value.

Even this protection is not always available to the lessee, for the ground landlord may obtain possession, *inter alia*, where he can show that he proposes to demolish or reconstruct the whole or a substantial part of the premises for redevelopment. There is no provision requiring the landlord to find alternative accommodation for the lessee. Speculators have not been slow to take advantage of this loophole.

In many cases the protection offered by the 1954 Act has caused serious hardship to lessees who have lived in the house for decades, many of whom are aged and have limited financial resources. This would not, of itself, be a reason for introducing leasehold enfranchisement. However, it will be shown that, on balance, the occupying tenant usually has a better right to claim the land than the freeholder.

As long ago as 1884 a Royal Commission on the Housing of the Working Classes commented: "The prevailing system of building leases is conducive to bad building, to deterioration of property towards the close of the lease, and to a want of interest on the part of the occupier of the house he inhabits . . . legislation favourable to the acquisition on equitable terms of the freehold interest on the part of the leaseholder would conduce greatly to the improvement of the dwellings of the people of this country."

The problem has been recognised for many years, and this century has seen between 30 and 40 parliamentary attempts to reform the system. So far, apart from the 1954 legislation, all attempts to introduce a just solution have been abortive. Among the supporters of ground landlords even those who are prepared to accept that there may be an argument for leasehold enfranchisement cannot accept any financial formula other than the *present* market value of the freehold interest. Any other solution, it is argued, would be a confiscatory measure which would rob ground landlords of their true. property rights. This argument must be examined in its proper perspective, that is, the whole 99 years' period; only that way can one assess the fair price of the freehold. Nobody denies, of course, that ground landlords must be fairly compensated for the loss of their interest.

The latest unsuccessful bill for leasehold enfranchisement was introduced as a Private Member's measure in December 1962. It provided that the ground lessees of residential property should have the right to enlarge their interest into a freehold interest. The price for the enfranchisement would be such sum as will be agreed between the parties or, in default of agreement, determined by a County Court on the following principles:

"The said sum shall not exceed an amount equivalent to twenty-five times the annual rent payable under the tenancy, unless the court, in all the circumstances, deems it just to determine a price in excess of such amount, having regard to:

(a) the date at which the tenancy was granted and the consideration, if any, paid by the tenant for the grant of the tenancy at the commencement of the tenancy;

(b) the date at which and the consideration, if any, for which the tenant shall have acquired the tenancy from his predecessor (if any);

(c) the length of the unexpired term of the tenancy;

(d) any dwelling house or other building erected on the land which is the subject of the tenancy;

(e) the state and condition in which such dwelling house or other building has been maintained by the tenant or his predecessors in title (if any);

(f) the extent and value of any improvement or improvements carried out by the tenant or his predecessors in title (if any);

(g) changes in the value of money at the date of the expiry of the notice as compared with the value of money at the date when the tenancy was granted."

These principles might give rise to a certain amount of confusion in cases where the lease has only a few years to run; for then it could be argued that the price must be something approaching the current market value of the house and land. But here again one has to look at the historical perspective. An unreal example might effectively indicate how the principles should be applied in some cases. Using modern figures, let us assume that $P$ takes a 99 years' lease of a property and pays a premium to $F$ of £4,500. Had $P$ been able to acquire the property from $F$ as a freehold interest, the market value would be, say, £5,000. Thus, when $P$ acquires the lease, he has paid 90% of the value of the house and land as it then stands, and $F$ retains a capital interest worth 10% of that value. Ninety-nine years later, assuming only a very mild inflationary tendency, the property is worth, say, £10,000 freehold. Under the present system $F$'s successor would be entitled to a 100% interest in the land, together with the benefit of a dilapidations claim against $P$'s successor; all that $P$'s successor now has is the right, subject to exceptions, to security of tenure, provided that he is willing to pay the full market rent. Clearly, the system is blatantly unfair. When the lease is granted it matters little to the purchaser whether he acquires the freehold (if available) or the leasehold. In either case he is able for a time to sell the property fairly easily and the price of the leasehold would not be much less than the freehold price. However, as the lease runs on, the capital value of the interest drops sharply. The leaseholder is unable to sell the house so easily, because mortgages become increasingly difficult to obtain. The value of $P$'s 90% interest is rapidly decreasing, and, correspondingly, the value of $F$'s 10% interest is rapidly increasing.

If one looks at the interests of the freeholder and the lease-holder in this light, then it follows that the price which the leaseholder should pay for the freehold interest is the current market value of the percentage interest which the freeholder originally had. Thus, in the above example, the current market value of $F$'s original 10% interest is now £1,000. This is a fair price in the circumstances, for it recognises and reflects the true interests of each party; but even this is possibly an under-statement, for it was the lessee who had been spending money on the property over 99 years. A saving provision might well be necessary to protect persons who acquired the ground rent, before the enfranchising legislation was passed, at an inflated value.

Obviously it is difficult for the parties, or the court, to assess accurately what the freehold interest of the property would have been at a time which may go as far back as 99 years. However, it is hoped that if the principle suggested above were adopted, justice would be done to both parties. Slightly different factors would have to be taken into account where the freeholder granted a 99 year lease of a plot of land, and the house was erected later.

The introduction of the proposed system would inevitably create certain difficulties. First there is the problem of the property speculator who might find it profitable to assume the opposite role to his present one. By buying the "fag end" of a lease from the leaseholder he could compulsorily acquire the freehold reversion for a relatively low sum, and sell the unencumbered freehold at a substantial profit. Why should a speculator-lessee make a profit instead of the freeholder? Such a person should be required to pay the market value of the lessee's interest, which would include the right to acquire the freehold at a fair price.

Next, the Leasehold Bill of December 1962 provided that a person who purchased the leasehold interest within the last ten years of the term should not have the right of leasehold enfranchisement. There is no real justification for this limitation; the reasons were mentioned earlier. The Bill also provided that the right of enfranchisement could only be exercised by a tenant while there was at least five years of the term unexpired. This, too, would work unfairly; many people who had less than five years of their lease to run at the date when such a measure became law would not obtain any benefit at all.

A further serious problem would arise if a tenant who wished to acquire the freehold interest, found that he was unable to pay the price determined by the County Court. Mortgage facilities might be curtailed, or the age or financial circumstances of the lessee might make a mortgage unobtainable.

A solution to this problem would be for State funds to be made available to lessees who wish to pay a reasonable price for the reversion but cannot find the funds through normal channels. The State loans should carry reasonable rates of interest repayable over a term of years suitable for the case of the particular lessee.

This reform would be only the beginning. As for the future, prevention is better than cure. In recent years the leasehold system of building development has become very popular. Purchases of houses, and more often of flats and maisonettes, are arranged by granting 99 year leases at a premium and a ground rent. Often the premium is not much less than the value of the freehold itself. The time is ripe for legislation preventing such leases being granted. The prevailing system of creating a delayed social problem should not be allowed to continue without some sound argument for its continuance. The argument usually put forward by supporters of the lease-hold ground rent system are the following:

(a) Any legislative interference with existing or future leases would be against the hallowed principle of sanctity of contract. This argument is emotive and irrational. Each year the statute book provides examples of legislation which interferes compulsorily with contractual relation-ships. This is a normal feature of modern society.

(b) A system of leasehold ground rents is essential if, par-ticularly in the case of flats and maisonettes, lessees are to be protected by a set of mutually beneficial and enforceable covenants between all members of an estate. To that, the real answer is, surely, to change the law relating to covenants, instead of using this defect in our law as an excuse to perpetuate the leasehold ground rent system.

(c) A leaseholding system will enable a landlord to re-develop an estate to the benefit of everybody at the right time; and some large landlords with a firm sense of social responsibility do in fact exercise a beneficial control over estates during the subsistance of the leases, and do re-develop at the end.

This is an important but not convincing argument. The first point is that the majority of landlords have no intention of re-developing at the expiration of a lease. Secondly, if this argument is sound, large areas of free-hold land in England and Wales could never be satis-factorily re-developed. The answer is that comprehensive re-development can be carried out by, or under the direction of, local authorities who have wide powers of acquisition. These authorities, if necessary, could be given further powers to encourage re-development, subject to adequate compensation and/or the provision of suitable alternative accommodation.

(d) A person sometimes prefers to take a lease rather than buy the freehold, since he can obtain it at a cheaper price at a time when his resources are stretched to the limit. This is no convincing argument for enabling a freeholder to increase his capital interest as the lease progresses.

Legislation should therefore be introduced prohibiting the grant of these long leases at a ground rent. Alternatively, if it is felt that the leasehold system is desirable from the point of view of community control and covenants, then such leases should all be granted for periods of 999 years and not 99. The problems of 1,000 years hence can be dealt with if and when they arise.

# VI

## FAMILY LAW

### INTRODUCTORY

MORE PEOPLE ARE affected by some provision or other of family law than by any other branch of the law. And while all law ought to be certain and ascertainable, fair and commanding of respect, even greater importance attaches to these attributes being applicable to family law.

Since the publication in 1956 of the Report of the Royal Commission on Marriage and Divorce,[1] there has been a massive crop of legislation—some 12 important statutes[2]—in the field of family law. These have undoubtedly done useful work in improving the law relating to children, particularly to children of broken marriages; in tidying up some anomalies in the field of separation and divorce; in permitting former spouses to apply for maintenance from their deceased spouses' estates; and in enabling spouses to sue each other in tort.[3] The courts, too, have been very active in recent years, bringing about some dramatic changes in the field of matrimonial property law.

### A Family Charter

However welcome may be some at any rate of the changes in the law, the manner in which they have come about have made the law even more unwieldy and unmanageable than it was before. Reforms are still urgently needed in several fields of family law (these will be set out below); and we think that the time has come for the whole body of the existing law to be reviewed and re-enacted, with the appropriate changes, in

[1] Cmd. 9678.

[2] Maintenance Agreements Act, 1957; Affiliation Proceedings Act, 1957; Matrimonial Causes (Property and Maintenance) Act, 1958; Maintenance Orders Act, 1958; Matrimonial Proceedings (Children) Act, 1958; Divorce (Insanity and Desertion) Act, 1958; Adoption Act, 1958; Legitimacy Act, 1959; Marriage (Enabling) Act, 1960; Matrimonial Proceedings (Magistrates Courts) Act, 1960; Adoption Act, 1960; Law Reform (Husband and Wife) Act, 1962.

[3] As we go to press the Matrimonial Causes and Reconciliation Bill (introduced by Mr. Leo Abse, M.P. in November 1962) is before the House of Commons.

what we might, for the sake of convenience, label a new "Family Charter".[1]

Care must, however, be taken that, once the Family Charter has found its place on the statute book, legislators should not sit back complacently. The working of the Family Charter must be kept under constant review and amended in the light of experience and current trends.[2]

Every lawyer is aware of the serious limitations of family law: no legal provision, however ingenious, can *create* a happy family relationship; the best that a Family Charter can do is to alleviate some of the hardship that has arisen and caused one or another member of a family to invoke the law.

We believe that the provisions of the new Family Charter should clearly reflect those general principles of family life on which our modern society is based. At the risk of restating what to most must be obvious, we would summarise those principles as follows:

(1) Men and women are equal before the law.
(2) Marriage is neither an insurance policy for women, designed to keep them in economic security, nor is it a conveyance of property.
(3) Marriage imposes rights and duties on both spouses; marriages break down because one spouse is (more usually both are) in breach of some of those duties.
(4) So far as the law is concerned, marriage is dissoluble. Parties to a marriage which has completely broken down should never find themselves irretrievably tied to each other.[3]
(5) Children are entitled to a special protection and are not to be treated as pawns in a battle between their parents.

*A Family Division of the High Court*

Before considering in detail the reforms called for in the substantive part of family law, let us turn to the question whether any change ought to be made in that part of procedural law

[1] The Rules of the Supreme Court (Revision), 1962, which will come into operation on 1.1.1964, have gone some way towards reducing the volume of the "over-elaborated, anachronistic, tangled web" of rules of court evolved since 1883. There is every reason to perform a similar task in the field of family law.

[2] For the urgent need of having available information and statistical data on the effects of the law on family relations, see pp. 141, 148, *infra*.

[3] At present the courts can and do sometimes hold that even though the marriage has hopelessly broken down neither party is "guilty" of a matrimonial "offence".

which regulates the tribunals having jurisdiction in family matters.

We do not advocate any change so far as the jurisdiction of County Courts and Magistrates' Courts is concerned; but we do want to see the structure of the High Court recast.

The fate of a marriage is often intimately bound up with that of the children, and *vice versa*; it seems therefore nonsensical to continue the present practice (which owes its existence to historical reasons) of having proceedings relating to the same family pending in two different Divisions before two different judges of the High Court. We see no good reason why the Divorce Division should be bracketed with Probate and Admiralty; and why children should be the concern sometimes of the Divorce Division, sometimes of the Chancery Division and even, in habeas corpus proceedings, sometimes of the Queen's Bench Division. Instead, we suggest that a "Family Division" of the High Court be set up. The judges assigned to this Division should deal with *all* matters affecting spouses and children, both at first instance and on appeal from Magistrates' Courts.

The Family Division should possess all the inherent powers of the present Chancery Division; and it should be presided over by a judge of equal standing to the Lord Chief Justice. As a corollary, the expert knowledge required of the judges in the Family Division should be reflected also in the Court of Appeal and (so long as it survives[1]) the Appeal Committee of the House of Lords. Not less than three Lords Justices and three Lords of Appeal in Ordinary with specialised knowledge of family matters should at any one time be attached to the Court of Appeal and the Appeal Committee respectively.

MARRIAGE

## Requirements Prior to Marriage

Society has in recent times shown great concern over the increased birthrate of illegitimate children and the increase in teenage marriages which all too often end, after only a short time, in divorce. The very young, whose economic status today is frequently far above their emotional maturity, can and do rush into marriage without adequate consideration for the consequences.

[1] See p. 16, *infra.*

The primary remedy lies in education: in the extension of the present, often rather unsatisfactory, sex education in schools to such matters as the responsibilities (moral, financial and legal) of husbands and wives, both towards each other and towards their children.

However, the law could and should do something even now. Only minor amendments to the existing law would be required to ensure that no marriage is solemnised until the parties have had time to consider, or reconsider, their position. Couples who agree to marry should be required to give notice of their intention to the superintendent registrar (or clergyman) and their marriage should be solemnised only after a period of, say, three months.

This provision may well meet with opposition from those who fear that the number of illegitimate children would increase if "shotgun marriages" ceased to be a practical possibility. We do not think that this would be so. In fact, we are optimistic enough to think that the reform would have the opposite effect. For the young (and the not so young) may well be induced to think twice before starting a pregnancy if they knew of the delay imposed by the law.

## Void and Voidable Marriages

As the law now stands, parties to a void marriage need not have their marriage judicially annulled: they can contract a subsequent marriage. Parties to a voidable marriage, on the other hand, are married in the eyes of the law until and unless a competent court annuls the marriage. On this we would make the following comments:

(1) Now that Parliament has recognised that even void marriages can have important legal effects (the courts have power to make maintenance orders after decree[1] and children may be legitimate[2]), all marriages should be deemed to be valid until and unless judicially annulled (or dissolved).

(2) A certain amount of confusion has arisen as to whether duress renders a marriage void[3] or voidable[4]; and whether a

[1] The latest statutory provision is s. 1 of the Matrimonial Causes (Property and Maintenance) Act, 1958.
[2] S. 2, Legitimacy Act, 1959. Children born of voidable marriages have been legitimate since the Matrimonial Causes Act, 1937; now s. 9, Matrimonial Causes Act, 1950.
[3] E.g. *H.* v. *H.* [1953] 2 All E.R. 1229; [1954] P. 258.
[4] *Parojcic* v. *Parojcic* [1959] 1 All E.R. 1.

void marriage can, like a voidable marriage, be approbated.[1]
The so-called "sham marriages" (where the parties go through
a ceremony of marriage for the sole purpose of deriving some
political advantage—e.g. the wife acquiring the nationality
status of the husband for the purpose of leaving one country[2]
or emigrating to another[3]) require similar clarification.

Here again, a clear statement in the Family Charter, that all
properly conducted wedding ceremonies are deemed to create
valid marriages until a court pronounces otherwise, would help
to resolve the present confusion. With the exception of bigamy,
consanguinity or lack of form, only the parties themselves
should be entitled to have the marriage avoided, and their
proceedings should be taken within a reasonable time (we
would suggest a period of two years from the ceremony) and
while both spouses are still alive.

(3) The comparatively simple expedients advocated in the
preceding paragraphs would also cure the anomaly that now
arises in connection with applications for maintenance: it
would not be open to either party to resist the other's claim in
the Magistrates' Court by raising an issue of nullity.

(4) At present, the Divorce Court can make an order for
maintenance ancillary to a *decree* of nullity; it has no such
power on making a *declaration* of nullity. We see no reason why
this distinction should continue.

(5) The decree now pronounced on the annulment of a
marriage, whether it be void or voidable, reads alike; it pronounces the marriage "to have been and to be absolutely void
to all intents and purposes in law whatsoever". As we have
seen,[4] even void marriages do not always lack all legal effects;
and the wording of the decree plainly contradicts the true legal
character of a voidable marriage.

We suggest therefore that the decrees should be rephrased
accordingly.

### LEGAL EFFECTS OF MARRIAGE

We are concerned here only with those effects which we
consider in need of reform.

---

[1] See Lord Merrivale in *Valier* v. *Valier* [1925] 133 L.T. 830, 832.
[2] *H.* v. *H.*, *supra.*
[3] *Silver* v. *Silver* [1955] 2 All E.R. 614.
[4] See p. 125, *supra.*

*Domicile*

Under the present law, on marriage the wife automatically acquires the domicile of her husband; and until the termination of the marriage she cannot, under any circumstances, acquire (or retain) a domicile other than that of her husband. Once we recognise that men and women (including husbands and wives) are equal before the law, it becomes difficult to justify this remnant of wives' subjection to husbands. On the other hand, it is plainly desirable that so long as there is in fact a unity between husband and wife they should be subject to the same personal law.

The simplest answer to this problem is to allow a wife to acquire (or retain) an independent domicile whenever either spouse emigrates to another country in circumstances which in the case of a man of full age would amount to acquisition of a domicile of choice. To simplify the ascertainment of a married woman's domicile in such circumstances, she should be enabled to place on record (e.g. with the Registry of the Family Division of the High Court) her intention to remain domiciled in England. Similar provisions for the recording of her intention should be made for a wife who intends to abandon her English domicile by emigrating to another country; and for the wife of a man domiciled abroad who comes to England with the intention of making this country her permanent home.

In the matter of the English court's jurisdiction to entertain a suit for nullity, or divorce, or presumption of death and dissolution, statute law already recognises, and attempts to remedy, the inequality between husbands and wives;[1] if married women were enabled to have a domicile independently from their husbands, then the need for this kind of exceptional legislation would disappear. The English court should have jurisdiction to entertain matrimonial causes whenever *either* spouse is domiciled in England.

Recognition of foreign decrees would also become simpler: a foreign decree would deserve recognition in England if pronounced by the competent court of the domicile of either spouse or if recognised by such a court.[2] In this connection we would emphasise that we do *not* advocate the recognition of foreign decrees granted by courts which, under their municipal law, assume jurisdiction solely on short residential qualifications,

---

[1] Matrimonial Causes Act, 1950, s. 18, sub-sections (1)(a)–(b), and (2).
[2] *Armitage* v. *Attorney-General* [1906] P. 135.

Comity and reciprocity in matters of recognition should be governed by statute; and recognition should be extended so as to make unnecessary the institution of divorce proceedings in England in cases where the husband has already obtained a decree in the country of which the wife is a national and where both spouses reside.

## Taxation

Considerable publicity has been given recently to the disincentive effect of joint income assessments between husband and wife. The effect (where the husband is on the border-line of surtax if his wife does not earn, but above it if she does) is said to be to discourage the wife from earning. It is difficult to know how real this effect is. In any event the argument affects fewer people since the lower limit of surtax was raised to £5,000 and increased reliefs for earned income were granted in 1961. The principal argument against separate assessment is, as the Royal Commission on Taxation said in 1955,[1] that it would largely defeat the progressive nature of income tax (and the same applies to surtax while we continue to use two separate names and two sets of rules for what should be one progressive tax). A compromise solution might be to provide that separate assessments on husband and wife should be obtainable for all earned income; but in the case of such separate assessments, no married man's allowance should be granted. In view of the enormous advantages which separate assessments would give to wealthy couples faced with a progressive system of taxation, there seems to be no alternative to continuing with the joint assessment of husband and wife for all unearned income, until such time as an effective capital tax will supplement the present income tax and surtax. But in such cases it should be provided that the joint income tax return must be signed by both husband and wife.

In general, there is a strong case for reducing the possibilities at present available for tax avoidance through the payment of substantial salaries from company profits to wives, sons, daughters and grandchildren, and through covenants, particularly in favour of grandchildren.

## Matrimonial Property and Maintenance

These two subjects are so closely allied that it seems con-

[1] Cmd. 9474.

venient to deal with them together. The observations that follow are restricted to the financial relationship between husband and wife. Maintenance for children—which should never be ancillary to a parent's maintenance—is dealt with elsewhere in this chapter.[1]

The present law is an amorphous mixture of old principles and modern thinking. The rule that a husband must maintain his wife stems from the ideas of the common law which vested all the property of the wife in the husband, in return for a right to be maintained by him so long as she did not forfeit this right by committing a matrimonial offence. As spouses could not sue each other, the wife had no means of enforcing her right to maintenance; all she could do was to pledge her husband's credit for necessaries if he failed to supply them. However, for more than 80 years now[2] wives have had legal capacity to own separate property and to enter into contracts with their husbands. Nonetheless, their right to be maintained by their husbands and to pledge their husbands' credit is still in existence; but not in a form well suited to deal with present-day situations.

Modern thinking has been the result of the war-time and post-war practice of married women to augment the family's income by earnings of their own. Wives have shown themselves far less egotistical than the law would have entitled them to be: instead of keeping their earnings for themselves and looking to their husbands for maintenance, they contributed to the family budget, whether it was a question of day-to-day expenses or the purchase of a family home. Thus the rigid doctrine of separate property introduced by the Married Women's Property Acts had to be adapted to deal with situations where property was not in fact separate, but joint. In the absence of definite rules, judges have during the past ten years resorted to equitable concepts; by and large, these have produced just results, but the law is far from being certain or ascertainable, and clear-cut reforms are overdue.

These reforms can go in either of two directions: one would be the retention of the doctrine of separate property with improved rules on maintenance; the other a combination of

---

[1] See pp. 144–6, *infra*.

[2] The Married Women's Property Act, 1882, the Law Reform (Married Women and Tortfeasors) Act, 1935, and the Married Women (Restraint upon Anticipation) Act, 1949, recognised that marriage did not render a married woman less able to manage her financial affairs than her unmarried sister.

separate property with a community of gains, maintenance
playing a less important role.

## The first alternative

This would be an approach to the problem on the footing
that since 1953 the courts have proved themselves well qualified
to do justice between the parties, and that only a few glaring
defects of the present system call for a change.

*Concerning property*, there are at present two sets of procedures:
first, during the continuance of the marriage, either spouse
may apply to the court to decide any question between husband
and wife as to the title to or possession of property[1]; but this
procedure is not available on or after a decree of divorce or
nullity.

On the other hand, after pronouncing a decree for divorce
or nullity, the court may "enquire into the existence of ante-
nuptial or post-nuptial settlements made on the parties . . .
and may make such orders with reference to the application of
the whole or any part of the property settled either for the
benefit of the children of the marriage or of the parties to the
marriage, as the court thinks fit. . . ."[2] Although this provision
can be invoked by way of an interlocutory injunction to
prevent a threatened disposition,[3] no final order can be made
until after a decree of divorce or nullity.

We suggest that

(1) both of these provisions should be made capable of being
    invoked by either spouse during the marriage, and also
    either before or after a decree has been pronounced;
(2) both provisions should be amended to the effect that in
    making any order the court shall have regard to the
    interests of any dependent children[4] of the family;
(3) the court should be given power to make orders not only
    with reference to ante-nuptial settlements made in con-
    templation of marriage, but also in regard to settlements
    made by one of the parties for his or her own benefit
    before marriage was contemplated; this would prevent

---

[1] S. 17, Married Women's Property Act, 1882. This was amended by s. 7 of the
Matrimonial Causes (Property and Maintenance) Act, 1958, and the fact that no
specific property or fund is in existence no longer deprives the court of its power to
make orders under this section.

[2] S. 25, Matrimonial Causes Act, 1950.

[3] *Hindley* v. *Hindley* [1957] 2 All E.R. 653. *Cook* v. *Cook* [1962] P. 235.

[4] For a suggested definition of "dependent children" see p. 145, *infra*.

the wealthy from settling all their property on themselves immediately on reaching full age and in such a
way that it is not available for the maintenance of wife
and children.

The unsatisfactory state of the law relating to ownership of the
matrimonial home and its contents was recently highlighted by
the Court of Appeal in *Allen* v. *Allen*.[1] In that case the husband
purchased a bungalow with the aid of a building society
mortgage; the bungalow was conveyed into his sole name. The
wife went out to work and applied her earnings towards the
household expenses. After the dissolution of the marriage the
wife continued to live in the bungalow and the husband sought
a declaration, *inter alia*, that she was not entitled to remain in
occupation. The wife claimed that in equity she was entitled
to a half share in the bungalow, and to remain in occupation
until it was sold. The Court of Appeal took occasion to formulate the principles on which the wife's title depended: if
husband and wife put all their earnings into a joint pool, and
out of that joint pool paid all their expenses, including the
mortgage expenses, then the house would be regarded as a joint
venture and each of the spouses was entitled to one half; but if
the husband alone had to pay for the purchase of the house and
the wife was asked to earn money for other purposes, then the
house was not a joint venture and the wife could not be held
to have a beneficial interest in it.

To avoid any such artificial distinction, we make the further
suggestion that

(4) it should be expressly provided that whenever a wife has
made a substantial contribution towards household
expenses, a presumption shall arise whereby the
matrimonial home and its contents are owned jointly in
equity, regard being had (as in all other questions
between husband and wife) to the interests of the children
of the family.

The time is ripe to bury certain types of outmoded but still
operative decisions; for example that any savings from a house-
keeping allowance belong exclusively to the husband,[2] or that
without evidence of gift a surviving wife is not entitled to the

---

[1] [1961] 1 All E.R. 1186.
[2] E.g. *Hoddinott* v. *Hoddinott* [1949] 2 K.B. 406, (C.A.).

credit balance of a current account set up in the joint names of husband and wife. We recommend that

(5) it should be provided by statute that where any money or assets have been allocated for the joint use of husband and wife, any property or savings or residue originating from such money or assets shall be presumed to be the joint property of both spouses in equity.

In view of the precedence of a surviving spouse over all other dependants (including children) on an intestate succession, we take the view that the interests of dependent children of the family must be safeguarded. We suggest that

(6) the court pronouncing a decree of divorce or nullity should have power to order property to be secured for the benefit of any dependent children of the family and to make orders for their maintenance which after the parent's death will continue to be enforceable against his or her estate.

*Concerning maintenance*, we suggest that the following principles should be sanctioned by statute:

(1) *Prima facie* the husband shall be liable to maintain his wife; but he shall be under no such obligation if the wife has sufficient independent means, *or* if (and so long as) the wife has sufficient earnings to maintain herself, *or* if the course of dealing between the parties shows that the wife had undertaken to maintain herself.

(2) In the case of a consensual separation, the husband shall be liable to maintain his wife unless he can show that for the reasons indicated under (x) it would be unreasonable for him to do so.

(3) No husband shall be liable to maintain a wife who is in breach of a matrimonial obligation. But the fact that a wife has ceased to be entitled to maintenance shall never reflect on a child. Its right to be maintained shall be vested in the child itself;[1] this maintenance must include the cost of proper supervision and care by an adult (normally the mother); and there should be proper machinery to ensure that maintenance is in fact used for the benefit of the child.

(4) On pronouncing a decree of divorce or nullity, the court

[1] See pp. 136, 144, *infra*.

shall have power to order the husband to make a lump sum payment to the wife (particularly to a young wife) to enable her to undertake a course of training or to set up in business.

(5) A husband's duty to maintain his former wife shall in any event cease on her re-marriage.

One result of these principles will be to deny to a childless wife the right to be maintained in idleness after the dissolution or annulment of her marriage. We regard this as a socially and morally desirable result.

Conversely, there is the all too frequent situation where a husband makes no reasonable effort to maintain his wife or children, thereby forcing the wife to incur debts for necessaries (which will never be paid) and endure the humiliation of living continuously in debt. We submit that in all cases where at the time of the marriage the husband represented himself to be in a position to maintain his wife but for reasons which are not beyond his control fails to do so, the wife should be able to petition for divorce on the ground that a husband's persistent failure to make a reasonable effort to maintain his wife and the children of the family is a breach of a matrimonial obligation *sui generis*; or on the ground that such persistent failure constitutes cruelty.

## The second alternative

Turning now to a different way of regulating the financial relations between husband and wife, we must start by looking at the realities of the situation. Housekeeping has become so much easier as a result of pre-cooked food, washing machines, man-made fibres, and so on, that a large number of women find themselves under-occupied unless they have children to look after, or an outside job. The majority continue to go out to work during the early years of marriage, usually until the first child comes; and about one-third of all married women return to some income-producing work at a later stage, when the children no longer need full-time care.[1] But even when wives are engaged in the household and in looking after children, they make a contribution to the family's budget, partly by performing these necessary tasks and partly by their thrifty use of the house-keeping money. In many cases the result is the accumulation

[1] See the statistics published in January 1960 by the Institute of Personnel Management (survey by Dr. Viola Klein and Mass Observation Ltd.).

of some family wealth. There are certain types of assets, such as the matrimonial home and its contents, which would normally be regarded not as "mine" or "yours", but as "ours". But spouses will continue to regard as "mine" and "yours" such assets as they owned before marriage or have during its continuance received from their own families by way of gift or succession.

Our existing statute law[1] ignores the economic value of the time and work expended by a wife on managing the household and looking after the children, except in so far as it imposes a duty on the husband to maintain her. It has been left entirely to the courts to adapt and apply equitable principles in order to fill this *lacuna* and make some provision, on the breakdown of a marriage, for the ownership and distribution of those assets which we have termed "ours". A reform of this part of the law is, we think, overdue.

*Concerning property*, we do not advocate a system of complete community of property[2], primarily because difficulty problems are raised by the administration of such a community. Administration by the husband is incompatible with the idea of the equality of sexes; and joint administration[3] might induce spouses too frequently to seek directions from the court.[4]

We do, however, recommend the introduction of a system of "community of gains" or "community of surplus"[5], somewhat similar to those which have been in operation in the Scandinavian countries for many years[6] and in Western Germany since 1958.[7]

In such a community each spouse would retain his or her separate assets but neither of them could without the consent

[1] Married Women's Property Acts, 1870 and 1882; Law Reform (Married Women and Tortfeasors) Act, 1935. These were primarily intended to safeguard the well-to-do wife's assets against the husband and to ensure that her own earnings remained her own separate property.

[2] Such as is found e.g. in the French *Code Civil*.

[3] This was envisaged by the minority of the Royal Commission on Marriage and Divorce; see paragraph 652(ii) of the Report.

[4] Few things are more likely to break up a marriage than court proceedings; it should be a principal aim of the Family Charter to make it unnecessary to "go to law", save in very exceptional circumstances.

[5] See O. Kahn-Freund: "Matrimonial Property – Some Recent Developments" (1959) 22 Mod.L.R., 241.

[6] See Ake Malmström's chapter in *Matrimonial Property Law*, W. Friedmann (Ed.); p. 411.

[7] Under the Law on the Equality of the Rights of Husband and Wife in Civil Law. This was enacted pursuant to the Basic Law of 1949, which gave statutory recognition to the principle of the equality of spouses.

of the other (or of the court) dispose of the matrimonial home
or its contents, or of the whole of his or her separate property;
and on the termination of the marriage as a joint venture[1], any
excess of either spouse's separate assets (*plus* his or her share in
the assets held in common) over the separate assets owned by
him or her at the beginning of the marriage would have to be
shared out fairly.

In the recent case of *Hine* v. *Hine*[2] the Court of Appeal
applied this very principle: on the sale of the matrimonial
home it ordered the repayment to the wife of the deposit which
she had paid out of her separate assets and (notwithstanding
the fact that the husband alone had paid what was due to the
mortgagees) divided the surplus equally between the spouses.

This combination of separate assets with a community of
gains is what we should like to see on the statute book. For
until the principle receives legislative sanction, there can be no
certainty that the court will impute an intention to the parties
(which in *Hine* v. *Hine* they themselves do not appear to have
had!) that any particular piece of property or amount of
money shall be treated as "separate".

Thus, this type of limited community would not be contrary
to the spirit of the present law. By retaining the principle of
separate property, it would make no departure from existing
statute law; it would give statutory recognition to the principle
of equality laid down by the courts since 1952[3]; and to the
economic value of the wife's work in the household.[4]

One great advantage of this régime is the separation, as far
as possible, of the spouses' property rights from their matrimonial conduct. But the court should still have power to award
financial compensation to a spouse who has broken no matrimonial obligations[5]; this, however, should be the exception and
not the general rule.[6]

---

[1] By death, or a decree of divorce, nullity or judicial separation. In the case of a
separation order made by a Magistrates' Court, or of a *de facto* separation by agreement or otherwise, the High Court should have jurisdiction to dissolve the community upon the application of either spouse or both.

[2] [1962] 1 W.L.R. 1124.

[3] See *Rimmer* v. *Rimmer* [1953] 1 Q.B. 63, C.A.; *Cobb* v. *Cobb* [1955] 2 All E.R.
696, C.A.; *Fribance* v. *Fribance* [1957] 1 All E.R. 357, C.A.

[4] *Hoddinott* v. *Hoddinott*, p. 131, *supra*. The subtle and wholly artificial distinction
drawn by the Court of Appeal in *Allen* v. *Allen*, p. 131 *supra* would also disappear.

[5] See p. 137, *infra*.

[6] The Royal Commission, by a majority, rejected the view that a "guilty" spouse
should wholly forfeit his or her right to maintenance; see paragraphs 502, 503.

*Concerning maintenance*, it would follow, as a matter of principle, that during the continuance of the marriage both spouses would be equally liable to maintain the children of the family and, in case of need, each other.[1]

On the breakdown of the marriage and after the distribution of surplus assets, each spouse will be liable for his or her own maintenance and, in case of need, for the maintenance of the other. "Need" will be presumed to exist so long as a spouse is physically or mentally incapacitated from earning a living. A spouse who has remarried will have no claim to be maintained by a former spouse; and one who was solely responsible for the breakdown of the marriage may be refused maintenance at the discretion of the court.

In the case of a mother who looks after the children or of a father who employs someone for that purpose, the right to maintenance should be vested in the children and be enforceable against either or both parents.[2]

No financial limit should be placed on the maintenance that a court can order. The Matrimonial Proceedings (Magistrates Courts) Act, 1960, raised the upper limit of weekly maintenance payable to a spouse to £7. 10s. od. in view of the rising trend of prices. That ceiling is already too low; and the maximum of £2. 10s. od. a week that can at present be ordered for a child is ludicrous.

DIVORCE AND SEPARATION

### Jurisdiction

As regards the High Court, our views have been stated earlier on.[3] As regards Magistrates' Courts, we advocate the extension of their jurisdiction also: they should have power to make maintenance orders against respondents who are either resident or have assets in the petty sessional area concerned.

### Grounds of divorce and separation

We see no reason why the grounds on which a separation order is obtainable in the Magistrates' Court should be different from those on which the High Court can grant a decree of

---

[1] Even under the present law a wife may have to make payments to, or suffer her property to be settled for the benefit of, her husband: Matrimonial Causes Act, 1950, ss. 19(4), 20(3) (as amended) and 24(1); Matrimonial Proceedings (Magistrates' Courts) Act, 1960, s. 2.

[2] See p. 144, *infra*.

[3] See p. 127, *supra*.

dissolution or judicial separation. The observations that follow are directed to both sets of proceedings.

The time has come when we must realise that from the legal point of view marriage is a contract, the terms of which are contained in the mutual undertakings given at the time of the ceremony. Analogies with the criminal law ("guilty" and "innocent" spouse, matrimonial "offence") ought to be abolished.[1] It is wrong that, when a marriage breaks down (and this may happen for innumerable reasons), the facts should have to be "interpreted" so that they should fall within the four corners of the law, instead of being dealt with, freely and candidly, as concrete factual situations. In many (if not most) cases both parties have contributed to the breakdown; yet, one of them (the one who is quicker, or gets better legal advice, or has a more obliging spouse) will be the "innocent" and the other "guilty". Worse, "the party morally reponsible for the breakdown is sometimes, under the existing law, permitted to masquerade as the legally innocent party".[2] Again, marriages can break down without either spouse committing a matrimonial "offence"; and yet, in order to obtain a divorce, one of them is forced deliberately, and with the knowledge and consent of the other, to commit a matrimonial "offence". In cases of this kind, there is no intention to injure, no injury, no sense of grievance; the proceedings are a farce and the court is not in a position to concern itself with the true reasons for the breakdown.

On marriage the parties promise each other sexual faithfulness, cohabitation and loyalty; they also promise—to put it broadly—to stand by each other and to create for each other and for the children of the family a reasonably equilibrated life, in whatever circumstances life may bring. To put it another way, they undertake not to commit adultery, not to be cruel to each other, not to desert each other and to look after each other and the children. Any breach of these matrimonial obligations (which should be construed widely) may lead to a breakdown of the marriage. But married life may become intolerable also for other reasons. We agree with those nine members of the Royal Commission who said that

---

[1] There is no reason why these terms should not become as obsolete as has become the term "criminal c onversation".

[2] Paragraph 6 of Lord Walker's Statement attached to the Royal Commission's Report.

"Adultery or cruelty or desertion may make married life intolerable or offensive or impossible and it is right that a remedy should then be available to the aggrieved spouse. But there are many cases where marriage breaks down irretrievably and where, as the law stands, no remedy is available.

We think that the time has come to recognise that matrimonial offences are in many cases merely symptomatic of the breakdown of marriage, and that there should also be provision for divorce in cases where, quite apart from the commission of such offences, the marriage has broken down completely."[1]

In our view *any* breach of a matrimonial obligation leading to the complete breakdown of the marriage should be recognised as a ground of divorce.

It should also be recognised by statute that certain events (e.g. impotence or insanity) which do not involve any wilful breach of a matrimonial obligation may nonetheless bring about the frustration of the marriage contract; in such cases there should be a possibility of dissolution or judicial separation.

Moreover, the law should move towards recognising that marriage (and divorce) is the concern primarily of husband, wife and children.[2] There should be a different approach to the dissolution of a marriage where there are children, and of a marriage where there are none. In the latter case, dissolution should be made much easier than it is now, and presently we will put forward some concrete proposals.

As the chief sufferers from a broken marriage are the children, the law should cast a positive duty on spouses to maintain the parental home. In cases where there are dependent infant children, the court should not pronounce a decree of dissolution unless it is satisfied that the petitioner (and the respondent who cross-petitions) has made a genuine attempt at reconciliation[3] by seeking, and as far as possible complying with, the advice of a marriage guidance counsellor, probation officer, social welfare worker, clergyman or some other suitable person. Help from persons trained in the task of effecting matrimonial

---

[1] Report, sub-paragraphs 70 (vi) and (vii).

[2] "Children" in the present context means "children of the family".

[3] The provisions in the Matrimonial Causes and Reconciliation Bill (see p. 122, *supra* n.3) whereby resumption of cohabitation for a period not exceeding one month shall not constitute condonation of a matrimonial offence or terminate desertion, is meant to assist efforts aimed at reconciliation.

reconciliations is just as important to the community as the medical help provided by doctors. We recommend that marriage guidance should be part of the welfare services supplied by the State.

It follows from what has been said already, that dissolution or judicial separation should be granted whenever there is proof of a serious breach of a matrimonial obligation or of frustration of the marriage contract. Words such as "cruelty", "desertion", "adultery" all advert to a breach; we would retain them, but we think that the courts should receive more comprehensive statutory guidance on the following matters:

*Cruelty.* The court's concern should not be to punish the guilty, but to give relief to the victim. Accordingly, a defence based on insanity within the M'Naghten Rules is wholly out of place; it is irrelevant to the welfare and safety of the other spouse or the children. The effect on children of cruel conduct in the home is invariably grave, and wholly unaffected by the question whether the cruel conduct is due to a parent's insanity.

A spouse who is cruel to a child is in clear breach of an important matrimonial obligation. Such cruelty should be a ground for divorce, provided the petitioner had no part in the cruelty.

The classic definition of cruelty refers to "reasonable apprehension of danger to life, limb or health (bodily or mental)". This should be construed more widely than at present. Once a spouse is shown to have a definite intention to injure, or to behave in a manner which reasonable people would regard as cruel, it should be presumed that in due course actual injury will follow. Such a spouse should not be allowed to call into question the other's reasonable apprehension of danger.

*Failure to maintain.* It is normally the husband's duty to maintain the family, and the wife's duty to look after the home and the children; but if the husband's earning capacity is impaired through age or illness it may well be the wife's duty to provide for or contribute towards the maintenance of the husband and the children.[1] Persistent failure by either spouse to comply with these obligations should be a ground for divorce.

*Habitual drunkenness.* This was introduced as a ground for relief in the Magistrates' Courts in 1902. It is still being regarded as a vice of the poor, and has never *per se* been a ground for relief in the High Court. However, by that sort of mental

---

[1] See Matrimonial Proceedings (Magistrates' Courts) Act, 1960, s. 1(1)(i).

acrobatics which we should like to see eliminated, in some cases the High Court construed drunkenness as cruelty. This construction should become the rule and not the exception.

*Drug addiction.* This has been a ground for relief in the Magistrates' Courts since 1925; it is not in the High Court.

It seems right[1] that both habitual drunkenness and drug addiction, if persisted in by one spouse regardless of the other's protests, should be regarded as serious breaches; as such they should be recognised as grounds for divorce.[2]

The present definitions of "habitual drunkard" and "drug addict" in s. 16 of the Matrimonial Proceedings (Magistrates' Courts) Act, 1960, are too narrow. Their subjective test (". . . a person . . . who . . . so conducts himself that it would not be reasonable to expect a spouse of ordinary sensibilities to continue to cohabit with him") should be replaced by an objective test, focusing on the point of the drunkard's or drug addict's inability to control his faculties and his or her disregard of the other spouse's protests.

*Artificial insemination.* Submitting to insemination by a donor without the husband's consent is, in our view, a grave breach of a matrimonial obligation. The Royal Commission's recommendation[3] that this be a ground for divorce should become law. The husband, at his option, should also be entitled to a separation order in the Magistrates' Court.

*Supervening insanity.* This is a recognised ground for divorce, but it is much too narrowly defined. Relief should be granted if the respondent has been under continuous treatment for three years. It ought not to be necessary to prove that the disease is incurable.

*Breakdown of marriage.* Once it is more widely realised that though "divorce is a confession of failure, it is not necessarily an unrelieved disaster"[4], there will be, we expect, less opposition than there is now to divorce on the ground that the marriage has broken down irretrievably. Where spouses have lived apart for five years[5], either party should be entitled to present a petition—the length of the separation being sufficient evidence

---

[1] The same view was taken by the Gorrell Commission in 1909.

[2] Habitual drunkenness has been a ground for divorce in Scotland since 1903.

[3] Paragraph 90.

[4] Prof. C. M. Carstairs, in his fourth B.B.C. Reith Lecture, broadcast on 2nd December 1962.

[5] The Matrimonial Causes and Reconciliation Bill (see p. 122, *supra* n.2) envisages seven years' separation.

of the breakdown. If there are no children, a decree should be granted as of right; if there are children, the court should have a discretion, the sincerity of the efforts at reconciliation made by the petitioner being the touchstone of the matter.[1]

Where the marriage breaks down without any breach of a matrimonial obligation and a divorce is pronounced notwithstanding the objection of the respondent, the latter should receive some compensation for any financial damage he or she may suffer (e.g. loss of pension rights, or no share or a reduced share in the petitioner's estate). In these cases the court should have a discretion to order increased maintenance payments or a lump sum payment or (if a system of community were introduced) make a suitable adjustment when distributing the excess of gains.

The working of such a radical reform as the acceptance of "breakdown" as a ground for divorce would have to be watched with special care. The statistics should show the number of decrees granted, the duration of the marriage, the age of the parties on marriage, and, in broad categories, the nature of the causes of breakdown.

*Adultery*. Although actions for "criminal conversation" were abolished over a century ago,[2] a husband (but not a wife) still has a right of action for general damages from an adulterer. This is a remnant of the wife's servitude and should be abolished.

## CHILDREN

*Domicile*

The established rule that a legitimate child takes the domicile of its father, while an illegitimate child that of its mother, is defective; for the question whether a child is legitimate may, in its turn, depend on the child's domicile. The way out of this vicious circle is to enact that all children (whatever their legitimacy status) should acquire, on birth, the mother's domicile.

Again, the present law is not clear in the matter of an infant's change of domicile. It is still open to controversy whether a widowed mother who, on remarriage, acquires a new domicile can change her child's domicile; or whether a legitimate child,

---

[1] See pp. 138–9, *supra*.
[2] Matrimonial Causes Act, 1857.

the marriage of whose parents is dissolved abroad without an order for custody being made and who thereafter resides with its mother abroad, continues to be subject to the father's personal law. Questions like these could and should be clarified by a few relatively simple rules[1], as follows:

An infant under the age of 16 should have the same domicile as the person entitled to its custody. If each of two persons domiciled in different countries is equally entitled to custody, the infant's domicile should be that of the person having actual care and control. If custody has been granted to a public authority (and not a natural person) the infant's domicile should be in the country under whose law the authority is established. Where the person entitled to custody changes his or her domicile, or custody passes to a person whose domicile is not the same as the infant's, the infant should not acquire a new domicile unless there be also an actual change of residence.

It is implicit in the rules we have suggested that a child above the age of 16 should have capacity to change its own domicile. There is no reason why the law which at the age of 16 confers capacity to marry should not at the same age grant a capacity to change one's own domicile.

### Custody

Today the court, when it pronounces a decree of divorce, nullity or judicial separation, has wide powers to award the custody of any children of the family to either of the parties, or to a third person (even a local authority) and to order that the child should be under the supervision of a probation officer or local authority. But the position is not at all clear when that parent who was awarded custody dies without having appointed a guardian. In most cases the other parent becomes automatically entitled to custody, without any further investigation by the court. From the child's point of view this may be unsatisfactory. We think it should be provided that on the death of the parent who has custody, the child's custody vests automatically in the President of the Family Division of the High Court. The court will then have an opportunity to inquire into the circumstances, and make a fresh order for custody, due

[1] See s. 6 of Lord Meston's first Domicile Bill of 1958, and s. 4 of the second Domicile Bill of 1959.

weight being given to the report of the appropriate social worker or children's officer.[1]

The manner in which parents fight battles over children in wardship cases, in cases under the Guardianship Acts, and after decrees of the Divorce Court is, in many instances, to be deprecated. The mutual spite and bitterness of spouses is often the predominant element in these proceedings; if not in the first then in the last resort the children are the principal sufferers.

To avoid this, it is necessary that whenever parents disagree on custody or care and control, the matter should at once be taken out of their hands, and become the concern of a social worker or children's officer. One or the other would then see and talk with the child in its home, listen to the parents, inquire into their circumstances, consult the child's school and doctor and, if necessary, refer the case to a child guidance clinic; in due course, he would report to the court. The court should be directed by statute to sanction the recommendations made in the report, save in specific cases, e.g. where the recommendations are *prima facie* unreasonable, or go against the weight of the evidence collected by, or offered to, the author of the report.

This procedure would entrust to non-lawyers certain functions which hitherto have been reserved to judges. That, we believe, is as it should be. Judges are trained to be the final arbiters of law. They are not trained and ought not to be the final arbiters of child welfare; this is a matter that requires specialised training in disciplines and techniques to which the law is not decisively relevant.

The social worker or children's officer should not fade out of the picture once a court order has been made. On the contrary, he should remain in continuing contact with the case and seek a variation of the court order whenever its practical effects do not work out in the best interests of the child.

### Parental Power

We do not wish to see this power reduced, but we think that those of its elements which in a modern society are mere relics of a father's proprietary right to his child's services should be

---

[1] One can easily think of circumstances in which the deceased mother's second husband, in whose household the child may have lived for years prior to the mother's death, would make a better guardian than the natural father.

abolished. Actions for enticement, seduction, or a tort committed against *the child* illustrate this point. These rights of action are vested in the parent and turn on his ability to prove that, as a result of the defendant's act (enticement, seduction or tort), he was deprived of the child's services.[1] In future, all such rights of action should be vested in the child itself; they should be enforceable solely for the child's benefit, and solely on the ground that something injurious was done to the child.

At present, a parent cannot effectively prevent an infant child from continuing an undesirable association or contracting an undesirable marriage without first making the infant a ward of court, and then obtaining an injunction which will put an end to the undesirable association or prevent the marriage. This is an expensive procedure. We suggest that where all that is needed is an injunction, "wardship" should be dispensed with.

*Maintenance*

At present, maintenance of the wife is the husband's primary obligation; his obligation to maintain the children is regarded as (and is, indeed, called) "ancillary". We regard this as quite wrong. Every child, whatever its status (legitimate or illegitimate, adopted or recognised) should have a right to be maintained. This right should be vested in the child, and be exercisable by either of its parents or by a third person, including a local authority. So long as the right remains vested in a parent, many children will suffer through the parent's neglect or reluctance to enforce obligations which, though relating to the children, are owed merely to the parent as a spouse or former spouse. The child should be entitled to claim maintenance from either parent, and also from the estate of a deceased parent.

However, this right to maintenance should be vested in dependent children only. The definition of a "dependant" in s. 16(1) of the Matrimonial Proceedings (Magistrates' Courts) Act, 1960, is unsatisfactory in that it limits maintenance to infancy, i.e. until the magical 21st birthday. We suggest that

---

[1] As far back as 1844, Serjeant Manning, in a note to his report of *Grinnell* v. *Wells*, criticised the anomaly of the law. He said:

"It may be observed . . . that the quasi-fiction of *servitium amisit* affords protection to the rich man, whose daughter occasionally makes his tea, but leaves without redress the poor man, whose child . . . is sent unprotected to earn her bread among strangers".

both for purposes of maintenance and for the purposes of the Inheritance (Family Provision) Act, 1938, (as amended) "dependent children" should mean: any infant under the age of 16; and any child who, having attained the age of 16, is incapable of maintaining himself either because he is engaged full time or for a substantial part of his time in educational training, or because of any physical or mental disability, or because of necessary full-time household duties or the care of incapacitated relatives.

We are anxious to put all children on an equal footing, irrespective of the circumstances of their birth. The moral stigma attaching to the word "illegitimate" is gradually disappearing; but the economic position of a fatherless child is still very much worse than that of a "child of the family".

Many Continental systems[1] have introduced the status of a "recognised" child, which is half-way between legitimacy and illegitimacy. We recommend the introduction of this new status into English law.

The recognised child is one that was not born in wedlock and cannot be legitimated by its parents' subsequent marriage. Nevertheless, its father recognises it as his own; such recognition vests in the child all those rights in relation to the father and his estate which are enjoyed by a child of the family.

Jurisdiction to declare the status of a child to be that of a recognised child should be given to the Family Division of the High Court; the father or the mother or any other person (including a local authority) should be allowed to make the necessary application on the child's behalf. It is desirable that a child's status should be determined as soon after birth as possible; applications should therefore be made either within one year of the child's birth or within one year of the termination of voluntary maintenance payments by the father (whichever the later). The death of the father or the mother should not to be a bar to a judicial declaration.

The point we have already made about the need to vest the claim to maintenance in the child itself is particularly important in the case of illegitimate children. Under the Affiliation Act, 1957, only the mother can apply for an affiliation order. Since the mother is frequently very young and inexperienced, it is usually a simple matter for her seducer to persuade her to

[1] Denmark, Norway, Greece, Holland, France, Italy, Spain, Portugal and, to a limited extent, Switzerland.

take no action within 12 months after the child's birth (or, if he is a visiting foreigner, until after he is out of the jurisdiction). Moreover, the mother is frequently ill-equipped to conduct the application and too inexperienced to realise her inadequacy. The recent successes of the National Assistance Board in obtaining affiliation orders in cases where the mother had failed to do so underline this point. We suggest that local authorities should have a general supervisory function, including the power to institute affiliation proceedings where the mother does not take them within a very short period after the child's birth.

The local authority should also be placed under a duty to see that maintenance payments are in fact used for the benefit of the child.

It is undesirable that the right to apply for an affiliation order should be confined to single women (even though this phrase now includes a married woman living apart from her husband). The overriding purpose of affiliation proceedings is the welfare and proper maintenance of the child. If the mother can satisfy the court as to the child's paternity, then the child's right to maintenance should not be defeated by the fact that the mother is living with her husband (who is not the child's father).

One final, but important, point. Every illegitimate child should, of course, be entitled to share in the estate of its mother and of its putative father.

### SUCCESSION TO PROPERTY ON DEATH

Under the Intestates Estates Act, 1952, the surviving spouse takes the first slice from the estate, even if husband and wife were not living together at the time of the death. This is unjust where, e.g. the wife left the husband many years before and is at the date of his death living with someone else.

The law should be changed so as to restrict the surviving spouse's right to the first slice to cases where the spouse was "living with" the deceased at the time of his or her death, i.e. was not living apart *animo separandi*. Claims of surviving spouses living apart should be met by an application under the Inheritance (Family Provision) Act, 1938 (as amended).

At present the law includes a "limping" provision whereby, after a decree of judicial separation, any property which is acquired by, or devolves upon, the wife while the separation continues, falls to be distributed on her death intestate as though her husband were dead.[1] We recommend a similar provision in relation to the husband's estate. Claims of surviving spouses whom the law deems to be dead should be met by application under the Inheritance (Family Provision) Act, 1938 (as amended).

The Inheritance (Family Provision) Act, 1938 (as amended), has functioned satisfactorily within its restricted field, and has completely belied the opposition put up by the majority of the legal profession at the time the Bill passed through Parliament. The extension of the Act to former husbands and wives by the Matrimonial Causes (Property and Maintenance) Act, 1958, appears to be working satisfactorily, but the interrelation between the two Acts should be clarified.

The two major defects of the 1938 Act (as amended) are the ease with which it can be avoided, and the very restricted class of dependants to which it applies. Reform is called for in the following directions:

First, the Act can be avoided by such relatively simple expedients as entering into covenants for the transfer of property on death, taking out insurance policies, or settling property on trustees. The courts should be given power to override all covenants, insurance policies and settlements if that is necessary in order to make adequate provision for the maintenance of dependants.

Secondly, no application can at present be made for the maintenance of a son over the age of 21 (although higher education frequently continues beyond this age), while applications can be made on behalf of an unmarried daughter of any age; the presumption being that an unmarried woman is entitled to be maintained in idleness by her parent. The meaning of the word "dependant" as used in the Act should therefore be extended to include

> any infant child of the family within the meaning of the Matrimonial Proceedings (Children) Act, 1958;
> any other infant child of the deceased (including an illegitimate or recognised child);
> any child of the family or of the deceased, being a child over the age of 21, who is engaged full time or for a substantial

---

[1] Matrimonial Causes Act, 1950, s. 21(1)(a); the position is the same in the case of a separation order made by a Magistrates' Court.

part of his time in educational training; or cannot maintain himself by reason of some physical or mental disability, or by reason of necessary full-time household duties or care of incapacitated relatives;

any aged or incapacitated parent or relative;

any person who immediately preceding the death had been living with the deceased for at least one year as the deceased's husband or wife and who by reason of physical or mental disability is incapable of maintaining himself or herself.

Persons within the last three categories should be eligible only if during the year preceding the death they had been wholly or largely maintained by the deceased and if having regard to all the circumstances it would have been reasonable for the deceased to have made provision for them *mortis causa*.

Yet another defect of the present law lies in the requirement that applications under the 1938 Act go to the Chancery Division, while former spouses must, under the 1958 Act, apply to the Divorce Division. This anomaly would be cured automatically if all applications could go to the proposed Family Division.

### INFORMATION AND STATISTICS

The statistical information at present available with regard to family relations leaves a great deal to be desired; the whole procedure is thickly encrusted with bureaucratic barnacles. The Home Office statistics are especially in need of reform. The Royal Commission on Marriage and Divorce noted the grave gaps in our knowledge, but missed the opportunity to recommend a drastic expansion of the information now available. Clearly, some of the information we require *can* be made available; this has been shown by papers such as *The Resort to Divorce in England and Wales* 1858–1957, by Griselda Rowntree and Norman H. Carrier.[1] At present, meaningful conclusions can only be extracted by highly-trained statisticians. This is wrong. The information should be available to and readily understandable by anyone looking at the published statistics. In particular, the presentation of the annual statistics should be revised so that it should be possible to discover at any time what the answers to the following questions are:

[1] Population Studies, Vol. XI, No. 3, March 1958.

(1) How many married couples are living apart under a decree of judicial separation or a separation order made by Magistrates' Courts? It should also be possible, by an appropriate sampling procedure, to arrive at a reasonable estimate of the number of couples living apart under separation agreements.

(2) What kind of orders are made in the Magistrates' Courts, on what grounds, and in what numbers?

(3) What proportion of matrimonial orders made in Magistrates' Courts lead eventually to divorce in the High Court?

(4) How many attachment of earnings orders are made, what sums do they produce, and in how many cases do they fail to produce the required maintenance? The Home Office appears to possess no sufficient information.

We also need to know much more about the circumstances in which marriages break down, and in this connection a clear distinction should be made between the initial breakdown and the circumstances which subsequently lead to proceedings in the courts. Much of the evidence before the Royal Commission and, indeed, many of the Commission's own findings, were based on the assumption that it is divorce which marks the final breakdown of a marriage. That is not so. Normally a divorce is only sought when a new marriage is to replace the old one, which was finally broken *before* the divorce proceedings were taken.

We should also be placed in a position to discover from the statistics the proportion of broken marriages in which children under 16 are involved; the proportion of first, second and subsequent marriages that end in breakdown; the age at the time of marriage of the parties whose marriage subsequently breaks down; and generally, all factors relevant to the problem of broken marriages.

Information of this kind is not provided by the statistics at present available. Action is urgently needed to improve the knowledge upon which our legislation should be based.

# VII

## COMMERCIAL LAW AND COMPANY LAW

THE TITLE OF this chapter has been chosen deliberately for the purpose of underlining the importance of the company in the modern commercial build up, for company law is of course part of the general commercial law. It is largely the creation of modern statute law, virtually over the last century, and has as a result required pretty constant development and reform. It therefore calls for special treatment here. The other subject which is dealt with in this chapter in similar detail is sale of goods, partly because of its intrinsic importance to the citizen and partly because the recent detailed survey of the subject by the Molony Committee made an assessment of the proposals put forward in their report necessary.

This observation involves the further preliminary point that we do not propose in this chapter to attempt a survey of the whole area of our commercial law, even within the narrower limits assigned to it in some legal textbooks. Outside those limits (which may be taken as covering agency, partnership and company law; sale and hire purchase of goods; bills of exchange and negotiable instruments generally; services in relation to goods, involving such matters as warehousing and transport; insurance and bankruptcy) other writers include within the subject such branches of the law as patents, copyrights, trade marks, and other aspects of what is often described as industrial property. These subjects are certainly of great importance and will have eventually to be rationalised by a Labour Government. We do not however propose to discuss them in this chapter.

Even in the narrower field just delimited there are some aspects in which the call for reform is not so urgent as to demand priority of treatment, and others where, although the argument for early revision of the law is strong, the points at issue are of a highly technical character, hardly suitable for treatment in this volume. Thus in discussing company law we have made no attempt to deal with all those useful reforms proposed in the recent report of the Jenkins Committee[1], the desirability of

[1] Report of the Company Law Committee (1962) Cmnd. 1749.

which will be mainly apparent to lawyers, secretaries and others primarily engaged in company administration.

Most of our commercial law is concerned with the application of the principles and rules of contract law to the particular circumstances of specialised types of business such as merchanting, transport, banking or insurance. Even in company law, where the rules are primarily concerned with the operational and administrative arrangements within which these important commercial institutions should work, some of the aspects most vital to the ordinary citizen, such as the terms on which he becomes a shareholder, are primarily governed by the law of contract, though there have been important statutory modifications.

We draw attention to this point which is one of a basic character because many of the most glaring defects in our commercial law stem directly from the *laissez faire* philosophy which played a governing part in the minds of our judges when they were building up our contract law, often in relation to the problems of particular types of business, a development which in many of its major principles, and in almost all its detailed rules, coincided with the period during which the doctrines of Adam Smith were dominant in our bourgeois society. As has been made clear in the chapter dealing with contracts, the effective removal of these blemishes often calls for major reforms in contract law rather than, or in addition to, the detailed remodelling of the subsidiary rules in particular branches of commercial law. Much of the more detailed discussion with which the remainder of the present chapter will be taken up will be found to be in the nature of illustration to the points of principle there underlined.

In particular, we would emphasise here the pretty consistent handling of the public policy doctrine in support of the so-called freedom of contract; under this, in large areas of commerce and industry merchants and manufacturers have been allowed to contract themselves out of responsibility for exercising due care in carrying on their businesses, and of this we shall find a number of instances in the following pages. The policy of the English courts in this regard has been in marked contrast to that pursued in some other common law jurisdictions such as the U.S.A., where both judges in many of the individual States and also the federal legislature have set their faces against "negligence clauses". Even in this country the widespread

6

abuse of this so-called freedom among company directors by means of protecting articles in the articles of association, which was pinpointed by the well-known case *Re City Equitable Fire Insurance Coy. Ltd.*,[1] was eventually put an end to by the Companies Act, 1929, a valuable reform which unfortunately has not been followed up in other branches of commercial law.

Another aspect of commerce in which general contract law has become of peculiar importance in modern times is the continuous growth of the use of standardised contracts. These can obviously be of considerable advantage, especially when all the parties concerned are experienced businessmen, as with charter party contracts in sea transport; but they may be used to take the ordinary citizen at a disadvantage, as in many sales and insurance contracts.

The successful conduct of business depends to a very large extent on mutual confidence, and many judges have underlined the importance of this. Yet the common law in its development has done little to restrain the unscrupulous businessman in the exercise of cunning, provided he stops short of actual fraud. "Let everyone look out for himself" is a hard doctrine, and one which should be out of date in the modern age; yet it too often indicates the line of approach taken in commercial law.

### SALE OF GOODS AND HIRE PURCHASE

The first thing to notice in this section is that hire purchase is in reality only an exceedingly artificial method of selling goods. It originated in a decision of the courts that a person who had agreed to buy goods and to pay the price by instalments could, if he had obtained the possession of them (as normally in the circumstances of such a contract he would be expected to do), transfer the full ownership to a *bona fide* purchaser, notwithstanding the fact that he had paid only part of the purchase price or even nothing. A system under which such a transaction could be regarded as a hiring right up to the stage at which the final instalment was paid, not only prevented a *bona fide* purchaser from the hirer from obtaining ownership, but had the additional advantage from the original seller's point of view of enabling him to re-possess himself of the goods in the event of the hirer making default in carrying out the contract. But of course, to the ordinary citizen, hire purchase is

[1] [1925] Ch. 407.

simply a method of buying goods by instalments, and we propose here therefore to deal with these two sections of the law together. Indeed, we take the view that the law relating to sale and hire purchase should be brought into line so far as there are not good reasons to the contrary. If our proposal for the modification of the rule of *nemo dat quod non habet* is accepted one of the main reasons for the invention of hire purchase will have gone. However, much of the protective legislation in the Hire Purchase Act, 1938, is of its nature only applicable to instalment buying, and we favour not only the preservation of this, but its extension.

## Sale of Goods

The law as to the sale of goods is obviously the section of commercial law which impinges most directly upon the life of the ordinary citizen as he deals with retail shopkeepers. It is, of course, also the basis upon which the great wholesale operations of big merchants and international traders are carried on. In this section we have concerned ourselves primarily with retail trade, though the changes in the law which we suggest might well in a number of respects be applied generally. We have not, however, found it possible here to examine how far this will be practicable.

It should be said at once that there is no other branch of commercial law in which the weaknesses of the common law, already referred to, give such advantages to the unscrupulous businessman. The reforms in the law suggested in the chapter on contracts, particularly a stronger enforcement of public policy and a tightening up of the rules relating to misrepresentation, would undoubtedly be of great advantage in improving the practice in relation to sale. It is of some significance that it is in connection with sale of goods that the American Restatement of Commercial Law (which is, in effect, a model code, and which has been adopted already in a majority of the individual States) gives the courts full power to deal with "unconscionable" contracts. The Restatement puts into the terms of a statute the rules developed by many of the American courts on the basis of public policy for restraining the more unscrupulous activities of businessmen: they provide a welcome contrast to the attitude of English judges.

The inadequacies of the existing law of sale have in recent years been underlined by the growing use of clauses exempting dealers from liability for supplying defective and even dangerous goods. There has also been widespread use, by manufacturers in a number of industries, of limited and unsatisfactory guarantee clauses (called by lawyers "warranties") in their sales contracts. During the same period the astonishing and valuable growth of the so-called consumer protection organisations, such as the Consumer Advisory Council and the Consumers' Association have brought the importance of these matters home to larger and larger sections of the public. It is no doubt this which has brought consumer protection into the field of national politics, if not yet quite into that of party politics, though it may well be that that development is not far away.

This resulted in 1959 in the appointment by the President of the Board of Trade of a committee to review the whole field of the existing law of trade marks, merchandise marks, and other aspects of consumer protection in relation to the sale and purchase of goods. This committee, officially known as the Committee on Consumer Protection is generally called by the name of its chairman, a distinguished lawyer, Mr. J. T. Molony, Q.C.

The Molony Committee has issued two reports; an interim one, dealing with dangerous goods, and a final one (1962) dealing with the subject generally.[1] This latter document provides an able and detailed survey of the whole subject; it runs to well over three hundred pages and makes a substantial number of proposals for the reform of the law. Although the Committee has been criticised for timidity, and very properly criticised[2], some of its proposals are far-reaching and are to be welcomed. It should be noted that these reforms are proposed to be confined to sales of consumer goods. It seems to us, however, to be obviously undesirable to have different sets of legal rules applying to different sections of goods, and we think that as far as possible the new rules should apply throughout.

The Committee did not by any means regard itself as limited to the use of legal weapons in its efforts to devise methods of consumer protection. Some of its most important recommendations, such as that for setting up a Consumers'

---

[1] Cmnd. 1011 and 1781.

[2] See, for example, the most effective and informative speech by Baroness Burton in the debate on the Molony Report in the House of Lords: Hansard Vol. 244, col. 605 (14 November, 1962).

Council (accepted by the Government) are extra-legal, and these aspects of the subject we shall not discuss.

It will be appreciated that the appearance of the Molony Report has made the writing of this section both easier and more difficult. It has brought out most, though not all, of the important legal matters involved in consumer protection, thus obviating the need for detailed analysis. On the other hand it discusses so many points of interest and importance that full consideration of them would overload this section seriously; as it is, we have felt compelled to give more space to this subject than we had originally hoped would be necessary.

And first of all we will refer to what seems to us to be the main gap in the Molony survey, that is its failure to deal with the position of the *bona fide* purchaser of goods where the seller from whom he bought had no title or a defective title.[1] The general rule in cases of this kind is that the buyer cannot take a better title than the seller had, so he will have to give up the goods to the true owner; and if he has sold them on, he will not only have to pay their value to the true owner, but may also be liable in damages to his own buyer. He has a right against his own seller to be compensated, but the latter is often a fraudulent person who may well have been sent to gaol, and in any case is probably not "worth powder and shot". This is the rule of *nemo dat quod non habet*—a man cannot give what he has not got.

As was pointed out in "The Reform of the Law", wholesalers may and actually do take advantage of this rule to protect themselves against retailers by means of the freedom of contract principle. Thus it is common in the jewellery business for wholesalers who supply retailers on "sale or return" terms to insist on a clause being put into the contract whereby the goods are to remain the property of the wholesaler "until settled for or charged". This means that a person who buys a piece of jewellery from a retailer may, if the retailer becomes insolvent, find himself faced with a demand from the wholesaler to give it up to him, notwithstanding that he paid cash for it over the counter at the retailer's shop. Even at common law there have been some exceptions to the *nemo dat* rule, and in commerce it caused so much trouble that from the early nineteenth century

---

[1] This was the main section of the law of sale selected for reform in "The Reform of the Law". The other reform proposed, that of getting rid of the need for written evidence in contracts of sale when the value of the goods is £10 or upwards, has since been achieved.

onwards a number of statutes, the Factors Acts, have been enacted to modify it, as well as important sections in the Sale of Goods Act, 1893. These are, at the best, only of partial application, and the administration of them by the judges has been almost uniformly obscurantist. The result is a situation which, from the point of view of consumer protection, is both unsatisfactory and highly complicated.

Generally speaking, the *nemo dat* rule does not apply on the Continent, and a purchaser is entitled to assume that the person he finds in possession of goods is entitled to dispose of them. This certainly is a fairer rule than the English one, since the original owners will in the majority of cases have enabled the intermediary to operate by entrusting him with the goods. It has, therefore, often been proposed to introduce the Continental rule here, and this was the view taken in the "Reform of the Law".

However, in the great majority of cases both the original owner and the present possessor are innocent parties (or at any rate neither of them has been guilty of a high degree of culpability) and if the rule were changed, as proposed previously, it would often work great hardship to the original owner. In all the circumstances we think it would be equitable to give to the courts a discretion to divide the loss between them as seems just in the circumstances. There is distinguished judicial support for this proposal, that of Lord Devlin; it is in accordance with recent developments in negligence cases where the "all or nothing" rule has been abolished; and it can be supported from the action of Parliament in the Law Reform (Frustrated Contracts) Act, 1943, under which, when a contract fails because of commercial frustration, the loss no longer "lies where it falls"; the court may order the repayment of any moneys which have been paid under the contract, to the extent that it considers just.

The Molony Committee was concerned with the character and quality of goods sold under contracts of sale and hire purchase, and with the protection of the consumer in respect of these matters. It approached the legal aspects of the subject (very properly, we think) on a basis much wider than that provided by the Sale of Goods Act, 1893, and took the view that the criminal law, the law of torts (liability for wrongful acts and omissions) as well as the law of contract (sale of goods) should be brought into play.

This involves the categorisation of goods. In respect of dangerous goods it is reasonable to require by penal sanction that in extreme cases they shall not be sold to the public at all without a special permit, as in the case of some poisons and drugs. The law in respect of goods of this kind has been effectively built up during the present century, largely in the Home Office, and does not call for further treatment. There are other types of goods which can be made reasonably safe by the exercise of proper care and safeguards in their manufacture. In some of these cases (perhaps in all the more important of them) the situation can to a certain extent be handled by requiring, under the sanction of the criminal law, conformity to certain specifications. Thus at the time of the appointment of the Molony Committee there was widespread disquiet at the number of accidents caused by defective oil heaters, a danger which is susceptible of control by this method. Largely as a result of the Committee's interim report, new regulations were introduced which do appear to have substantially reduced this evil.

The Committee investigated three other types of particularly dangerous goods, viz. electrical appliances, inflammable clothes, and certain classes of toys, particularly those made of celluloid. It found that to a greater or less extent all these could be effectively handled by the same type of punitive regulation. It further considered that under modern conditions other types of goods might well begin to appear which needed control in similar ways, and it advocated that general powers should be conferred upon a designated Minister to deal with these problems as they arise. We are in general agreement with this proposal.

There are, however, numerous other sorts of goods which would not be considered to be of a dangerous character by the ordinary man but may certainly become harmful, if not actually dangerous to life, under certain conditions or in the case of peculiarly susceptible people. There have been numerous cases before the courts arising out of injuries caused by e.g. defective hot-water bottles, unwholesome food and drink, irritating underclothing which has been treated with chemicals, hair washes to which some people are allergic; many other examples could be given from court decisions founded on commonsense. Frequently in such cases the rules of the Sale of Goods Act, 1893, have proved adequate, at any rate to secure compensation for the buyer.

These rules, the more important of which we shall now look at, apply generally in sales of goods, so it would not be at all easy, legally speaking, to define the category of goods which we have just mentioned (those containing, as it were, only the seeds of danger) and to separate them off from consumer goods at large. However, the fact that this type of goods does exist and that it is an important type provides an additional reason for tightening up the rules.

There are four of these. The first provides that goods sold by description must answer to the description; the second, which concerns goods sold for a particular purpose by a seller who deals in such goods, lays it down that such goods must be reasonably fit for that purpose; the third provides that goods sold by description by a dealer who deals in such goods must be of merchantable quality; the fourth is concerned with sales by sample, and this we do not propose to discuss. The second of these rules is subject to various provisos, one of which makes it necessary that the buyer should have made known to the seller the particular purpose for which he requires the goods, so as to show that he relies on the seller's skill or judgment to provide suitable goods.

None of these rules is altogether easy to apply. The second and third, which are most important in retail trade, are unnecessarily complicated, though the liberal attitude adopted by the judges in most of the cases has prevented the hardship which a more rigid construction would undoubtedly have caused. However, we think that the rule which at present applies only to dealers in goods of a particular description should apply to *all* dealers in goods who are in business as such. Also, goods sold under a patent or a trade name are at present exempt from the rule; we think that this exemption should go. It is more difficult to say, particularly with reference to retail trades, whether we should abandon the requirement that the buyer must show his reliance on the seller's skill or judgment. There must be quite a number of cases where it would be unfair to a seller to exclude this requirement, especially in the not uncommon case where goods may normally be supplied for purposes of a rather general character—sometimes described as the "normal" use—though there may be particular uses for them as well; it would be wrong to hold the seller liable to supply goods suitable for a particular use unless the point had specifically been brought to his attention. On the whole we think that this proviso should be maintained, and this view is supported by the fact that the proviso is in line with the requirements of the Hire Purchase Act.

In regard to these rules and their modification we are in general agreement with the Molony Committee. There is a strong case for not applying these rules to second-hand goods, especially if the rules are to be modified against the interests of the seller. We agree with the Molony Committee that the Sale of Goods Act should be brought into line with the Hire Purchase Act in this regard, but we do not agree that the rules should not be applied in auction sales, at any rate when these are of new goods.

We think that the reforms proposed in connection with misrepresentation in the chapter on Contract[1] would go far to give the purchaser of second-hand goods a reasonable amount of protection. More likely than not there will have been some misrepresentation (i.e. that the goods are in working order or otherwise better than they in fact turned out to be) which will have induced him to make the purchase.

An important point noticed by the Molony Committee relates to the application of the "reasonable fitness" rule to purchases made in self-service stores. Although the courts have not yet apparently been faced with this problem, it is obviously going to be difficult to fit this type of transaction into the framework of s. 14 (1) (the reasonable fitness rule) of the Sale of Goods Act, 1893. No doubt the third rule, which implies a condition of "merchantability", would be easier to apply to self-service sales, but even here it could be argued that in the circumstances which are typical of such sales goods are not bought by description. If and when statutory effect is given to the recommendations made in this chapter this problem will have to be tackled and we would propose to place upon self-service stores the obligation to supply goods which are not only merchantable but are reasonably fit for the general or normal purposes for which they could reasonably be expected to be used. We see no reason why a dealer in goods, who is in business as such, should not be required to supply goods of merchantable quality except in cases where the goods are bought by description.

The main problem which has arisen in connection with all these rules has been the growing tendency by sellers to contract

[1] See pp. 64 and ff., *supra*.

out of them. This practice was strongly criticised by the
Molony Committee which proposed that such devices shall in
future be inoperative. This, too, would bring the law of sale into
line with that of hire purchase. In respect of fitness for a particular purpose the Molony Committee took the view that
contracting out could be allowed, provided the provisions were
brought to the notice of the buyer and its effect made clear to
him (the onus of proof being presumably on the seller). And
with this too we are in agreement.

If the above suggestions are adopted, the law will become
much more protective of the buyer, but it will still remain
defective as long as he remains defenceless against the manufacturer. Generally speaking the buyer is not in contractual
relationship with the manufacturer. This appears clearly
enough in the Sale of Goods Act which is silent as to the rights
and duties of consumer and manufacturer *vis-à-vis* one another.
In so far as the buyer has any rights against the manufacturer
they arise at common law in tort.

At first sight it might appear that a buyer does not need any
right over against the manufacturer, especially if his position
*vis-à-vis* the seller is improved in the ways that have been proposed. Retailers are often small men, however, and even when
substantial, may be unable to meet the large number of heavy
claims which can result from one large consignment of defective
goods. It can therefore be valuable (and the case law shows that
it has in fact been so from time to time) for the consumer to
have rights against the manufacturer.

It is not at all easy, however, for a consumer to establish a
right of action against a manufacturer in tort, even since the
noteworthy decision of the House of Lords in *Donoghue* v.
*Stevenson*,[1] perhaps the outstanding example in the present
century of "judicial valour" in making new law.

In our view a sufficient nexus should be established between
consumer and manufacturer to enable the former to sue the
manufacturer direct in all cases where he has used or consumed
the goods in a reasonable and proper manner. This would cover
such matters as the use of poor materials, faulty construction,
and inferior design. The Molony Committee shied off from the
legal radicalism involved in this proposal.

Quite apart from its intrinsic desirability in the conditions of
modern life, our proposal can be supported on the ground that

[1] [1932] A.C. 562.

many manufacturers already recognise their responsibility to consumers by giving so-called guarantees, particularly in respect of the replacement of defective parts and the repair of faulty workmanship. It is true that these guarantees are often worded in such a way as to deny any legal liability, but their very existence recognises a moral responsibility. It is one which should be given a legal basis. The position is the more absurd owing to the qualification placed upon the existing liability of manufacturers in tort, which is limited to cases where physical damage has been suffered by the consumer. We are unable to see any common sense in this restrictive rule, and if no other step be taken to widen the responsibility of manufacturers, we suggest that the reform here indicated should be regarded as a minimum: the compensation recoverable should not be restricted to physical damage.

It is worthy of note that this problem seems to have been dealt with successfully in the U.S.A., where the courts found implied warranties of merchantability by manufacturers and extended them to cover other persons using the goods with the buyer's consent. If British judges are not prepared to show the valour of their American brethren, we hope that Parliament will intervene to extend to British citizens the protection which has been extended to their American cousins.

The Molony Committee stressed the fact that it was appointed to report on consumer protection, and not to initiate reforms of the law. In the result they took a somewhat narrow view of their field, omitting to deal with the *nemo dat* rule, passing lightly over other matters which were perhaps peripheral to their main concern, or only dealing with them in a cursory manner. Some of these matters are, however, of quite substantial importance.

One of these is the buyer's right to reject goods which are not in accordance with the contract of sale: this is referred to in two paragraphs of the Molony Report (460–461). This is a point which goes far beyond the consumer interest. The judicial interpretation of "acceptance" of goods under s. 35 of the Sale of Goods Act is a highly technical one. Not only does it preclude a consumer buyer who has accepted delivery from returning the goods when he finds that they are all wrong; it also operates against a merchant who has made a sub-sale of goods which he has bought but has been unable to inspect.

We do not like the Molony Committee's proposal for handling this problem. In effect, it proposes to enable the buyer to
return unmerchantable goods (even after they have been used)
but not goods which are found to be unfit for the purpose for
which they were bought. This seems to be a most unsatisfactory
compromise, and we are very doubtful of the wisdom of allowing the return of goods which have in fact been used by the
customer; a line would have to be drawn somewhere, and the
drawing of it would give rise to numerous acrimonious disputes.
We propose that the right of rejection for breach of condition
should last as long as the goods can be returned to the seller in
the same condition as at the time of delivery or acceptance;
once this has ceased to be possible, we think that the only really
practicable course is that of an award of damages. There is also
in these cases very often a problem of the property having
passed to the buyer before he has had a reasonable opportunity
to inspect the goods and satisfy himself that they are in accordance with the contract. In such cases too, he may be deemed to
have accepted. In our view the right to reject should continue
until such time as the buyer has had a reasonable opportunity
to inspect.

### Hire Purchase

The Molony Committee seems to have been satisfied with the
general structure of the law of hire purchase, though it made
some recommendations for its improvement, and, as we have
already seen, wished to see it made uniform with the law of sale
in respect of the implied conditions as to fitness for purpose,
merchantability, etc. We have already indicated that we regard
a separate system for hire purchase sales as a highly unrealistic
and even anomalous development in the law. The Committee
rejected as unnecessary any drastic attempt to remodel the law.
We would like to see a re-integration of the law of sale, though
with a number of added safeguards (which would be mostly
taken from the law of hire purchase) for consumers under
transactions in which the possession of goods passes before the
price has been fully paid. However, in view of the vested
interests which have been built up round the institution of hire
purchase, we appreciate that a drastic recasting of the law is
unlikely, and we have accordingly concentrated on an attempt
to eliminate the principal defects in the existing law. As we have
said, hire purchase sales are essentially sales by instalments, and

genuine sales by instalments of consumer goods should not be deprived of the protection afforded to hirers under the Hire Purchase Acts. In the preparation of any remedial legislation therefore care should be taken that such instalment contracts are effectively covered.

The law of hire purchase was, to a considerable extent, brought into line with the need for consumer protection in the Act of 1938. Labour lawyers can take pride in this, as it was to them that the late Miss Ellen Wilkinson, to whose enthusiasm and energy the Act was due, turned for advice as to the drafting, and, to some extent, as to the contents of her bill. The law was amended in 1954, to take some account of the fall in the value of money which had made the £100 limitation of the statute unrealistic; and it is a further reform in that direction which is now urgently called for. There has been controversy as to whether the money limit should be abolished altogether (which is the view favoured by the Molony Committee) or raised to a sum of £1,000. On the whole we think that the £1,000 limit should be adopted.

There is no question that many housewives have been induced to sign hire-purchase agreements without realising what they were doing. The Molony Committee proposes to guard against this by a requirement that the buyer's signature must be placed in a box which will also contain a statement that the hirer understands that by signing he is committing himself to a hire-purchase transaction. We accept this proposal, but do not think it goes far enough. We think there should be another box to contain a certificate by the seller's representative that he has explained that the transaction is one of hire-purchase: a breach of this obligation should result in the forfeiture of the owner-seller's special rights under the contract. We also agree with the Committee's proposal for a cooling-off period of 72 hours in the case of agreements obtained by doorstep canvassing.

Of all the causes of heart-burning which arise in connection with hire purchase sales, "snatching back" is undoubtedly the chief. The whole development of this branch of business has turned on the seller-owner's ability, both in fact and law, to take back the possession of the goods if and when the hirer-buyer makes default. No doubt, in the majority of cases the retaking is fair enough; but the number in which it amounts to sharp practice is substantial. In Scotland an order of the court is required in all these cases, instead of only in those cases where under one-third of the total has been paid. We would favour the introduction of the Scottish rule. The Molony Committee reported that in England and Wales it found no demand for such a concession; but then those affected would be unlikely to give evidence. The Committee also saw no reason for reducing the figure of 50 per cent. as representing the minimum level of payments at which the buyer is given the right to cancel the agreement (subject to payment of damages as provided in the 1938 Act, s. 4). This minimum payment clause often gives rise to hardship[1] and legal difficulty. Consideration should be given to its abolition and the substitution of a provision along the lines of the Australian Uniform Bill.[2] We also think that a strong case can be made for introducing the mortgage principle into securing the repayment of what is after all a loan. This has been done in some of the Dominion legislation to which we shall be referring, and has been recently illustrated in *Overstone Ltd.* v. *Shipway*.[3]

Legally, one of the most unrealistic aspects of hire purchase (at any rate in respect of the more valuable sort of article, such as motor cars) is the fact that the actual seller, always called the "dealer" in these cases, usually drops out of the transaction as soon as the contract is completed. This is because of the way this sort of business has developed, with finance companies stepping into the shoes of the dealers and becoming technically the owner-sellers. This is quite bewildering to the layman and often deprives him of rights which in common sense should be his. In most of these cases the dealer does not even become the agent of the finance company; this again makes for a most unsatisfactory position. The Molony Committee, which took up a most unhelpful attitude on the subject, seems to us to have allowed the technical difficulties to weigh too heavily with it. We see no reason why statute should not put on to the dealer the normal obligations of a seller, as provided in certain cases by the Hire Purchase Act of 1938 itself (e.g. s. 8). The finance company should be made the dealer's principal, and also his surety. In this way if legal action becomes necessary both dealer and finance company can be brought in together. At the same time the technical difficulties which arise in connection with

---

[1] See *Campbell Discount Co., Ltd.* v. *Bridge* [1961] 2 W.L.R. 596.
[2] See p. 165, *infra*.
[3] [1962] 1 All E.R. 52.

establishing the liability of the dealer under the present law would be removed.

It often happens in hire purchase transactions that the hirer wishes to transfer the agreement, together with the possession of the article which is the subject matter of the transaction, to a third party. This may prejudice the position of the owner-seller, and it is usual to insert a term in the agreement which not only makes such subsidiary transactions void, but gives the owner-seller a right to bring the main contract to an end, recover the article and nevertheless retain the instalments paid. We think that these clauses go further than is necessary for the reasonable protection of the owner-seller, and indeed, we understand that they are not infrequently waived by agreement. In the Uniform Hire Purchase Bill which has been adopted by most of the States in the Commonwealth of Australia[1] the sting is taken out of such terms by a provision that the owner-seller cannot unreasonably withhold his consent to such transfers, provided all instalments have been paid up to date. We see no reason why this policy should not be adopted here.

In a number of American States, legislation has been enacted to prevent exhorbitant interest being charged by finance companies engaged in hire purchase work, and this line seems to be being followed in Australia[2] and also in Quebec. In spite of the fact that the Molony Committee deliberately refrained from going into the matter, we think that the overseas experience to which we have just referred establishes a strong *prima facie* case for similar action here.

We also think that there is much to be said for a policy such as the one pursued by the Australian Uniform Bill, under which the hirer, if he pays all the instalments before the due date, becomes entitled to a reduction of the finance charges provided for in the hire purchase agreement. And on the same kind of principle, in cases where the goods have been forfeited or for some adequate reason have been returned by the hirer to the owner after substantial payments of hire have been made, the court should be given power to order the repayment to the hirer of such an amount as it may judge to be over and above the amount required to give the owner-seller reasonable compensation in the circumstances.

---

[1] See e.g. the New South Wales statute of 1960 which is the subject of an article in (1962) 25 Mod.L.R. p. 687.

[2] E.g. in New South Wales: see Mod.L.R. *ibid.* p. 694.

## CONSUMER PROTECTION

The largest part of the Molony Report is devoted to other methods of consumer protection than those adopted in the Sale of Goods Act, 1893, and the Hire Purchase Act, 1938. These consist partly in proposals for laying down special rules for certain categories of goods (a method already used in earlier statutes, such as the Fertilisers and Feeding Stuffs Act, 1926, the Anchors and Chain Cables Act, 1899, the various Food and Drugs Acts) and partly of more general proposals relating to the establishment of standards of quality wherever practicable, the introduction of standard systems of labelling, the extension of the law relating to merchandise marks, improvements in the trade marks system, the placing on a proper basis of the nascent system of seals of approval, and some tightening up of advertising methods (though this important matter is left very much in the air). The Report also gives its approval to the system of comparative testing of consumer goods which, originating in the U.S.A., has of late years been successfully used by the Consumers' Association and the Shoppers' Guide organisation; but the Committee considered that these methods should remain voluntary.

Although many of these recommendations of the Committee involve the amendment of existing statute law or the introduction of new statutory rules, and will require to be buttressed by penal rules, we do not feel that it would be appropriate for us to go further into these matters in this chapter. But we have no doubt that it will be to a considerable extent along such lines of a rather particularist approach that the problem of consumer protection will be solved, in so far as it is capable of solution in a society which bases its economic organisation upon a system of private profit.

## NEGOTIABLE INSTRUMENTS AND BANKING

We do not think that reforms in this branch of commercial law are urgently called for. Commercial bills of exchange are now little used outside certain limited branches of commerce. Cheques, which are of course bills of exchange, have become the predominantly important type of instrument. The Cheques Act, 1957, carried through a useful reform of an administrative character by doing away with the need for endorsements on cheques passing through bank accounts.

Probably the main defect in the law of bills of exchange (and this applies to negotiable instruments generally) arises from the application of the *nemo dat quod non habet* rule that we have already discussed in connection with sale of goods and hire purchase. One of the great values of negotiability is that by commercial usage the Continental doctrine had become firmly attached to these instruments before the judges could apply the narrow common law doctrine; but the common law was brought in by a side-wind in connection with instruments passing under forgeries. When a bill of exchange is made payable to order, it cannot be transferred without an endorsement. Should it be stolen, the thief, if he is to gain anything from his theft, will have to forge an endorsement; but as regards the passing of the property in the instrument, such a forgery is a nullity in law, and a *bona fide* transferee obtains no title. This typical common law rule has not been applied in Continental countries. It obviously works hardship, though in the case of cheques the extensive use of crossings does in practice give a limited degree of protection; for a crossed cheque must pass through a banking account, and this will in many cases deter the thief. We think that in this branch of the law too, the fairest rule would be to give to the court discretion to divide the loss between the innocent parties in a way required by the circumstances of the individual case. Indeed, as far as we are able to judge, it would be helpful to create a general rule of this kind to operate in all branches of commercial law and of the common law.

There is, however, one argument against this proposal as it applies to bills of exchange which we ought to mention. Various conventions[1] have been adopted in civil law countries for the establishment of uniform rules in connection with these instruments. This country, and indeed the common law countries generally, refused adhesion to these conventions on the grounds of the differences of the rules laid down in them from those operating here. The most obvious of these differences is the one just referred to. Now, if the recent negotiations in connection with the application of the United Kingdom to join the Common Market had succeeded, the case for adhesion to the Geneva Conventions would clearly have become much stronger. Even without the Common Market, we think that the argument in favour of adhesion is made out. In all the circumstances it would be of considerable practical convenience to adopt the

---

[1] Notably the "Geneva Convention" of 1931.

Continental rule in relation to forged endorsements, rather than the more equitable one which we have proposed above.

The law of cheques is a very important part of the law of banking. There are certain other parts of the latter branch of law which we think call for reform. Some of these are highly technical, and cannot be satisfactorily discussed here. There is one matter which has recently been before the courts in which the law is quite unsatisfactory and where substantial injustice is not infrequently done to innocent traders. This is the rule that a bank is not responsible for the accuracy of its "references", however careless or even fraudulent its officers may have been in giving them. This arises chiefly from the fact that the banker is not in contractual relationship with the person to whom he gives the so-called reference. Since bankers' references are very much in use whenever a businessman is contemplating opening up relations with a new customer, the matter is one of importance. This is one aspect of a much wider subject, that of responsibility for representation, to which reference has already been made.

## TRANSPORT AND WAREHOUSING

We deal with these two subjects together because the reform which we put forward applies equally to both branches of business, indeed to bailments generally—that is to all cases where one person has the custody of the goods of another.

The common law rules in relation to the responsibility of a bailee (custodian of goods) are reasonable enough, except perhaps in the case of the common carrier and the common innkeeper; here they have generally been regarded as over-severe. In other cases the obligation is to exercise reasonable care which is the same as the position under the civil law rule, and this we regard as proper.

But carriers, and bailees generally, have for many years been accustomed to make use of their freedom of contract to exempt themselves in greater or lesser degree from the general rule of law; thus it is common to find a term in contracts of this description that the goods are to be at "owner's risk".

This has been a substantial cause of grievance to merchants and others for many years, and in the case of railway transport, where the State intervened at an early stage, a reasonable compromise was arrived at by giving the owner of the goods a choice of two alternative forms of contract: transport at carrier's risk and transport at owner's risk. Under the first of these the railway, while not accepting the extreme liability of the common carrier, which is virtually that of an insurer, does take upon itself liability for negligence, while in the second it is not so liable, though it accepts responsibility for misconduct. As one would expect, freightage rates are higher in the case of consignment under the first set of terms than under the second, though, as control has been exercised over railway rates, this has not operated unfairly. Broadly speaking, this modus operandi was carried forward into the nationalised transport system, and while there are some criticisms which could be advanced against it, they are of a technical character. On the whole, we think, the position is satisfactory.

In connection with sea transport, a compromise was also arrived at, though much later and of a rather different kind. Since this was embodied in an international convention[1] we do not propose that it should be amended. There are in sea transport a number of anomalies in respect of rules not governed by the convention which will eventually have to be dealt with. These, however, are concerned with highly technical matters and relate to a rather limited field of business, so we have not felt it necessary to deal with them here. Air transport is in much the same position as sea transport. Even locally, it is largely governed by the Warsaw Rules, which were modelled on the Hague Rules.

There remains, however, a considerable section of transport where complete freedom of contract still exists, and in which it is general practice for carriers to disclaim all responsibility even for gross negligence on the part of their employees; and this is even truer in respect of contracts for the custody of goods generally. Thus cases come before the courts from time to time, not only where failure to take obvious precautions to prevent the theft of property has led to its loss, but even where the goods have been handed back to the wrong person, which amounts to the tort of conversion; yet the bailees have been exempted from liability, because such was found to be the effect of the relevant contract, often contained in small print and handed to the depositor under conditions where he had no proper opportunity of reading it.

As we have already indicated, we do not think that these negligence clauses ought ever to have been upheld. They are

[1] The Brussels Convention of 1924, ratifying the Hague Rules.

particularly obnoxious in these bailment cases, since their existence is a direct incentive to bailees not to concern themselves with organising their business in such a way as to prevent carelessness on the part of their employees, and are really therefore contrary to public policy. It is in that light that they have generally been regarded in the U.S.A., and the model Restatement, to which we have already referred, makes them ineffective. We think that their abolition should be given high priority in English law.

Apart from the sacredness of free contract, the normal defence of these exception-clauses is that the goods owner can insure himself, and that if he does not choose to do so it is his own look-out. It is further argued that if this liability is placed on the bailee as proposed, the bailee will have to provide insurance and the premium will be added to the cost of transport or custody (as the case may be). This strikes us as more specious than realistic. In the first place, many of these bailments take place in circumstances in which it is quite unrealistic to suggest that a depositor could effectively be expected to insure. In the second place, economically speaking, it is obviously preferable that the total risk should be covered by one policy rather than by the hit or miss method of leaving it to the depositor to insure; an insurer providing a substantial block of cover of this sort is well placed for ensuring that his assured is not careless in the conduct of his business. It would be reasonable enough that the bailee should increase his charges to the extent of covering his premiums; but he should be prevented from taking advantage of the insurance to make unreasonably heavy charges. Indeed, we think that depositors should have the right to insist on a reasonable scale of deposit charges in all cases where the bailee holds himself out to take the goods of everyone who comes to him. This was the rule laid down for common carriers, and we understand that in the U.S.A. the charges which may be made by storekeepers and similar bailees in respect of insurance are controlled.

The result of changing the law in the way we propose might well bring about a system of alternative contracts, at any rate in connection with transport services; a company's risk form and an owner's risk form such as we have already noted exists in connection with railway transport. Provided that the bailee is required to bring the resulting position clearly to the notice of his customer, we see no objection to this.

The considerations above apply to the transport and cartage of goods, not of passengers. Except in the case of cheap excursion fares and free passes, we are not aware that a policy of exempting themselves from responsibility for negligence has ever been pursued by carriers. In public service transport the cheap fare can no longer be clogged with a term of this kind, but in the case of passengers carried free of charge, as under many service agreements, exemption is possible. The position here is not as clear as it ought to be because the B.T.C. (Passenger) Charges Scheme, 1954, pursues a somewhat different policy from that of the Road Traffic Act, 1930. At common law any passenger who is injured through the negligence of a carrier is entitled to be compensated, provided he was lawfully in the vehicle and was not a trespasser; and we think that the traveller on a free pass should be placed in at least as good a position, at any rate when he is properly using his free pass. Further, we think that carriers of passengers for reward, other than in public service vehicles, should not be allowed to contract out of their common law obligation to exercise a high degree of care in relation to the safety of such passengers.

## INSURANCE

Commercial insurances are contracts of a rather special nature, since the business of insurance can only be efficiently conducted on the basis of a very high degree of honesty on the part of the insured person. From early times therefore the obligation of utmost good faith was laid down by the courts.

This is in principle reasonable enough, but partly because of rather technical extensions of this principle, and partly because of occasional practical difficulties in the way of enforcing it, insurers took to bargaining for even stronger rights. A position has now been reached which is far from fair to the insured, and this in our view calls for remedial action.

In the first place the "utmost good faith" principle requires that a would-be insured must disclose to the insurers every fact which it is material to them to know, and that every representation which he makes in regard to such matters must be true. A failure to disclose, or a misrepresentation, provided these are concerned with material matters, gives the insurer the right to avoid the policy of insurance.

The first point to notice is that insurers, when faced with

a claim, are apt to contend that matters which would appear to the ordinary citizen to be of no great moment, such as conviction of a crime of dishonesty many years before taking out an insurance, are in fact material. In the case suggested, they will say: "If we had known that the man was dishonest we would not have accepted him, or at any rate would have required him to pay a higher premium." Judges now tend to decide these points in favour of insurance companies, and it is perhaps right, good faith being so important, that insurers should have the benefit of the doubt.

Nevertheless, we think that something can and should be done to help the insured. The problem is, to a substantial extent, one of bringing home to the mind of the proposer the matters to which he must direct his attention, and of ensuring that he deals with them accurately and fully. For a long time now, in certain types of insurance, such as life, accident, and motor vehicles, insurers have required the proposer to answer a number of questions on a form: this is the so-called proposal form on which, in the majority of cases, the proposer asks the insurer to grant him the cover or insurance required.

These proposal forms may be drafted in such a way as to be traps for the unwary,[1] so much so that distinguished judges have warned the public from the bench "against such practices on the part of insurance offices"[2]; or they may be "framed in such a slovenly way" as to be equally misleading.[3] The remedy seems to us to lie in the use of standard proposal forms drafted appropriately for different types of insurance.

Properly drafted we think that the proposal form provides a useful means of bringing home the position to persons seeking insurance. The need for full disclosure and complete accuracy of representation should be drawn to their attention in large type at the top of the proposal form, the use of which in life, industrial, fire, motor vehicle, and perhaps accident insurance should be made compulsory. It is common to make the truthfulness of the answers the basis of the policy, but we doubt very much whether the average person appreciates what the legal

---

[1] So described by Lord Greene, M.R., in *Zurich Insurance Co.* v. *Morrison* [1942] 1 All E.R. 529 at p. 537.

[2] Fletcher Moulton, L.J., in *Joel* v. *Law Union* [1908] 2 K.B. 863 at p. 885.

[3] These words are also taken from the judgment of Lord Greene in the case previously cited; he described the practice as a "vicious one".

effect of this is. In any case, we think that there is a strong argument in favour of providing that the right of the insurer to avoid the contract for breach of good faith shall be limited to cases where the questions have been answered falsely and it is clear that the insurer was induced to grant the cover by such false answers. Perhaps an overriding sanction might be allowed in cases where fraud can be clearly proved. As we understand it, the law has been altered so as to establish such a position in Ontario, Canada, and we think that it should be amended in the same way here.

Difficulties have arisen in some cases because the agent of the insurer has filled in the proposal form for the insured, and has been held to have acted as the insured's agent in doing so, so that the insurer was still entitled to avoid the policy. We think that this highly technical ruling should be reversed by statute. The insurer's agent, who is paid by commission, is anxious to effect an insurance and if doing so he acts fraudulently or even mistakenly, his principal should accept responsibility for his actions.

In the absence of fraud, insurers should only be entitled to repudiate liability in respect of untruthful answers to questions put on the proposal form, and the good faith rule should be narrowed to this extent.

We limit what we have just said to the position as between insurer and insured. In many of these cases it is a third party, injured by an insured, who is the person to suffer. The kind of case which may arise is illustrated every day in motor car accidents. A pedestrian is seriously injured and is awarded very heavy damages, far beyond the ability of the driver to pay. His only chance of redress is that the driver's insurance company will pay up. But when called upon to do so, the latter may claim to avoid the policy for non-disclosure or misrepresentation, and if it succeeds the injured man may get nothing.

So obvious is the interest of third persons in these insurances under the conditions of modern life, that, when motor vehicle insurance was made compulsory by the Road Traffic Act, 1930, an attempt of sorts, described by one judge as a "half way house",[1] was made to protect the third party victims of accidents. Although the policy introduced by that statute has been carried further by later statutes,[2] the position of the third

---

[1] Stable, J., in *Merchants' Insurance Co.* v. *Hunt* [1940] 4 All E.R. at p. 207.
[2] See particularly the Road Traffic Act, 1960.

party is still far from being completely safeguarded. In particular, the insurer may take steps to have the policy avoided on grounds of non-disclosure or misrepresentation, provided he does so within three months.

We think that these qualifications upon the rights given by statute to third parties should be removed, without, of course, interfering with the statutory obligation of the insured, whose non-disclosure or misrepresentation has caused the trouble, to indemnify the insurer.

The Road Traffic Acts have enabled third parties to look directly to the insurers, instead of having first to take proceedings against the insured. This policy could with advantage be extended to other branches of insurance law where appropriate, and notably to accident insurance generally; that a pedestrian's rights should depend on whether he was knocked down by a motorist or a horse and cart is an indefensible position. Careful consideration should also be given to the advisability of applying the same principle to all cases where third parties acquire *bona fide* interests under insurance policies. We have in mind particularly life assurance contracts, where a person who has, for example, advanced money on the security of a life policy may find the security worthless because of some failure to disclose or some misrepresentation that occurred when the insured took out the policy. We appreciate that such an alteration of the law might lead to an increase of fraudulent insurances, but the possibility of these is already evident, and the fact that they do not seem to be common in practice suggests that the danger is not substantial. An analogous problem in life assurance is raised by the suicide of the assured. Even when the policy contains a promise to pay on "sane suicide" it is not certain since *Beresford* v. *The Royal Insurance Co.*[1], whether an assignee can enforce the policy, and without such a clause it would appear that he cannot do so.

The Road Traffic Acts make provision for safeguarding the procedural position of insurers in cases where third parties are interested in the ways indicated above. Thus insurers who are made directly responsible to third parties are in justice entitled to be brought in as quickly as possible, so that they may take steps to defend their position. As, however, the insured (who is, of course, the person liable in the first instance) is in between, the situation is a little complicated, and the administrative

[1] [1938] A.C. 586.

arrangements made under the Acts have in a number of cases led to insurance companies escaping liability; see *Cross* v. *British Oak Insurance Co. Ltd.*[1] If our proposal for eliminating the right to avoid policies so as to defeat third parties is accepted, it may be that these difficulties will largely disappear. But we think that the situation, which is highly technical, should be carefully examined. It is important that injured third parties should not go remedyless through the operation of technical points which may protect insurers, who, in justice, have no good reason for avoiding liability.

We have already referred to the existing practice by which the truth of the answers given to questions in the proposal form is made the basis of the contract of insurance, so that if there is any incorrectness the insurer is discharged from his obligation. This is really just one important example of the use of warranties by means of which insurers have for many years been accustomed to strengthen their position as against the insured. Thus, a sympathetic jury might be ready to find that some matter not disclosed or misrepresented was immaterial, so that the insurer would not succeed with his claim to avoid the insurance. But if the matter is covered by a warranty, materiality ceases to be relevant; or to put it another way, the materiality is conclusively established by the warranty. Thus, although the actual loss for which a claim is made may be quite unconnected with the breach of warranty, the insurer is nevertheless entitled to be discharged from his obligation. We think that such a rule of law is quite unjust, and we believe that the better class insurance companies, and Lloyds underwriters, are more and more ceasing to take advantage of it. The time has come when it should be laid down that only when the loss claimed for has been caused by the breach of warranty, should the insurer be entitled to claim discharge. We have already suggested a substantial inroad into the materiality doctrine with our proposal to apply the Ontario rule in this country, and we think that serious consideration should be given to the question whether it would not be in the public interest to make it generally impossible to establish materiality by the terms of a contractual warranty in cases where it does not exist in reality. We consider further that unless the breach of warranty alleged against the insured can be proved to have injured the interests of the insurer (as by causing the loss for which the claim is

[1] [1938] 2 K.B. 167.

made), the insurer should be precluded from relying upon it as a defence to a claim for indemnification.

In "The Reform of the Law" it was proposed that in some of the commoner types of insurance the policy should now be standardised. In marine insurance a form of policy already standardised for long years was adopted by the statute of 1906, though the addition of further clauses is not prohibited. In practice, however, these additional clauses are also standardised. Life (including industrial life), motor accident (and probably accident generally) and possibly fire insurance have all reached a stage of maturity where there seems to us to be a strong argument for enacting forms of policy. A powerful argument for regulating the terms of policies in this way is the fact that in very many cases the insured does not get the policy issued to him until long after he has been at risk, and he may well find then that the policy contains terms which are not intelligible to him or, alternatively, are much more onerous than he had any reason to suspect. Such standardisation would have the additional advantage of eliminating many of the existing unnecessarily complicated and often ambiguous forms of policy which are used by the less reputable insurers.

There are many other aspects of insurance law in which technical improvements, some of them of substance, could be suggested, but the above proposals seem to us to be those in which the ordinary citizen is mainly concerned. We feel, however, that we should not leave this subject without drawing attention to certain suggestions of a much more fundamental character, which are beginning to be more widely accepted and with which we have considerable sympathy.

In the conditions of modern life many accidental misfortunes occur which cause great hardship, and for which no compensation is obtainable. Thus, in motor vehicle accidents no insurance may be available for one reason or another; a common example being that which occurs when a thief is driving away a car that he has stolen. Or a man falls down some steps and breaks his leg, or the victim of a cosh attack is badly injured.[1] The position in relation to uncovered motor vehicle accidents has been realised for a long time to be one of such seriousness that the insurance companies have established a Bureau to which

---

[1] The Government is known to have this particular case under consideration, following the proposal of the late Miss Margery Fry that special statutory provision should be made for compensation in such circumstances.

claims can be submitted for ex gratia payment. In some countries, we understand, the government has already stepped in to provide State compensation. While the Motor Insurers Bureau no doubt provides a useful stop-gap, we think that such an important risk of hardship ought not to be left on an insecure basis like this, and we think that some, at any rate, of the more obvious forms of common accidental misfortune should be covered by a State scheme of insurance. It does not seem to us to make sense that a man who breaks his leg by a fall while at work should receive compensation, but not if he breaks it by slipping on the pavement on his way home.

We appreciate that with existing actuarial knowledge it would not be possible to introduce a full-fledged scheme at once, but we would certainly advocate that a start should be made with a few well-defined types of casualty, such as the uncovered motor vehicle accident and the case of the victim of violent crime. The experience gained from the operation of such schemes over a number of years would enable further desirable extensions to be made. With these proposals we are, of course, leaving the narrow area of law reform proper, and entering the field of social legislation. We do not, therefore, propose to discuss this matter further.

Finally, there are certain procedural aspects of insurance claims which require careful consideration with a view to possible legislative action. In certain types of insurance, e.g. fire, an arbitration clause is often inserted under which the insured is required to submit any dispute which may arise to arbitration rather than to a court of law. This has the effect of preventing publicity, and this is solely in the insurer's interest; when he is relying upon a highly technical point in an attempt to defeat a claim. Arbitration may also add considerably to the expense, a particularly objectionable example being a clause which insists that the arbitration shall take place within a certain distance of the insurer's place of business. We propose that in drawing up the standard-form policies which we have suggested this type of arbitration clause should be eliminated.

## COMPANIES[1]

The corporation with limited liability has, despite the short time it has been in existence, become an integral part of the

---

[1] Unless otherwise stated, all references in this section to the "Companies Act" are references to the Companies Act, 1948.

commercial system and is today recognised as a right rather
than as a privilege. It was created by statute law just over one
hundred years ago. The private company as a distinct entity is
even younger than the company with limited liability. It was
created by statute just over sixty years ago and, at the time,
there was a good deal of doubt whether it should be created at
all. In fact, the forgotten Limited Partnership Act was passed
in 1907, the same year in which the second statute affecting
private companies came into force. As the result of the work of
many committees the company is surrounded by a mass of
legislation. This, says the introduction to the Jenkins Report[1]
has become necessary "in order to keep effective control over
the growing and changing uses of the company system as an
instrument of business and finance and the possibilities of
abuse inherent in that system".[2]

The possibilities of abuse are those with which the Jenkins
Committee and all previous committees have been most concerned. Limitation of liability, in its inception a convenient
method of joining a number of small investors with a common
interest in a particular venture and insulating them from the
risks of the venture and the travails of management, became a
means to defraud investors, bilk creditors and evade taxation.

Committees and legislators have overlooked the differing
motives for the formation of companies and also the fact that the
function of private and public companies is not the same; they
have also failed to note that practice has deformed the administrative machinery originally devised for the formation and
control of private companies. In real life, the members of a
small private company look upon the formalities required with
regard to directors' and shareholders' meetings as a nuisance,
and do everything they can to get over them. Very few formal
directors' meetings are called; they can be conducted by
telephone. The annual general meeting is disposed of by
circulating documents for signature and often it is forgotten
altogether. The filing of returns with the Registrar of Companies is frequently overlooked.

Not all the law relating to companies is found in the Companies Acts themselves. Some of it is found in legislation concerned with the prevention of fraud (the latest being the
Protection of Depositors Bill (1962) and in the Income Tax

[1] Cf. p. 150, *supra.*
[2] Para. 6.

and Finance Acts. In this legislation too, the different functions of the public and private company have been either overlooked or muddled. Legislation concerned with the prevention of fraud has been mainly directed against the activities of the promoters of public companies and is not really adequate to deal with the types of fraud which can be and are committed through the use of the private company. Conversely, the prevention of tax evasion has concentrated upon evasions open to promoters of private companies, without much regard to similar possibilities of evasion that present themselves to promoters of public companies.

### Private Companies

The private company differs from the public company in the amount of publicity required for its business and accounts, the restrictions placed upon the transfer of its shares and the minimum number of members (seven in a public company, two in a private company).

Concentration on these statutory differences has so far inhibited any radical reform of the law. Therefore, before making any recommendations for reform, it is desirable to analyse the motives which lie behind the formation of private companies on the one hand and public companies on the other, and the different ways in which each of them is used or abused.

It is not usual for a businessman to instruct his lawyer that he wishes to conduct his business through the medium of a private company because he hopes in this way to avoid payment of his debts. This advantage may be a factor when launching a new and speculative enterprise; but even in such a case limitation of liability is not a necessity and may become a trap. The promoters of speculative enterprises can by limitation of liability be tempted to overreach themselves and run into debt (for which they are under no personal liability). The risk of bankruptcy involving the loss of personal possessions will limit the extent of speculation. It is strange how gullible traders are, and how ready to give credit to companies which are not always creditworthy.

Although the private company has no direct access to the public for capital, this disability is evaded by means of credit obtained over a long period and such devices as the "mushroom farm", "pig ownership" and the soliciting of deposits in hire-purchase and other finance companies. Out of moneys obtained from trade creditors and the general public, other businesses can be financed and the directors can enjoy high salaries and expenses until the company finally goes into liquidation after having lost all its assets.

The perpetration of fraud is made more attractive by the divorce of management from capital liability. Directors are not, unless the articles of association so provide, required to hold any shares and thus they may have nothing but their job to lose if the business of the company fails.

The private company is also used as a means of carrying on a complicated business through an association or partnership of companies. By separating such parts of the enterprise as may be temporarily profitable from those which are not, credit can be obtained for the profitable units. This credit will then be used to finance and keep afloat the unprofitable. This method of carrying on business by the transfer of assets from one private company to another often takes place when a public company with access to public funds has acquired a number of private companies, whose businesses were not previously correlated. This use of private companies as subsidiaries of public companies makes the accounts of the public company more than usually incomprehensible to its shareholders. In a recent and well-known case of fraud more than one hundred private companies were used to shuffle the assets of an enterprise fast enough to deceive the eye of the investor. The demand for private companies for this and other purposes has now become so large that it pays to keep a stock of them, ready-made for sale.

There are, of course, penalties enforceable against directors who are guilty of fraudulent trading or do not keep proper books of account; but in practice these are seldom imposed on directors of private companies and certainly inadequate to achieve their purpose. The assets available to creditors on the liquidation of a private company are often small or nothing. Creditors are therefore loth to throw good money after bad by spending it on the heavy costs of investigating the conduct of directors merely to have them prosecuted. The police only intervene where there is a widespread scandal, and while the Companies Fraud Department at Scotland Yard has been assiduous in requesting lawyers and accountants to report suspected cases of fraudulent trading as early as possible, it is difficult to discover evidence on which to found a prosecution or to persuade the Director of Public Prosecutions to institute one at public expense.

The directors of a company which has traded in a fraudulent manner are, in theory, personally liable for its debts if in a liquidation the creditors cannot be paid in full; so also, in theory, are the directors of a company which continues to trade when it is, to their knowledge, not in a position to pay its debts as they fall due. This liability is rarely enforced because creditors are not usually willing to risk heavy costs in suing directors who may themselves turn out not to be worth powder and shot. Consequently, directors who are also the main shareholders of a private company find it profitable to continue to trade so long as they can obtain credit; for once all the capital of the company has been lost they are gambling with the creditors' money, in the hope of turning a losing enterprise into a profitable one and recouping some of their own capital.

A very important motive behind the formation of a private company is the tax advantage. In fact, the existence of the private company has been the cause of much complicated tax legislation, dating back, so far as income tax and surtax is concerned, to the Finance Act, 1936, and straying into the field of estate duty in ss. 46 and 55 of the Finance Act, 1940.

While the sole trader or the partners in an unincorporated partnership are liable to pay income tax and surtax on the whole of their profits, company profits are, in principle, subjected to income and profits tax only. Surtax is payable by shareholders only if their income, including dividends, is sufficiently large. The private company is therefore very convenient to the trader because (subject to the provisions of s. 245 of the Income Tax Act, 1952) very little of the profits need be distributed by way of dividend, and liquid reserves can be accumulated out of profits which carry only income and profits tax. They are subjected to surtax only if the distribution made to shareholders is not, within the meaning of s. 246 of the Income Tax Act, "reasonable". To decide what reserves are reasonable for the satisfactory conduct of a company's business is a game carried on between the Inland Revenue on the one side and the company and its shareholders on the other.

The first post-war Labour Government took the view that it was socially desirable to limit the distribution of profits by companies; but it failed to distinguish between public and private companies. Profits tax on distributed profits was made higher than on retained profits in all companies. It may be that the publicity given to large dividends distributed by public companies might have had an undesirable social effect; but no such publicity is given to the distribution of dividends by private companies. Their profits would have been subjected to surtax either if they were distributed to shareholders or if the company failed to make a "reasonable" distribution (the definition of which was not strict enough). The Inland Revenue had to find a compromise between the provisions under which private companies were liable to pay surtax and the Chancellor's direction requiring limitation of dividends. This particular compromise became known as the "Chancellor's umbrella"—a rule under which the profits of private companies were not subjected to surtax so long as they distributed a proportion of profits comparable to the years preceding the Chancellor's direction. This encouraged the use of the private company structure because it was suitable for the accumulation of cash reserves upon which only income tax and the lower rate of profits tax had been paid. Eventually, by means of the purchase of suitable private companies by public companies, all this facilitated the evasion of the orders attempting to control capital investment.

The methods of saving estate duty and income tax by gifts *inter vivos* and the settlement of shares in private companies have caused a running battle between the Revenue and the lawyers. It has been going on for over thirty years and the lawyers are always a short head in front.

The private company has a number of disadvantages for the businessman. A partnership involves control by discussion and consent (and not, usually, by a vote the weight of which depends on the amount of capital paid in). When a joint venture is converted into a private company, the difficulties which confront the practitioner are considerable. He must provide adequately for the varied interests of the members, keeping in mind also the estate duty payable on the death of a shareholder and the protection of widows, children and minority interests. Because votes are attached to the shares, elaborate articles of association are often required to deal with the problem of control. Voting agreements are sometimes used to protect the rights of small minorities. To be a minority shareholder in a closely knit family company, even if one has a right of representation on the board, is not an enviable position. The chances of extracting anything from the investment depend upon the goodwill of the directors. It is mandatory for the articles to restrict the transferability of shares and, unless elaborate precautions are taken, the restriction can be enforced by the directors in an arbitrary manner. The reduced value of a minority share in a private company is recognised by s. 55 of the Finance Act, 1940, which, for the purposes of estate duty, directs a higher valuation to be put upon a share forming part of a controlling interest in a private company. No such provisions apply to shares in a public company quoted on a stock exchange.

The private company, however small the number of its shareholders, has to set up the same elaborate machinery by way of statutory books, directors' and shareholders' meetings and the filing of documents with the Registrar (other than a statement in lieu of prospectus) as a company with many hundreds of shareholders. Usually these requirements are carried out perfunctorily. All the elaborate machinery designed to prevent fraudulent activities and enable minority shareholders to be kept informed of the progress of the business is often ignored, precisely because of its complicated design. The oppression of minorities is most glaringly facilitated, and most frequently made use of, through the medium of private companies.[1]

The protection of the successors of deceased partners is more easily dealt with in partnership deeds. The restriction placed on the transfer of shares in a private company makes it difficult to sell them to obtain cash generally or for the payment of estate duty. Liquidation of a company in order to distribute its assets involves expense, and in any event for all practical purposes it is not within the powers of minority shareholders. Elaborate arrangements for the purchase of shares of a deceased shareholder in a private company can be made by special agreement and in the articles, but these are frequently a burden on surviving shareholders who by law cannot buy the company's shares out of the capital of the company. The survivors are therefore left either to use their own capital (if they have any outside the company) or to pay out of taxed income (if any) distributed by the company.

The memorandum of association, originally designed to protect the investing public from having its money used for purposes other than those publicised, has become an unwieldy and repetitive document (the Jenkins Committee recommended that a standard form shall be incorporated in future legislation); with the consent of three-quarters of the

[1] *Scottish Co-operative Wholesale Society Ltd.* v. *Meyer* [1958] 3 All E.R. 66.

7

shareholders it can now be changed completely and without difficulty. The *ultra vires* rule can be a trap for creditors[1] and a means of defeating them. It is a trifle absurd that a private company cannot, for instance, grant pensions to directors or employees or exercise powers which are not contained in its memorandum; no such restriction is placed upon a trading partnership concerning whose powers the outsider need not enquire before making a contract, provided that the contract is signed by a partner or someone who is held out to be one.

Even the most assiduous and knowledgeable creditor or employee who would wish to know about the creditworthiness of a private company cannot find out very much from published records. Balance sheets are only filed by public companies and non-exempt private companies. The Jenkins Report has recommended that all companies should file them. But this may be of little use in some cases. The period of 15 months, which is allowed between the filing of successive annual returns with accompanying balance sheets, is often exceeded, particularly in cases of fraud; and even when filed, balance sheets are not always co-terminous with the period covered by the annual return. Penalties for not filing an annual return are no real deterrent to the fraudulent director; the Board of Trade cannot adequately supervise the files of the approximately 400,000 companies now in existence. Penalties are enforced only in the most flagrant cases and then only a long time after notices requiring compliance have been sent to the directors and ignored. It is quite possible for the period elapsing between the filing of one balance sheet and the next to exceed three years; during that time the finances of a company may have completely altered. By means of those provisions which are theoretically designed to protect the creditor he has really no adequate opportunity of ascertaining what is the financial position of a private company.

## Public Companies

The object of creating a public company was at first to canvass the public to subscribe for shares, to find risk capital for a new enterprise and to pool a number of small investments. As late as the 1920's shares of 1s. each in wholly untried enterprises could be offered for subscription and bid up to a high price on the London Stock Exchange long before publication of

---

[1] *Anglo Overseas Agencies Ltd.* v. *Green & Another* [1960] 3 All E.R. 244.

the first accounts. Speculation of this nature resulted in a tightening up of the regulations relating to prospectuses, both in the Companies Acts and by the Share and Loan Committee of the London Stock Exchange. The latter will not now as a general rule grant a quotation for shares of an untried enterprise, and thus the principal function of the stock exchange has become to find buyers for shares in established enterprises; the only exceptions are general investment companies and unit trusts with managements of proven experience.

The modern businessman, when for the first time he considers a stock exchange quotation for the shares of his company, does not do so because he hopes thus to find additional capital for his enterprise. He is not in any event likely to get a quotation unless he can publish accounts showing a handsome profit earned over a period of at least five years. Quotation of shares is a great advantage for the investor, because he can thus easily ascertain the price at which he can sell and change his investment.

There are in the formation of a public company a number of valuable tax advantages. No tax is imposed by the Finance Act, 1962, on the profit made by the sale of shares in a public company, representing shares in a private company which the vendors have held for more than six months or before the 9 April, 1962. The provisions of s. 256 of the Income Tax Act, 1952, regarding surtax do not apply to a company which is under the control of more than five persons and of which 26% or more of the shares are held by the general public. The provisions of s. 55 of the Finance Act, 1940, regarding valuation for estate duty do not apply to the shares which control a public company.

Flotation is therefore a means by which surtax on undistributed profits can be avoided and cash reserves built up; the promoters can still keep control of the company, for 30% of the votes at general meetings is in practice sufficient for this purpose where the shareholding is otherwise widespread. On the death of a controlling shareholder his shares are assessed for estate duty on a valuation based on the middle price ruling on the stock exchange at the time of his death, and the money required to pay the duty can be more easily obtained than in the case of a private company whose shares are to all intents and purposes unsaleable.

The profits of a public company not being (unlike those of a private company) subject to surtax even if no reasonable distribution is made, public companies are able to accumulate handsome liquid assets and reserves which are subjected only to income and profits tax. If such profits are distributed they may, in the hands of shareholders, be subjected to surtax. They can, however, be capitalised by the issue of bonus shares and these can be sold by the recipient shareholders without payment of either surtax or the capital profit tax imposed by the Finance Act, 1962 (provided in the latter case that the shares in respect of which the bonus shares were issued had been held for six months or more).

Promoters of a public company enjoy the further advantage of being able to acquire additional companies, too small to warrant a separate stock exchange quotation, for shares saleable on the market. The "takeover bid" which in recent years has become so fashionable was fostered after the war by (i) dividend limitation and capital investment control and (ii) nationalisation. Public companies could do without the consent of the Capital Issues Committee if they found the new capital needed by acquiring, against shares quoted on a stock exchange, the shares of private companies with cash reserves accumulated under the "Chancellor's umbrella" or with assets which were readily saleable. Companies whose assets were, on nationalisation, acquired for cash could have gone into liquidation and distributed the cash; but the directors might then have been left without a job. The cash was therefore used to acquire control of other businesses, and the board of the original company remained in office. This began the fashion of the "ragbag" holding company which, unlike the vertical or horizontal merger, has no real social or economic value; it only serves to maintain directors in office and increase their prestige. The facility with which successful enterprises can be purchased for quoted shares assists the fraudulent use of the assets of a successful enterprise in making good the losses of an unsuccessful business, managed by the board of the same holding company.

The sale of shares to the public is the subject-matter not only of statute law and regulations made by the Board of Trade but also of rules made by the London Stock Exchange and the Association of Provincial Stock Exchanges. These rules do not have the sanction of law but they must be complied with before a quotation can be obtained. They are interpreted by a body which is elected and answerable only to Stock Exchange members. While there is no doubt that the rules are commendable and in the interests of the public (particularly as regards the information required to be given in prospectuses and advertisements, and by the directors after a quotation has been granted) there is no appeal against the manner in which the rules are interpreted. Shareholders can, for instance, suffer considerable damage if the Committee of the London Stock Exchange decides to suspend the quotation of their shares. Usually the shares then become to all intents and purposes unsaleable; if a purchaser can be found, the price is likely to be far below that which he would have paid for a quoted share. What is the remedy at law of a shareholder injured by a suspension of quotation has yet to be decided by the courts.

## Recommendations of the Jenkins Committee

The Jenkins Committee made a number of recommendations which, if adopted and passed into law, will to some extent improve the law in the interest of shareholders; but it took a very narrow view of its task, particularly on the subject of take-over bids, company accounts, shareholders' votes and the duties of directors.

Takeover bids were one of the principal grounds why the Jenkins Committee was appointed; but the Report contains little more than recommendations concerning the information to be given. No recommendations can be found with regard to the economic effects of, or the duties of directors towards shareholders in, a takeover bid. And yet, these are matters of great consequence. Mergers which have the effect of greater efficiency in production are in most cases desirable. There is, however, no general control in the public interest over mergers and takeover bids; the freedom with which these can be effected permits such ill-effects as the artificial inflation of share prices caused by competing bids and (as in the case of the *News Chronicle*) the closing down of a business which may result in loss of employment without adequate compensation and also the disappearance of a public service.

Negotiations for a bid to take over the whole share capital of a company are usually carried on in secret at board-room level. They are relatively easy when large blocks of shares are held in a few hands. The outside shareholders are then usually asked to make a decision with few facts upon which to judge the issue. S. 209 of the Companies Act provides that if 90% of the shareholders have agreed to sell out, the remaining 10% can be compelled to sell at the same price.

Concerning the right of holders of equity shares to attend and vote at general meetings, the Jenkins Committee merely recommended that the assistance of the stock exchange and other means of publicity should be enlisted to draw the attention of shareholders to their position. This is hardly adequate. Equity shares without a vote are usually created when the reserves of a company are capitalised by means of a distribution of bonus shares. A quick profit not subjected to tax is thus provided and as a result there is no widespread opposition to the voteless equity share even though by its existence it enables a small circle of shareholders, often the original founders of the business, to control the enterprise. Nobody minds so long as the business continues to be satisfactorily conducted; but if something goes wrong, the equity shareholder is the first to suffer a loss, and if he has no vote he has no say as to who is to manage the company.

Failure by shareholders to take an active interest in the affairs of the company encourages the contempt in which the management holds them and the lack of information found in the accounts; and accounts which are not informative do not serve to encourage the shareholders to take an intelligent interest in the affairs of their company. The Jenkins Committee made a number of recommendations for improvements in the accounts, but refused to recommend that banks and discount houses should give full information to their shareholders. This may encourage public companies generally to give as little information as possible. Some members of the Committee dissented and pointed out that the method of accounting used by bankers and discount houses was not devised especially for them but was an adaptation of a form of accounting presentation widely used for public companies many years ago; they recommended that the exemption granted to bankers and discount houses should be withdrawn, but the Board of Trade should have power to grant exemptions to the extent to which this might be necessary in order to preserve public confidence. The dissentients drew attention to the amount of reserves which banks and discount houses under their present form of accounting keep hidden from shareholders. This defect also appears to a lesser extent in the accounts of trading companies, and is well illustrated by the disclosures made by Courtaulds as a counter to the I.C.I. takeover bid. This happened after the Jenkins Committee had reported and it might well have altered its views about general improvements in company accounting if it had seen that the shareholders of Courtaulds were, after the I.C.I. had made their bid, shown that the accumulated reserves alone were enough to cover the price put upon the ordinary shares by the Stock Exchange. In fact, the Courtaulds directors found that they could distribute a bonus of ten shillings worth of 7% loan stock to each ordinary share. The directors even went further; they promised larger dividends in the future, and a capital distribution free of tax to each ordinary shareholder in each of the next three years. All this was made possible out of reserves which had not been apparent from the company's earlier published accounts.

Periodic revaluation of assets is a practice adopted by some of the larger public companies, the surplus being capitalised and forming the basis for a distribution of bonus shares. But it is an open question whether shareholders would be satisfied with the dividends they receive if they had a clear picture of the company's real surplus assets. Obviously, every well-administered company requires an adequate trading reserve, but there is no justification for hoarding assets unless they are being accumulated for the purposes of a definite investment or trading project. And yet shareholders who are dissatisfied with the amount of dividends distributed have no remedy other than to replace the directors, and that they are not likely to do in the case of a company whose business is successfully conducted.

By law, directors owe no duty to shareholders; their duties are to the company and have never been clearly defined, either by statute law, or by decisions of the courts. One of the reasons why the company has become a favoured instrument of fraud is just because the duties are so vague.

The structure of, and the law relating to, private and public companies is out of harmony with the needs of the modern State and the progressive businessman. In particular, the public company and the way in which shares are dealt with on a stock exchange (such as artificially high prices encouraged by the small number of shares made available on a placing, and the peculiar relationship between jobbers and brokers) has encouraged shareholders to gamble for a capital profit and not otherwise to take an interest in the business in which they have invested. The result is a real gulf between them and the management (which is interested in prestige and power) and the employees (who are scarcely recognised by the company law at all).

The Jenkins Committee has merely touched the surface of those problems by reason of which our existing company law requires radical reform for social and economic reasons. Limited liability, which has become a right, should once again become a privilege. The private company has ceased to have any useful function as a separate form of organisation. This was to some extent recognised by the Jenkins Committee, but it has stopped far short of recommending (as we do) that the distinction between the private and the public company should be abolished.

### Proposed Reforms

*The company generally.* The Jenkins Committee has recognised that the memorandum of association in its modern form is cumbersome and recommended a standard form which could be adopted by all companies; thus it would still be necessary to file a memorandum setting out the chief objects of the company. As it is now so easy fundamentally to alter a memorandum of association by special resolution, the original reason for its adoption has fallen to the ground. It is, however, important that investors should know what are the limits of the business in which they are risking their money. There is no reason why these limits should not be clearly defined in some document other than the memorandum, and the law amended to abolish the memorandum of association and to provide that all companies have certain general powers.

The Jenkins Committee also recommended that s. 109 of the Companies Act should be repealed. We would maintain that section and, indeed, extend and strengthen it, by providing that no company should be given a certificate to commence trading until the promoters have filed a very strict statement in lieu of prospectus, including a statement of the intended business of the company, along with a statutory declaration that the paid up capital is adequate for such business. If at a future date it is desired to alter or extend the principal business of the company, it should be possible to do so on condition that a certificate to commence the new trading is granted; and this should be granted only if the change had been previously approved by a special resolution of the shareholders and the directors have filed a new declaration that the available capital of the company is adequate. Any radical change or extension of business without a certificate to commence trading should involve the directors in personal liability for all the debts of the company.

It is a matter of dispute whether a company should be permitted to be registered unless it had a minimum paid up capital. The Jenkins Committee rejected this proposal, mainly because it took the view that evasion would be easy. Another objection is that the requirement of a minimum capital might prove to be a brake on enterprise. We suggest that the Board of Trade should be given powers to require by Order in Council a minimum capital to be paid up before a company is given leave to commence trading. This would enable a restriction of this nature to be tested, and to be abolished if it proved to be undesirable.

If reforms of the nature above set out were extended to the promoters of all companies, and the liability for fraud now only applicable to public companies made applicable to all companies, businessmen might think twice before using the privilege of limited liability. This might slow down the proliferation of subsidiary and interlocking companies.

*Directors.* The Jenkins Committee was content to make the somewhat obvious recommendation that in future legislation there should be contained a provision that directors must observe the utmost good faith towards the company in all transactions with it or on its behalf and that they must act honestly in the exercise of their powers and the discharge of the duties of their office.

Directors with powers of management are in most substantial companies employed under a service agreement setting out their duties and powers. Future legislation, we propose, should provide that all directors engaged in the day-to-day management of the company's business must be designated as such and that (with the exception of a director appointed because of his professional qualifications and not engaged in the day-to-day management of the business) the duties of a director are those which are contained in most service agreements; in particular a director who is also a manager must not take part in a competing business. Directors engaged in the management of the company's buiness should be referred to in letter-headings and business documents by their special designation.

The law should also be amended to provide that directors

7*

negotiating for the transfer of all the assets or the majority of the shares of their company are the agents of the shareholders, to whom they are under an obligation to report on all stages of the negotiations.

The Jenkins Committee has recommended that the personal liability of directors should extend to "reckless trading". The onus of proving that the directors were guilty of reckless trading would be on the creditor or shareholder concerned. This is often a difficult and expensive task, particularly because the directors have all the evidence in their hands. It seems right, therefore, that in certain circumstances the onus of proof should be shifted. The law should be amended to provide that there is a presumption of reckless trading against a director concerned with the management of a company which, on liquidation, is unable to pay some minimum proportion of its debts, or which has not carried out its statutory duties. The onus would then be on such a director to prove (in the same way as a bankrupt can prove) that what has occurred was due not to recklessness but to misfortune. Only a certificate of misfortune granted by the court should exempt the director from personal liability.

*Shareholders.* S. 28 of the Companies Act[1] should be repealed. A similar protection for a small circle of shareholders against the type or number of persons who can become members of a company can be achieved by special agreement between them, including such devices as pre-emption rights, without giving the board what is, as the law at present stands, a veto which can prevent a shareholder from disposing of his shares. There would then be only one form of company with, as recommended by the Jenkins Committee, a minimum of two members.

Shareholders should be encouraged in every way to take an active interest in the affairs of their company and given every opportunity to protect their interests. Therefore the creation of equity shares without vote should be forbidden. The occasions upon which shareholders of a special class can vote should be extended to cover, for example, the sale of all the assets of the company or a radical change in its business.

Shareholders should be able to obtain a complete picture of the assets of a company. The recommendations of the Jenkins Committee do not go far enough to prevent that kind of sup-

---

[1] By this section the transfer of shares in a private company is restricted, the number of members is limited to 50, and any invitation to the public to subscribe for shares or debentures is prohibited.

pression of the truth which was so vividly exemplified by the disclosures made in some recent takeover battles. It is still possible for all companies to hide in their accounts an accumulation of reserves. Some companies, particularly those wishing to distribute bonus shares, have their assets periodically revalued. The Companies Act should require a periodic revaluation of assets by an independent valuer; this would help shareholders to find out if the management is making full use of the company's assets and, incidentally, the Treasury would also get a better idea of the size of assets available for investment.

In special circumstances, e.g. where the number of shareholders exceeds a certain number, or the capital exceeds a certain figure, and the shares of the company are quoted, the shareholders (including those of a special class) should have the right to appoint to the board a person whose duties will be to look after their interests generally and to report to them; he would be acting like a kind of "ombudsman".

The procedure for the protection of the rights of minorities is expensive and slow. The power of shareholders to requisition meetings is strictly circumscribed and this can lead to delays and assist fraudulent directors to cover their tracks. The law should be amended to enable shareholders wielding a certain number of votes to requisition a meeting without first having to request the directors to do so. The procedure now available under s. 210 of the Companies Act for the protection of oppressed minorities should be made cheaper, and with suitable safeguards the Board of Trade should be given power to intervene and, if necessary, to appoint a receiver to manage the affairs of a company in which minority shareholders get no fair deal.

Access to the books of a company is at present granted only to its directors. The enforcement of the rights of shareholders can be made very difficult by this restriction. The law should be amended to give the holder or holders of a minimum proportion of the issued capital access to the books for specified purposes and on a restricted number of occasions during the year.

The method of changing the registered ownership of a share should be simplified. Anyone who works in the City knows how cumbersome and expensive is the machinery at present involved in distributing transfers, having them stamped and completed, and later collected and presented to the company for registration and the issue of new share certificates. Transfer by endorsement of the share certificate itself, with suitable safeguards against fraud, might be well worth considering.

Shareholders should be given the right to appeal to the courts against any suspension of quotation and the courts should have power to require the Committee of the Stock Exchange to give reasons for its decisions. Consideration should also be given to legislation entrusting the powers of the Share and Loan Committee of the Stock Exchange to a statutory body.

*Employees.* S. 319 of the Companies Act is the only one under which the existence of employees of a company is recognised. This section, in delightfully old-fashioned language, gives priority in a winding up to the wages or salary of a "clerk or servant" and the wages of "any workman or labourer" for services rendered in a period not exceeding four months before the winding up (and not, be it noted, exceeding £200 in all— a top salary of £12 a week!) The section also refers to "a labourer in husbandry who has entered into a contract for the payment of a portion of his wages in a lump sum at the end of the year of hiring"; this sounds like a quotation from the Old Testament. The anomalous position of employees was brought to public attention in the case of *Parke* v. *Daily News*.[1] This case was launched by a shareholder, to prevent payments being made out of the proceeds from the sale of the company's assets to those who would, as a result of the takeover bid for the *News Chronicle*, lose their jobs. The judge, although he expressed the view that the company and its directors were prompted by motives which were laudable from the point of view of industrial relations, was constrained to find that the law did not recognise such motives as a sufficient justification for using, against the wishes of a shareholder, part of the proceeds from the sale of assets as compensation for displaced employees. In contrast, compensation for loss of office payable to directors *is* recognised in the Companies Act (where it is the subject-matter of certain restrictions) and also in the Finance Acts. The standard form of memorandum of association that we have recommended earlier on should contain a power for all companies to pay compensation to employees out of the selling price of assets. It should also be a part of the law that on an amalgamation or on the sale of all the assets or shares of a company, there should be a duty upon the directors adequately to compensate employees

[1] [1962] 2 All E.R. 929.

for loss of employment; and, where the assets themselves are not sold, an obligation to pay such compensation should be placed upon the shareholders receiving cash or shares.

In certain circumstances, to which reference will be made in the next section, the employees should be given power to appoint a person to the board (or to be concerned with management) whose special duty it should be to look after their interests.

*Taxation and control of investment.* The manner in which the extensive current reserves of public companies are invested is entirely a matter of decision by management. The orthodox manipulation of the money market has little effect on the investment policy of such companies; and wholesale nationalisation may not commend itself to the majority of voters. Other means must therefore be found to make the central planning of investment more effective. Nationalisation involves the nomination by the Minister of the whole board of an enterprise; but this need not always be done to obtain control. It would in many cases be sufficient if there were in existence an ultimate sanction to remove the management and put another in its place. The pool of trained managers is not inexhaustible and it is therefore in the interest of efficiency to make use of their knowledge as long as possible.

The Companies Act should therefore contain powers for the Board of Trade by Order in Council to declare any enterprise to be an Enterprise of National Interest. The board of directors or, in the case of a corporate partnership, the managing partners of such an enterprise, should be put under an obligation to negotiate, with any Government department or other public authority concerned, the contracts covering the type of goods to be manufactured, the price and quality of such goods, any requisite scheme of investment (or reduction in investment), the location of the industry, the terms and conditions of employment, and so on. Employees should be given suitable power to appoint representatives to the board (or, in the case of a corporate partnership, persons having powers equal to those of a partner) to watch the interests of staff. The Board of Trade should be able to remove, at the request of the department or authority concerned, any person who, in the exercise of his managerial power, impedes the negotiation or performance of any contract made with the appropriate Minister or other public authority. This power of the Board of Trade should be subject to suitable safeguards, including a right of appeal to the courts. Provision should also be made for compelling the Government or other public authority concerned to buy at a fair price the shares of any substantial minority of shareholders who desire to sell them. Public money nowadays is frequently lent to private enterprise and a residual control of the type set out above would be particularly useful in such cases.

Taxation has not in the past been effectively used as an instrument of central planning and investment. Limitation of dividends facilitated the accumulation of assets and the investment of these was outside the control of the State. Profits tax was used to discourage distribution, and surtax, generally speaking, is only payable on the incomes of individuals. In the battle between the State and business, the company is being used as a protective cloak and as an instrument to accumulate, out of profits, assets on which income tax and profits tax only has been paid. Taxation should encourage and even force companies to distribute profits which are not required for investment or reasonable reserves, and such profits should be subject to progressive taxation in the hands of shareholders. In order to prevent the distribution of profits to directors as "earned income", the preferential treatment of earned income should be limited to a maximum amount. Investment and depreciation allowances do not by themselves encourage new investment at the right time. It is the present practice to grant an investment allowance at the date of the contract made for the new investment. In the interest of central planning it would be better if such allowances were granted at the time when it is desired to encourage new investment. Any such allowances found to be retained in the business, distributed as income or not used for new investment within a given period of time should be subjected to appropriate taxation. As a corollary to this, and to encourage economically desirable investment, any enterprise undertaking to carry out an approved scheme of investment should be entirely relieved of the burden of taxation in respect of its profits required and used for the approved scheme.

Mergers and takeover-bids are not always socially or economically desirable. They should be subject to approval by a central authority, at any rate if they involve more than a fixed ceiling of assets or capital.

## PARTNERSHIP

Company law enables a number of people to organise so

tightly for the purpose of carrying on business that the law has always been ready to treat them as if they were in fact one person: a legal person or "corporation". The much looser organisation of the partnership was, however, until quite recently the dominant form used for collective business action. The legal rules governing partnerships were laid down at common law and in equity, and were naturally formulated at a much earlier period than those of company law, which is substantially the creature of statute; they are much less formal or detailed. They were codified in the Partnership Act, 1890, so successfully that little further has been heard of them in the law reports.

However, the fluidity and formlessness of partnership law have their draw-backs in the conditions of modern business. In practice these difficulties can be overcome by the partners themselves laying down a fairly elaborate code of rules dealing with such matters as how the relationship is to be brought to an end, what is then to happen to the firm's assets, and so on. In this way some continuity and stability is achieved. But to give an example of the unsatisfactory state of affairs: when there are no articles of partnership, then (under the old rule adopted by the Partnership Act) not only does the partnership come to an end when a partner dies, but the business itself has to be sold, so that the family of the deceased, or the beneficiaries of his will, may take his estate. The surviving partners have no right to take over the business at a valuation (which would be the sensible course, and is often provided for in the articles). Similar difficulties arise on the bankruptcy of one of the partners. Simple amendments of the law which would take care of such points are long overdue.

Since the informal partnership was never regarded by the law as having the attributes of a legal person, any right of action arising out of its transactions had to be brought against all the individual partners. The result of this was, and broadly speaking still is, that if the name of one partner was omitted from the writ for any reason (and there may have been good reasons) all rights against him were lost when judgment was obtained against the named partners. Morover, the procedural difficulties involved in pursuing a large number of partners are usually tiresome and may be formidable. To a considerable extent these have been overcome by a provision in the Rules of the Supreme Court, whereby action may be brought against a partnership in the firm's name. We think that this step should be pursued to its logical conclusion and the partnership be treated as a corporation in all respects; but it should be a corporation in which the personal liability of the individual partners is preserved. This would have the additional advantage of providing in itself a remedy for the difficulties to which attention was drawn at the beginning of this section.

The Limited Partnership Act, 1907, provided for the limited liability of dormant or inactive partners. We think that a system under which active partners remain fully responsible in law for the contracts and torts of the firm while the dormant partners cannot be made liable for more than the capital which they have put in, is much to be preferred to the limited liability doctrine of the private company; this, as we have pointed out, has many openings for evasion and unscrupulous conduct within the law.

Without going into full details, we suggest that the law should provide that the registration of a business name by at least two persons carrying on business in partnership automatically confers corporate status. Provided that at least two persons are personally liable, it should be possible for others, not exceeding a certain maximum number, to enjoy limited liability. Any agreement conferring limited liability should be filed and open to public inspection. "Limited" partners should be able to withdraw their capital without it becoming necessary to liquidate the partnership. An "unlimited" partner should be able to buy out a "limited" partner and thereby put an end to the privilege of limited liability attaching to that particular partnership share. The letterheads and publications of the partnership should disclose all partners, including those whose liability is limited.

Partnership agreements in these circumstances could conveniently provide that, so long as there remain two partners with unlimited liability, a widow of an unlimited partner can leave her husband's capital in the business without losing the privilege of limited liability. Registration of a corporate partnership should be made cheaper than that of a company and there should be no standard form of agreement appointing limited partners until some general practice concerning the form of such agreements has been established.

# VIII

## INDUSTRIAL LAW

### EMPLOYEE OR WORKMAN?

IT IS NECESSARY for the law to take note of the changing structure of the working population, and to remove some obsolete vestiges of class distinction. The law distinguishes between "workmen" and other employees and has given special protection to the former. Yet the changing social structure of the population makes it difficult to find a "working class" any more and this, together with the increased willingness of white collar workers and other salaried employees to resort to the more militant tactics of "the workers", makes the word inappropriate.

"Workmen", defined narrowly as manual labourers, are protected, with regard to the amount of deductions that may be made from their wages and to the method of wage payments, by the truck legislation.

"Workmen", defined a little more widely to cover persons employed in trade or industry (excluding local and central government employees, medical and educational workers, etc.), are the only persons protected under the trade disputes legislation.

It is vital that equal protection should be given to all employees. We recommend that all references to "workman" should be replaced by references to "employee" and that this word should be given the wide definition given to "workman" in the Industrial Courts Act, s. 8, which covers ". . . any person who has entered into or works under a contract with an employer, whether the contract be by way of manual labour, clerical work, or otherwise, be expressed or implied, oral or in writing, whether it be a contract of service or of apprenticeship or a contract personally to execute any work or labour."

Thus, "employee" would clearly include local government personnel, teachers, doctors, nurses, and other professional workers. It would still be necessary to exclude one group, namely certain civil servants, from some of the protective

measures provided for employees. It has now been determined
that civil servants do have a contract of employment (at one
time it was thought that they did not), but the contract has a
limited effect. Owing to the constitutional rule that the Crown
cannot by contract fetter its future action, any civil servant can
be dismissed without notice and without being given any reason.
On grounds of public policy it is essential that the Crown should
retain this power. But it is not necessary to apply this rule to
all civil servants, especially those who are employed on work
not connected with policy-making or security. We would
suggest that civil servants employed by the Crown in profit-
seeking enterprises, or the social services, or the industrial
services, or the Post Office should be treated in the same
manner as ordinary employees, and not have their job security
or right to strike or any other right restricted on the ground that
they are employed by the Crown.

### THE CONTRACT OF EMPLOYMENT

The first thing that strikes any foreign observer who looks
at English industrial law is the absence of legal protection
against arbitrary dismissals. As our law now stands, so long as
the employer gives notice as provided in the contract of employment he may dismiss any of his employees. There is no control
over the length of this period of notice; it depends entirely on
the contract. Of course, the employee has similar power to
terminate the contract and the period of notice again depends
on the contract; it need not be the same as that given by the
employer. A man who has given 20 years of service to his
employer can lose his job, with "the protection" of one week's
notice, or one week's wages, even though he has been a good
workman and has given no reason for the dismissal. No one
would argue that an employer should not be able to dismiss his
employees; but we do think that an employee, particularly one
who has been employed for a long period of time, should have
some assurance that he will not lose his job arbitrarily, and that
when his employment is terminated he will receive a definite
sum of money as compensation, a sum which does not depend
on the period of notice in the contract but on the period of
service.

Most Continental countries have legislation to give the
employee job security. Job security involves two distinct

problems: the selection of the employee to be dismissed, and the period of notice and amount of compensation.

## Selection

French law[1] gives the dismissed employee a right to apply to the courts for compensation, on the ground that his discharge amounted to "abusive dismissal". "Abusive" has been widely construed and covers unfair discrimination and hardship to the employee.

German law[2] gives all discharged employees aged 20 or over who have been employed for at least six months in an enterprise employing at least six employees a right to apply to the Labour Court on the ground that his dismissal was unjustifiable. German law goes further than the French and requires the employer to show that he dismissed "the right workman"; in deciding on this issue the court will consider many things, including length of service, size of family and other social matters, as well as the economic need to dismiss an employee at all. If the dismissal is found to be unjustified, the employee is reinstated or else awarded by way of compensation a sum assessed according to the length of employment. This sum may be as much as a whole year's wages.

## Notice and Compensation

In Germany the period of notice is fixed by the law itself[3] and ranges from two weeks for industrial manual workers to six weeks for technical and clerical salaried employees. Other salaried employees are entitled to a minimum of three months' notice, increasing according to the period of service until it reaches six months after twelve years. These periods can be lengthened or shortened by collective agreement.

Belgian law[4] also determines the period of notice for all employees except those salaried employees earning more than 120,000 francs a year. The period varies from two weeks' notice for manual workers (but they need only give their employer one week's notice) to three months for salaried employees. Collective agreement can only alter these terms by

---

[1] Code du Travail, bk. I, tit. II, art. 23.

[2] Law concerning Protection in the Event of Dismissal, 1951, Arts. 1–3, 7–8, 12, 21.

[3] Gewerbeordnung, Arts. 122 and 133a; Handelsgesetzbuch, Art. 67.

[4] Law of March 10, 1900, as amended by the Law of March 4, 1954; and Law of August 7, 1922, as amended by Law of March 11, 1954.

extending the notice to be given by the employer or reducing that to be given by the employee.

No Continental country has removed the employer's power to dismiss instantaneously for serious breach of contract, or the employee's right to leave when circumstances make it unreasonable for him to remain. But in France and Germany, if an employer wrongly dismisses a man without giving him the proper notice, the employee may obtain double compensation.

These Continental systems show how the two separate sets of rules, the one relating to the choice of a man for dismissal, and the other to notice and compensation, can exist side by side, and together provide effective job security.

The United States system of industrial law does not include any kind of job security legislation, but the development of grievance arbitration has more than adequately compensated for this. Under American law the collective agreement determines the terms of the individual contracts of employment of all employees covered by the agreement. These collective agreements invariably include a section on the procedure of arbitration that will be used to determine questions relating to the interpretation and application of the agreement; this type of arbitration is known as "grievance arbitration". Awards made by the arbitrators are binding and only limited appeals can be made to the courts. Normally the collective agreement also contains a set of complicated rules whereby employees are given degrees of seniority depending not only on length of service but also on skill and type of job. In the event of dismissals on the ground of redundancy the employer must dismiss in accordance with these rules (which often cover rights to promotion as well) and any alleged breach by the employer can be taken through the grievance procedure. The question of choosing the right man for dismissal is separate from that of the period of notice.

American law requires all employers to bargain in good faith with the union of their employees' choice, and though they are not compelled to make a collective agreement normally they make one. In this way all employees have job security. In his turn, the employer retains the right to dismiss summarily for cause.

One of the first requirements of any reform in the field of industrial law must be to provide some form of job security. No one would suggest that the right of management to select staff, or to dismiss employees summarily for serious misconduct, should be interfered with. But we feel very strongly that employers should be compelled to justify dismissals and their selection of the persons to be dismissed. This could be done by adopting either the Continental or the American system. The American scheme would probably fit into our system more easily than the Continental one. We will recommend later in this chapter that collective agreements should be incorporated into contracts of employment, and that the practice of some form of grievance arbitration should be adopted. If collective agreements also contained seniority clauses we would be much nearer to solving one of the problems relating to redundancy.

This leaves the questions of notice and compensation. The present Government is in the process of legislating to ensure that all employees obtain adequate notice of termination.[1] One would have thought that this legislation would alleviate some of the hardships caused by redundancy and mass dismissals. Unfortunately it fails to recognise or solve the problems involved in this type of discharge. Even on the narrow problem of ensuring reasonable notice the Bill is hopelessly inadequate.

The proposed legislation would merely lengthen the period of notice to be given by the employer (not radically; one month would be the maximum) without dealing with compensation or termination payments. It would give the employee no more than a couple of weeks security of employment. The Government also fell into the trap of assuming that both sides ought to be placed in the same position—that the employee should give the employer the same notice as the employer would have to give him. This would be justifiable if both sides were in an equally strong position; but they are not. The employer can well afford to give the employee longer notice; to make the employee do the same is to weaken his bargaining power by effectively curtailing his right to strike. It is generally supposed that a strike is a breach of the contract of employment and can only be "legal" (in the sense of not amounting to a breach of contract) if the strikers give notice to terminate their contracts. What the Bill proposes to do is to postpone strikes by the period of notice to be given by the employee with the longest period

---

[1] The Contracts of Employment Bill is at present being considered by a Standing Committee of the House of Commons. References to the Bill in this chapter are to the text as it stood early in February 1963.

of employment. Thus a Bill purporting to protect the employee in fact aids the employer. If the employee is required to give a notice equal to the employer's, then it should also be provided that a strike is not a breach of contract. This provision should not be limited to official strikes; the employer ought not to be able to take advantage of the union rules. But the Schedule to the Bill expressly states that if employees strike without first giving notice in writing (or without such notice being given on their behalf), this will amount to an interruption of employment and the employee will lose any increase in the period of notice that he has earned by length of service.

There is no need to put every employee's contract into writing and insist that only the written terms are effective. It would be almost impossible to reduce some contracts to writing, and it would reduce the strength of the collective agreement if it were unenforceable unless each employee covered by it had received a new document incorporating the new terms. To safeguard the employee's position it should be sufficient for him to receive a written payslip with his pay, indicating how the wages have been calculated, and a notice in writing when his employment is terminated.

### TRADE DISPUTES

The common law tried its utmost in the nineteenth century to make strikes both criminal and civil offences. In particular it utilised the crime and tort of conspiracy to such an extent that it appeared to be a crime and a tort to combine to strike, even though no criminal or tortious acts were contemplated or committed. Understandably therefore the history of legislation relating to trade unions in this period was one of continual attempts to give workers freedom to strike. The result is that the law is extremely confused and uncertain.

### Criminal Law and Strikes

It should be made absolutely clear that the mere act of striking is not a crime and that it is not a conspiracy to combine to strike. Criminal liability should only arise if some crime, e.g. riot, assault, malicious damage, is committed during the strike. As the law now stands this is only certain so far as strikes in contemplation or furtherance of trade disputes are concerned, and the definition of a trade dispute is too narrow.

It has been said by some that general strikes are criminal, and by others that they are not but ought to be. This is wrong; general strikes are not criminal and should not be made so. The only difference between a general strike and any other strike is that through size alone its chances of success are greater, and strikes can hardly be penalised on the ground that they are likely to succeed.

A considerable body of opinion holds the view that political strikes are criminal. It is very doubtful if that is so. Certainly it is not true of strikes which are concerned with terms and conditions of employment, even though such strikes may be directed against the Government; and the further the Government interferes with industrial policy, especially wage policy, the more likely it is that this type of "political" strike will occur. The only type of political strike which could possibly be criminal is one entirely unconnected with employment, e.g. a strike against nuclear armament or foreign policy. It is hard to see why this type of political pressure should be criminal while other types of pressure remain permissible. Is it because a strike is open and obvious and other pressures are more secret? So long as the method of the strike is persuasion and not force, it should not be criminal.

Certain acts are expressly declared to be crimes by the Conspiracy and Protection of Property Act, 1875. It is a crime for anyone to break his contract of employment when he knows that the effect of his breach will endanger life or injure persons or valuable property. This clearly affects strikes by e.g. nurses and doctors. But if the strikers give notice, then they do not break their contract and commit no crime. A similar provision expressly applies to gas, electricity and water workers. The police are absolutely forbidden to strike. It is vital that when the right to strike is taken away or limited, some form of effective machinery should be established to enable such employees to maintain fair and reasonable terms and conditions of employment. The employer should not be in a position where he can take advantage of the essential nature of his employees' work. The existing machinery does not seem to function adequately; see the recent unrests among nurses, doctors, postmen and police. It would be impossible to evolve one single form of machinery which would be suitable for all classes of employees. But one vital principle should be made clear, and this is that the person or body with ultimate power to determine the terms of employment, especially wages, should not be the employer, but some independent person or body agreed by the parties or nominated by the Ministry of Labour. Once the parties have failed to agree, either side should be able to refer the matter to this independent person or body. The Industrial Court would be a suitable organ for this function. A form of compulsory arbitration, such as once existed under the Conditions of Employment and National Arbitration Order, 1940, should replace the right to strike in the case of employees engaged in essential services.

### The Law of Tort and Strikes

When the Trade Disputes Act, 1906, was passed to give unions a reasonable degree of freedom to strike without interference from the common law, it was difficult to determine what precisely the common law was on this topic. But the common law continued to develop and now gives a fairly satisfactory degree of protection so far as the aims of strikes are concerned. So long as the predominant aim of the strikers is to improve their own conditions, to act in their own interests, there can be no action for conspiracy at common law unless the strikers resort to some unlawful method, e.g. riots or malicious damage. But in 1906 it seemed as if the very aim of a strike was unlawful, and that is why the Trade Disputes Act provided that no action for conspiracy would lie against any persons acting in contemplation or furtherance of a trade dispute unless the acts committed would be actionable if done by one person. The effect of this is that a combination to strike in which no torts or crimes (i.e. no "actionable" acts) are committed does not amount to conspiracy so long as the aim of the strike is connected with a trade dispute. The fact that it harms the employer or is in restraint of trade does not matter.

Yet another restriction which severely hampered strikers, namely the tort of inducing a breach of contract, was removed by the 1906 Act. Section 1 has the effect that no action will lie against any person acting in contemplation or furtherance of a trade dispute on the ground only that he has induced the breach of a contract of employment. This is important, for clearly, every time a person persuades an employee to strike without first giving the employer the necessary notice to terminate the contract, a breach of the contract of employment is, technically, induced.

All this protection given to the strikers is dependent upon the acts being done in contemplation or furtherance of a trade dispute. It has been decided that only the workers themselves and not the union officials may act in contemplation of a trade dispute, although union officials may further a dispute if it already exists: *Conway* v. *Wade*.[1] "Contemplation" and "furtherance" of a trade dispute are words which should be widely construed; it should be possible for workers and officials alike to act in contemplation of a dispute before the dispute is absolutely imminent.

"Trade dispute" is defined in the statute as a dispute between workmen and workmen, or workmen and employer, which is connected with the employment or non-employment, or with the terms of the employment, or the conditions of labour of any person. This includes secondary and sympathetic strikes, but not strikes supporting one employer in his battle with a fellow employer; this is treated as a matter between employers. In this respect the definition is far too narrow. It may be essential for the employer to be strengthened before he is in a position to grant his worker's demands and in such a case the workers are involved in a dispute which concerns, ultimately, their chance of obtaining better conditions for themselves. Protection is given to this type of dispute at common law, but not under the 1906 Act. This is unsatisfactory. The definition of a trade dispute should refer to the object of the dispute and not to the immediately apparent battle formations. Accordingly, it is proposed that the definition of a trade dispute should be widened to include disputes in which employees are participating in order to improve the terms and conditions of employment of any person.

There is yet another defect in the definition, and that lies in the use of the word "workman". For the purposes of trade union legislation a workman is a person employed in trade or industry, and this narrow definition excludes e.g. civil servants, local government employees, teachers, nurses and hospital employees. Any disputes which these "excluded" employees may have, are not trade disputes and are therefore outside the protection of the Act. These employees also require protection; one way of providing it would be to substitute "employee" for "workman", as proposed earlier in this chapter.

Even with this widening of the scope of the 1906 Act the problems do not end. There has recently been a shift of emphasis

[1] [1909] A.C. 506.

away from the aims of the unions towards the methods employed in achieving them. The protection only exists under s. 1 so long as no "actionable" act is done. The Court of Appeal, in a recent case[1] had to determine the meaning of this section. The facts of the case, much simplified, were as follows. Rookes was employed by B.O.A.C. as a draughtsman. His union had concluded a National Procedure Agreement with B.O.A.C. which forbade strikes until the procedure had been exhausted, and this agreement was incorporated into the individual contracts of employment of B.O.A.C. employees. The union also had an arrangement with B.O.A.C. that after a 100% membership declaration had been made by the union and accepted by B.O.A.C. in relation to any shop within the workplace, B.O.A.C. would only take on new employees who were union members; but present union members who resigned would not be affected. Rookes resigned from the union and after some dispute three union officials, two of whom were employed by B.O.A.C., threatened to strike if he was not dismissed. Rookes was given notice by B.O.A.C. and he sued the three officials for conspiracy. It was agreed that this was a trade dispute, so the aims of the union officials were protected; but were the methods? The court of first instance decided they were not. The employee-officials had threatened to strike in breach of their contracts of employment which included the National Procedure Agreement. If a breach of contract could be regarded as an unlawful act (on the ground that the law punishes breaches of contract) then the officials, by threatening to do an unlawful act, committed a tort, namely intimidation. This tort is actionable if done by one person and so s. 1 of the 1906 Act cannot apply; or, to put it differently, a conspiracy to intimidate is actionable despite the 1906 Act. But previously a breach of contract had not been considered to be an "unlawful" act; unlawful acts were restricted to crimes and torts. If this extension of the definition of intimidation had been allowed to stand, the protection afforded by s. 1 of the 1906 Act would have been effectively removed. However, the decision was reversed on appeal, on the ground that only crimes and torts are "unlawful" for the purposes of the section. Whichever way the decision may go in the House of Lords, it is vital that the tort of intimidation should be limited in its application to trade disputes. It has

[1] *Rookes* v. *Barnard* [1962] 2 All. E.R. 579; [1962] 3 W.L.R. 260.

been decided in *Gibson* v. *Lawson*[1] that the *crime* of intimidation is, in relation to trade disputes, restricted to threats of physical force. This should also apply to the *tort* of intimidation.

## Picketing

No part of trade union law is more confused than this. All the provisions on picketing should be repealed and re-enacted in clear language. There are at present two sets of rules relating to picketing. First, where there is contemplation or furtherance of a trade dispute, any person (whether involved or not, whether a "workman" or not) may attend or wait at any place to peacefully persuade people to work, or not to work, or to give and receive information. Secondly, where there is no trade dispute, only the giving of information is permitted, but no persuasion, however peaceful.

There are obvious defects in these rules. The law should be the same whether there is a trade dispute or not; it is very difficult to decide which disputes are trade disputes. Also, as the law stands, it is not permissible to persuade persons other than the *workers* and these can only be persuaded to work or not to work. Picketing outside a shop or restaurant to persuade customers not to enter, or not to buy certain goods is not protected by the statute. This is unrealistic. Subject to the laws relating to breaches of the peace any person should be able to wait at any place in order to give or receive information, or peacefully to persuade any person to do or refrain from doing any act which he may legally do, or refrain from doing.

## Trade Disputes Act, s. 4

With the object of protecting union funds, s. 4 of the 1906 Act provided that no action in tort could be brought against a union. This meant that the union could not be sued for torts committed by its members and officials during strikes or trade disputes, or at any other time. Clearly it is necessary to protect union funds from tort actions based on trade disputes; but it is not necessary to give them this extremely wide immunity. If a union employee negligently injures another person, why should the union not be liable for its employee's tort in the same way as any other employer would be? The immunity should be restricted to acts done in contemplation or furtherance of a trade dispute.

[1] [1891] 2 Q.B. 545.

We have already recommended an extension of the definition of a trade dispute and the removal of the restrictions preventing interference in a dispute between employers; these reforms should adequately protect the unions.

## COLLECTIVE BARGAINING AND THE LAW

The practical importance of the collective bargain in fixing the terms and conditions of employment can hardly be over-estimated. About 60% of all employees have their contracts settled in this way, and even employees who are not expressly covered by collective agreements may come within their ambit in either of two ways:

(1) Under the Fair Wages Resolution of the House of Commons (1946) which is incorporated in all Government contracts the contractor promises to "observe such terms and conditions as have been established for the trade or industry in the district by representative joint machinery of negotiation or arbitration". If terms have been fixed and the contractor fails to observe them, he may be removed from the list of Government contractors. This is a heavy sanction.

(2) Section 8 of the Terms and Conditions of Employment Act, 1959, gives trade unions (and employers' associations) the right to apply, through the Minister of Labour, to the Industrial Court when an employer in the industry concerned is not giving his employees terms and conditions of employment which are at least as favourable as those settled by collective agreements or awards. The employer need not be a party to the agreement or award. If he is found to give his employees less favourable terms and conditions, then the Industrial Court must order him to observe the collective agreement. This award of the Industrial Court becomes a term of the contract of employment and the employees can enforce it against the employer named in the award.

And yet, despite its considerable practical importance, the collective agreement has been granted no legal recognition and the courts have never treated it as an enforceable arrangement.[1]

[1] Agreements made between employers' associations and trade unions are, of course, affected by s. 4 of the Trade Union Act, 1871, but this is not the reason why collective agreements are treated as legally ineffective. Section 4 does not touch agreements made with *one* employer.

This means that an employee cannot legally compel his employer to pay him the wages allotted to him in the collective agreement, nor can he claim the holidays, hours of work and other conditions fixed in the same way. Yet the clear intention of the collective agreement is to alter the terms of the contract of employment of the workers within its ambit, and in practice this is what happens. It is only the law which is out of step. At present an employee can only sue his employer to enforce the collective agreement when an award has been made by the Industrial Court or where the collective agreement has been acted upon to such an extent that it has become a custom in the trade or industry concerned. In the latter case it is the *custom* which is incorporated into the contract and not the *collective agreement*, which in law amounts to nothing more than a convenient way of creating a custom. But no one knows how far, or for how long, or by how many people the collective agreement must be observed before it becomes a custom, and customs can easily be excluded from the contract by contrary customs, or express or implied terms. The Privy Council once suggested that collective agreements should be enforced by strike or lockout. Thus the giving of no legally binding force to collective agreements increases the likelihood of industrial disruption and contains the seeds of bad industrial relations.

It is quite obvious that the law must be brought up to date and the collective agreement given the legal effect of fixing the terms of the contract of employment. The collective agreement should automatically be incorporated in the contract of employment of all employees; for, whether they are union members or not, to provide otherwise might give an incentive to employers to engage non-union labour, which is employed by employers who signed the agreement, or belong to signatory associations. Employers joining signatory associations should be bound from the moment of becoming members of the association. The terms of the collective agreement should replace any contrary terms in the contract of employment, and it should be impossible for the parties to contract out of them to the detriment of the worker.

By virtue of s. 8 of the Terms and Conditions of Employment Act the collective agreement could be extended still further to cover "outside" employers. It would however be necessary to cure one glaring inadequacy of the section. At present, once the Industrial Court has made an award against an employer, the only method of enforcement is for the employees to bring actions for breach of contract. This fails to take account of an employee's obvious reluctance to put his job security in jeopardy by suing his employer, and is not therefore an effective method of enforcement. This problem has been solved in the Factories, Truck and Wages Councils Acts by the introduction of an inspectorate which is there to see that the employer is fulfilling his duties, and can institute proceedings on behalf of the employee where the employer is in default. Without this kind of administrative sanction the law cannot be adequately enforced. There must either be a Terms and Conditions of Employment Act Inspectorate or the powers of the Wages Act Inspectorate must be extended to cover s. 8.

It is not desirable that the collective agreement itself should become a legally binding *contract*. In their present form such agreements intend to affect the legal relationship between the employer and his employees, and not that between the em- ployers' association and the trade union. The difficulties involved in enforcing the collective agreement between the *signatories* would be very great. What, for example, does the union or the association promise to do? Does it promise to do its best to persuade its members to keep to the agreement? What would that mean? How could damages be assessed in the event of a breach? But these difficulties can be left unresolved. It is enough to give the employees the right, with the help of an inspectorate, to enforce the agreement.

### TRADE UNIONS

There has been recently a spate of court actions concerning the internal affairs of trade unions, one of which, the E.T.U. case, disclosed grave breaches of union rules. We do not think that such abuses are widespread, but none the less the necessity of joining a union in order to get or keep a job is now so great that it is essential for union members to have some guarantee that the union to which they belong is being properly run. Members should also have some security of membership, to ensure that they will not be expelled without a fair hearing and then only on reasonable grounds.

This poses two problems: should the rules of the unions be altered to guarantee, in particular, fair elections and fair expulsion procedures? and who should supervise the unions in order to see that these rules are being complied with?

At present there is no method of checking the rules of unions, nor are any minimum standards laid down, except in the case of political fund rules; there the Trade Union Act, 1913, lays down certain minima which must be incorporated in the rules to ensure that non-contributing members are not in any way penalised. The act does not insist that these minima should be guaranteed in any particular way; but it lays down the principle that if this protection is not afforded then the rules are void. This precedent could be usefully applied to elections and expulsions. It would be useless to draw up rules relating to all union elections and expulsions. For example it would not be reasonable to insist that every union election has to be by ballot; the expense would be enormous and the procedure might well be too cumbersome for local elections. To require ballots for regional and national elections would appear reasonable, but who can tell whether an election is regional or national where national officers are chosen by delegates elected locally?

It would be sufficient to provide for certain minima to be contained in the rules, e.g. that reasonable notice of elections must be given, and that all members should have a reasonable opportunity to vote. Failing adequate provisions, the rules would have to be replaced by others which contain the necessary safeguards. For expulsions the rules should provide that the member threatened with expulsion must be told of the charges against him, notified of the hearing and permitted to put his case. A member should only be expelled for cause and wide discretions ("should the expulsion committee think fit") should not be permitted.

These recommendations, it is submitted, have the advantage of raising no need to supervise or control unions. They leave the unions to put their own house in order, each in the way best suited to it; and only if a union were to fall down on this would the law intervene.

We recommend that complaints of non-compliance with the minimum rules should be made to the Registrar of Friendly Societies after the domestic procedure has been exhausted. Exhaustion should not be necessary if the domestic procedure is lengthy or dilatory; speed is essential in this matter, and elections and expulsions should not be in doubt for long periods of time. The Registrar's decision should be as binding and effective as that of a court, but we would not interfere with an aggrieved member's right to apply to the courts for damages for breach of contract if he has been wrongfully expelled.

The advantages of this procedure are that it is cheap, speedy and effective. The Registrar is experienced in union matters and has been dealing with similar matters under the political fund rules. The unions' freedom of action would not be unduly hampered, but members would be given power to see that their union is properly run.

## SHOP STEWARDS

The growth of the power of shop stewards has been both hailed and reviled. Whether liked or disliked that power is clearly here to stay and what is needed is some recognition of its place in industrial relations.

We do not see how the shop steward could at the moment be given statutory status, nor how his powers could be regulated by legislation. But should there arise in the future a need for this type of legislation, we feel that the following points will have to be considered. First, the shop steward would need some guarantee that he can carry out his job efficiently without resorting to strikes. In order to do this he must have proper opportunities to put cases before the management, and an assurance that his job as a shop steward will not imperil the security of his position as an employee. Legislation at some future date will have to deal with the following problems:

(1) no shop steward should be dismissed except for breach of contract, and the management should give reasons in writing; following the American example special seniority rights should be given to stewards;

(2) a steward must be free to argue with management without any fear that his job or his promotion will be placed in jeopardy;

(3) it *might* become necessary to ensure that shop stewards are elected by the men they represent, in which case the election procedure should follow those general principles which we have suggested for union elections.

## GRIEVANCE ARBITRATION

Many alternatives have been suggested to strikes as a method of enforcing collective agreements; these include compulsory arbitration and "cooling off" periods. Some, for example the authors of the pamphlet "A Giant's Strength",[1] would forbid unofficial strikes. We feel that none of these proposals would solve the problem and we would not recommend any legislation on this subject. The basic problem is one of industrial relations and if a relationship is bad no amount of legislation will improve it.

But we do feel that parties to collective bargains and negotiation procedures ought to consider some form of arbitration in preference to resorting to strikes. The interpretation and application of collective agreements are very suitable subjects for arbitration, far more so than the making of such agreements. Yet the Industrial Court seems to deal with more disputes relating to the making of new agreements than with disputes concerning their application.

As we have said before, in the United States the use of "grievance arbitration" to settle these types of disputes is widespread and most effective. Once the parties have agreed that disputes will be arbitrated, one side can force the other to accept arbitration, and the award will be binding and enforceable. We do not suggest that these rules, which give a compulsory effect to arbitration, should be adopted over here, but the principle of grievance arbitration ought to be accepted. It has many advantages, the most important being its character of self-regulation—the parties choose to arbitrate, choose the arbitrator or arbitrators, and also establish the limits of the arbitral jurisdiction by indicating the matters on which they wish decisions to be made; and those are the only decisions that may be made. Grievance arbitration is definitely no regulation by outsiders. The number of steps to be taken before the parties actually resort to arbitration, and the actual form of the arbitration, are entirely left to the parties who can tailor them to suit their own particular needs.

We emphasise that what we have just said is not a recommendation for legislation, but a suggestion that parties to collective bargaining should consider.

We have already recommended that collective agreements should be binding on the employer and that the individual employee should be able to enforce them in the courts. But this is a slow and expensive method of enforcement and entirely

[1] Published by the Inns of Court Conservative and Unionist Society in 1958.

8

unsuited to some terms, for example those relating to redundancy, which could be better enforced by speedy on-the-
spot arbitration. We do not recommend that there should be
an appeal to the courts from the arbitrator, or that his award
should be legally enforceable. Nor do we think that grievance
arbitration should be a compulsory term in every collective
agreement. Arbitration appears to work most successfully when
it is voluntary and we do not consider the courts to be the best
place for the interpretation of collective agreements; something
more speedy and less judicial is required. But as the arbitrator
and the courts would have overlapping jurisdiction, if the
employee decided to apply to the court, the matter would not
be heard by the arbitrator.

### THE PAYMENT OF WAGES

Parliament has long since been concerned to ensure that the
worker and his family do in effect obtain the benefit of the
worker's wages. It has done this in two ways, first by ensuring
that the worker does actually receive his wages, and secondly
by permitting only limited deductions. Unfortunately, not all
employees are protected and the protection that is given does
not cover all the abuses.

The main statutes safeguarding the payment of wages are the
Truck Acts of 1831, 1887 and 1896, and the Payment of Wages
Act, 1960. These provide for the workman to receive all his
wages in current coin of the realm (this now includes bank
notes) unless he has requested payment by one of the methods
permitted by the 1960 Act (money order, postal order, cheque
or payment into a bank account). Thus there must be no
payments in kind. The statutes also list those deductions which
the employer may make from wages, and although he has
retained the power to fine a worker for bad work or bad
conduct, this power is limited. But the statutes also prevent the
employer from making loans to his workers and deducting re-
payments from wages, even without interest being charged;
nor may workmen be given luncheon vouchers. In these
respects the statutes do not favour the workman.

Moreover, only "workmen" are protected under the Truck
Acts. This is by far their most serious defect, because "work-
man" is narrowly defined and includes only manual workers.
This definition has been a fruitful source of litigation, but many

of the reported cases are irreconcilable. This is not, however, the principal point we are seeking to make. The main point is that "workmen" are not a special section of employees who need special safeguards. *All* employees require a basic guarantee that they will receive the wages they have earned.

A recent committee on the Truck Acts (the Karmel Committee) recommended[1] that these statutes should be completely repealed and the whole topic thought out afresh. They propose that any new legislation should relate to all employees and not just to "workmen". On this point the Committee is indisputably right, in most of its other recommendations it is, we submit, quite wrong. The suggestion that we should return to the old "freedom of contract" between employer and employee is a retrograde idea which ignores the function of the collective agreement and the fact that the individual employee and his employer do not occupy positions of equal power. The Committee takes the view that the unions and wages councils will be able to counteract the economic power of the employers. But not all employees are union members and it is difficult to see how the wages councils could effectively supervise the formation and performance of all the contracts within their jurisdiction. The Committee would establish a special labour tribunal to which the employee could apply whenever the employer is in breach of contract in such matters as deductions or the method of payment. Although this tribunal would have to determine legal matters, the Karmel Committee, somewhat surprisingly, has not proposed that the tribunal should have even one member with legal qualifications. Also the whole burden of referring a contentious issue to the tribunal would be placed on the employee, who is less likely to be aware of his rights than his employer.

We regard the recommendations of the Committee as wholly inadequate and this applies in particular to the short section devoted to the proposed new tribunal. Should it ever be necessary to set up a court to deal with labour matters (and the need is not apparent at the moment) the type of court needed, and its procedure, will have to be thought out with the greatest care.

We would suggest that there should be legislation covering all employees which forbids the payment of wages otherwise than in cash and also prohibits deductions from wages except

[1] The report of the Committee was published by the Ministry of Labour in 1962.

for certain limited reasons (as at present). This rule should be compulsory, and any contractual term or payment of wages contravening it should be void. But we would give the unions power to alter these provisions by collective agreement. The union could agree to payments in kind, deductions, payments by cheque, etc., with the employer, and these terms would be incorporated in the individual contracts of employment. Thus the collective agreement would have the effect of modifying a rule of law. This recognises that the true balance of power lies between the employer and the union, and not between the employer and the employee. The collective agreement has already been given this effect, for certain purposes, in the Netherlands and in Germany.

In no circumstances should employer and employee have the power to derogate from the law. The employer should be required to deliver a written statement with each wage payment indicating in detail how it was calculated. The power of the unions to agree to deductions should be limited and there must be a basic level beyond which no deduction can be made. This level should be based on the employee's family commitments; the Maintenance Orders Act, 1958, would be a good guide here.

The right of employers to suspend employees for breach of contract has been decided by the courts to be outside the ambit of the Truck Acts.[1] Various reasons have been given for this, all of which ignore the one vital fact that the employer is punishing his employee not by suspending him from work but by reducing his wage packet; here again the function of the court to fix the "punishment" of the "guilty" party is being usurped by the employer. The affinity of suspension with deductions is so great that the power to suspend must be governed by the same principle, namely that the employer must have no power to suspend unless the union agrees.

None of the arrangements relating to wage payments or deductions made under collective agreements should be capable of extension under s. 8 of the Terms and Conditions of Employment Act, 1959.

Although workers within the ambit of the Truck Acts cannot assign their wages, they do have the right to instruct their employer to pay them to a third person (subject to the limitations found in the rarely used Shops Clubs Act, 1902). This

---

[1] *Bird* v. *British Celanese Ltd.* ,[1945] 1 K.B. 336.

does not give the third person a right to demand the payment but it does prevent the employee from obtaining the benefit of his wages; and there is no restriction as to the amount which can be dealt with in this way. The law should regulate this subject in a way similar to deductions: the instruction should be in writing, signed by the employee; the basic wage level should govern the amount of the payment, and the employee should retain the right to terminate the arrangement.

There is a general rule which provides that if a debt cannot be assigned it cannot be attached. The Wages Attachment Abolition Act, 1870, specifically prohibits the attachment of the wages of servants, labourers and workmen in certain instances. Wages should be made incapable of attachment as well as assignment, because the evils are the same in both cases. However, the exception to the prohibition of attachment created by the Maintenance Orders Act, 1958, should remain; for instead of allowing third persons to obtain the wages this Act preserves them for the family.

## PAYMENT DURING SICKNESS

It has now been decided, although only at first instance,[1] that at common law it is an implied term of the contract of employment that wages must be paid during sickness. Unhappily, as this implied term can be overruled by a custom in the trade or industry or locality or workplace concerned, or by a term in the contract itself, the common law rule provides but inadequate protection.

If the employer wishes to retain the services of the employee, then wages ought to be paid during illness; but the employer should be able to deduct half the National Insurance benefits received by the employee: as the employee has contributed also towards sickness benefit the whole payment received by the employee ought not to be deducted by the employer. However, it would be unfair to compel the employer to pay full wages throughout the illness of the employee. These should be paid for, say, four weeks; thereafter the wages should be gradually reduced to (after a maximum period) *nil*.

We consider that collective agreement should be the only way in which these rules can be altered to the detriment of the employee. The union alone should have the bargaining power,

[1] *Orman* v. *Saville Sportswear Ltd.*, [1960] 3 A.E.R. 105; [1960] 1 W.L.R. 1055.

not the individual employee; but the advantages obtained through bargaining with these rules should not be capable of extension by s. 8 of the Terms and Conditions of Employment Act, 1959.

## PAYMENT IN THE EVENT OF INTERRUPTION OF WORK

The law on this matter is still confused, but it would seem that if the interruption is outside the control of the employer he need not pay wages even though the contract of employment is not terminated. There is no reason why the employee should bear this burden. The employer is more capable of standing the loss and in many cases will have insured against it. Unless, therefore, the employee has broken his contract, the employer should continue to pay wages during the interruption.

But here again, the new legislation should give the union power to bargain and accept a gradual reduction of wages on lines similar to those that we have suggested for sick pay. Payment in the event of the interruption of work should also be subject to "guaranteed week" provisions and to the Wages Regulation Orders.

## INSURANCE PROBLEMS

There are three of these: the right of the employee to sue the employer's insurance company; insurance against accidents caused by the employee; and insurance against damage caused to the employer or third parties. These will be discussed in the following paragraphs.

It is usual for the employer to insure against claims for injuries caused to employees. Although employees will normally obtain compensation under the National Insurance scheme, this is not full compensation and the employee should retain the right to sue the employer. For this reason it is vital that the employer should be compelled so to insure that the employee can be certain of compensation, and it is also vital that the employee should have a direct claim against the insurance company (as in the case of road traffic insurance). This would have the additional advantage of protecting the employee where the employer goes bankrupt or into liquidation.

The accident injuring the employee may have been caused by himself, or he may have contributed to it. In this situation the employee has no claim against the employer, or only a reduced claim (as the case may be). The question of who ought to insure against this type of accident is a most difficult one. However, it would be better if the employer effected the insurance. The courts have already recognised that an employee's ability to take care of himself may be dulled by the nature of the work he is doing. This insurance need only cover accidents occurring in the course of the employment.

If the employer is insured, the employee causing the accident should be able to take advantage of the policy and be protected by it. Whoever may be injured can only recover one set of damages and it should not matter whether he elects to sue the employer or the employee. The policy should cover both.

INDEMNITY: *Lister* v. *Romford Ice Cold Storage Co.*[1]

In 1957 the House of Lords decided that there is an implied term in every contract of employment whereby the employee must indemnify the employer against all the damage caused to this latter by the employee's breach of contract, including acts of negligence. Liability for negligence was already well defined in the law of tort; *Lister's Case* added a heavy liability in contract.

First it undermined contributory negligence. Prior to *Lister's Case*, if an employee negligently contributed to his own accident, his damages in tort were reduced, but not lost. Under *Lister's Case* the employee may get nothing, for his negligence will be construed as a breach of contract, and the damages for which he will be liable may include the damages payable by the employer for the injuries suffered by the negligent employee.

Secondly, the Factories Acts have carefully laid a duty to take care on the owner or occupier; but if the owner or occupier happens to be the employer of the man causing the accident, then the employer can recover the damages from the employee. Thus the duty has shifted from employer to employee.

It is the same with the safe system of work. The courts made it difficult to delegate to servants the employer's duty to provide a safe system of work; but the rule in *Lister's Case* makes this delegation effective in practice.

Next, when a servant commits a tort he is a joint tortfeasor with his employer, and the loss caused is, in theory, apportioned

[1] [1957] A.C. 555.

between them. In practice, the rule in *Lister's Case* makes the employee bear the whole loss by way of damages for breach of contract.

To sum up: *Lister's Case* makes it more profitable to employ someone to work for you than to act yourself, because an employer will always be able to recover damages from his employee and will never have to bear the loss without recourse to an employee for reimbursement.

It is no answer to the problems raised by *Lister's Case* to insure employees. The employer is already insured and the risks have already been taken into account in fixing the premiums. Fresh insurance would only give insurance companies two premiums for the same risk. The answer is to remove the *Lister* rule completely and let the employer (or, by subrogation, his insurance company) rely on their ordinary remedies in tort against the employee as a joint tortfeasor. They will then get an award proportionate to his fault, and not a hundred per cent indemnity.

An Inter-Departmental Committee was appointed in 1957 to consider the effect of *Lister's Case*. The Committee rejected, without giving reasons, compulsory employer insurance and suggested, first, that an existing agreement between employers and the insurance companies to the effect that the latter would not exercise their rights of subrogation without the former's consent gave adequate protection, and secondly that the trade unions could use their bargaining power to compel employers to arrange for adequate insurance. These suggestions are hopelessly inadequate. There is nothing to prevent the employer from agreeing to proceedings being taken against the employee, and the second suggestion is of little help in the weakly unionised industries.

## ACCIDENT PREVENTION AND WORKERS' SAFETY

It sounds incredible, but there is no general statute relating to accident prevention and workers' safety. The Mines and Factories Acts lay down detailed rules for those who are fortunate enough to work in a place defined as a factory or a mine; but for those outside the scope of these statutes there is only the common law rule which requires the provision of a safe system of work. This is not enough. The provisions of the Factories Acts should apply to *all* places of work, whether factories or not; why should dangerous machines be fenced only in factories? All employees are entitled to equal protection. It should also be made clear that the manufacturer or supplier of inadequate machinery is responsible direct to the injured employee.

This in itself would not be enough, as the Factories Acts have been interpreted restrictively. This is shown by the fate of s. 14 which provides that dangerous machinery must be fenced. This provision has been so interpreted that there must be a fence to keep the workman from contact with the machine, but not to keep the machine in. The result is that if an employee is injured by something which flies out from the machine he cannot complain of a breach of duty by the employer. Further, only the employee himself is to be kept away from the machine; if a tool which the employee must use while operating the machine comes into contact with the machine and injures the workman,[1] there is no breach of statutory duty. Then again it is only a dangerous machine which must be fenced, and not a machine which is only dangerous when materials are being used in it; there is no duty to fence when the danger is caused by machine plus material. Section 14 must be amended to protect the workman in all these instances, and safety legislation of this kind should be liberally interpreted.

The problem of interpretation is not the only one which arises in the sphere of workers' safety. Another vital problem is that of causation, and this arises not only from the statutory provisions but also in relation to the employer's common law duty to provide a safe system of work. Often the employee has, in some way, contributed to the accident that has injured him. If he was solely responsible, the employer is relieved of liability; but where the employer was partly responsible, the damages are apportioned in accordance with the respective degrees of fault. Unfortunately, the courts have shown an increasing tendency to say that the accident was caused by the employee, even in situations where the employer was not altogether innocent of negligence. Also, the extent of the duty to provide a safe system of work apparently depends on the experience of the employee; if he is very experienced the duty is reduced. A change of attitude is required here. Employees are engaged to do possibly dangerous work for the profit of the employer and the duty placed on him to ensure their safety should not

[1] *Sparrow* v. *Fairey Aviation Co., Ltd.* [1962] 3 All E.R. 706.

be lightly cast aside. If the employer has not done all he should do to comply with the safety statutes or to provide a safe system of work, he should be responsible for *any* resulting accident. If the employee is an experienced worker who should have known better and taken more care, his damages should be reduced for contributory negligence; the experience of the employee should not alter the extent of the duty of the employer, but only the quantum of damages. In reducing damages for contributory negligence, great care should be taken to ensure that the employee is not over-penalised for taking risks while doing his work, especially when these are generally accepted risks.

One major defect of the present system is the lack of a scheme of accident prevention. The Inspectorate is the nearest thing to it, but it is not enough. More care should be taken in providing adequate training and supervision; employers should not simply tell employees what to do, but should make sure they can do it.[1] Employees, especially supervisors, should receive some form of training in accident prevention. Employers who have not provided this training should be fined when accidents take place.

The old plea for more Factory Inspectors still stands.


## PATENTS, INVENTIONS AND SPARE TIME

At common law these are covered by the duty of fidelity owed by the employee to his employer. This means that all inventions made by the employee, whether in his employers' time or not, belongs to the employer and may be patented by him if it is in some way connected with the employment. This is a very wide rule and can be made even wider by express terms in the contract. The basis of the rule is that it would be a breach of good faith on the part of the employee to deprive the employer of his invention. But the invention ought not to belong to the employer if the employee has made it in his own time and at his own expense, and not at the employers' request or using the employer's secret information. By an express clause in the contract and for adequate consideration the employee should be able to contract out of this protection, but such clauses should be treated in much the same way as contracts in restraint of trade and be deemed to be, *prima facie*, contrary to public policy.

[1] See *Barcock* v. *Brighton Corpn.* [1949] 1 K.B. 339.

A similar problem arises from spare-time activities. How far is an employee, during the time in which he receives no pay, free to do acts that may harm the employer? Clearly some duty of fidelity exists, for example a duty not to give away secret information. It has been said in the courts that *any* act harming the employer in his business may be a breach of fidelity. This goes too far. The duty should be restricted to secret information or processes and allied matters. There is no reason why an employee should not be at liberty, in his spare time, to work for a competitor of the employer, unless this is forbidden by express or implied terms in the contract; and these should be treated as covenants in restraint of trade.

The whole question of covenants in restraint of trade also needs an overhaul. It should be made absolutely clear that such covenants can only be legal when they are necessary to prevent the employee from divulging secret information or processes.

### CHILD LABOUR AND APPRENTICES

The law relating to child labour should be consolidated into one statute and the inspectorates operating under the Education Acts, Factories Act, and the Shops and Offices Acts given wider powers of supervision. At present many children under 14 are employed in part-time jobs, e.g. paper rounds, and there is no effective control. It would also be an improvement if all young persons (up to the age of 18) had to obtain a doctor's certificate to show that they are fit to undertake the work they are doing; at present this only applies in factories.

Apprentices have tended to be considered as a race apart and this has had disastrous results. The only real difference between a contract of apprenticeship and a contract of employment is that under the former the employer undertakes the added duty of teaching his apprentice. It should be recognised that apprentices are also employees; they should be paid a reasonable wage and should not be charged a premium. The inspectorate, recommended to be set up under s. 8 of the Terms and Conditions of Employment Act, should be given power to check contracts of apprenticeship and refer these to the Minister of Labour and the Industrial Court where the terms seem to be unreasonable. This should prevent the exploitation of apprentices as a cheap source of labour. The unsavoury remains of Elizabethan and seventeenth-century legislation found in the Employers and Workmen Act, 1875, under which apprentices who have paid less than a £25 premium may be apprehended and convicted for breach of contract, must go.

### REHABILITATION AND RETRAINING

The National Insurance system is something to be proud of, but it needs improving. It is not enough to give assistance to those out of work; it is better to give them employment. A more effective system of retraining is required—at present it is easier under the National Insurance Act to force someone to move to the same job in a different area than to retrain him for an available job in his own area. The same problem applies to injured persons. What they require most is rehabilitation in a new occupation. To achieve this we need regional hospital and rehabilitation centres for the retraining of injured employees, something along the lines of the rehabilitation centres set up for coal-miners in Belgium. These two types of retraining (the one for the out-of-work, the other for the injured) are vital and we cannot afford to do without them.

# IX

## CRIMINAL LAW

### FELONIES AND MISDEMEANOURS

*The Distinction an Antiquated One*

All crimes in English law are treasons, felonies, misdemeanours or petty offences; but since treasons are often classed as felonies, and petty offences as misdemeanours, the real distinction is between felonies and misdemeanours. There is no clear principle behind this classification, and indeed, one judge has even said that "a misdemeanour . . . means all those crimes and offences for which the law has not provided a particular name".[1] The truth is that the classification is historical, and formerly depended on the degree of gravity of a given offence. All those crimes which were so heinous as to be punished by death and forfeiture became felonies—the rest were misdemeanours.

We can see now why there is today no clear principle behind our classification, and why it is out of date; for as society changes so does its attitude to crime. A specific crime may be regarded as serious in one century, as slight in the next. Thus, when the Church was all-powerful in medieval times, blasphemy was a grave offence; when the landed gentry were the ruling class, poaching was considered one of the most serious crimes; with the growth of capitalism, private property was given more and more protection by the law, while, nowadays, the interests of the community are sometimes thought to be more important than the sanctity of private property.

So, today, because of the changes in the attitude of society, many crimes now accepted as serious are misdemeanours, while the reverse is equally true. For instance, in the eighteenth century, horses were more valuable than today, as the principal means of transport; and they were also easier to steal. Steps were therefore taken to prevent the disposal of stolen horses; and so it became a felony to keep a horse-slaughterer's yard without a licence (this offence ceased to be a felony in 1895, when the Slaughter of Animals Act reduced the punishment to

---

[1] *Pickup* v. *U.K. Dental Board* [1928] 2 K.B. *per* Shearman, J. at p. 462.

three months' imprisonment and a £50 fine.) But perjury, though it may lead to the death of an innocent person, has always been only a misdemeanour.

This anachronism in our law is not, unfortunately, merely academic, for certain important consequences follow from it. A felon, for example, may be arrested without a warrant by anyone; certain legal disqualifications attach to his person—he may lose any office or pension which he holds; and his trial will differ in certain respects that are still of importance. In addition there are many consequences of seemingly minor importance, which are nevertheless legal cobwebs and ought to be swept away.

## Proposals

Clearly, crimes must differ in three main particulars—the courts in which they are tried, the maximum punishments to which offenders are liable, and whether or not the offenders are liable to arrest without a warrant. Our classification, therefore, ought to be along these lines, but it will be seen that each of these distinctions is based on a different principle, the maximum punishment depending on the seriousness with which a crime is regarded by society at any given time, the allocation of jurisdiction both on this and on the difficulty of trying the crime, and the question of arrest without a warrant very largely on convenience. To take an example, a company director who fraudulently converts to his own use £50,000 is liable—and quite rightly so—to a higher maximum punishment than a tramp who steals an apple from a barrow in a crowded market place. Yet there is more need in the latter case for powers to arrest without a warrant, for the thief may be seen actually committing the crime—which is highly unlikely in fraudulent conversion—and if he is not stopped at once may be difficult or, indeed, impossible to trace subsequently, after a warrant has been obtained for his arrest. This is not so in fraudulent conversion, where the offender's identity, and probably his address as well, will be known.

Therefore, if the classification of crimes is to be of any value at all, it must be on the lines of the above distinctions. It is, in fact, impossible to draft a single classification which does not embody the faults of our present one. It is submitted, then, that the need is for three parallel classifications. For each crime the legislature should specify (1) the punishment, (2) whether it must be, can be, or cannot be tried summarily, and (3) whether there can be arrest for it without warrant. The distinction between felonies and misdemeanours should be abolished.

## THE AGE OF CRIMINAL RESPONSIBILITY

In English law, as in most other systems, the lower limit of criminal responsibility is fixed by statute. According to s. 50 of the Children and Young Persons Act, 1933, no child under the age of eight years can be guilty of an offence. In the light of our present knowledge of child psychology, this age limit seems to be too low. The heavy machinery of the criminal law, even if it is administered by juvenile courts with many safeguards designed to protect the juvenile from the full severity of adult criminal law and procedure, still remains psychologically unsuitable for children, involving a stigma which may prejudice the whole life of the young offender. Very few Continental countries have an age limit lower than thirteen years. This does not mean, of course, that nothing is done in the case of offenders who have not yet reached the lower age limit. They are taken in hand and dealt with (on lines similar to those used by English juvenile courts) by administrative agencies, in Scandinavian countries the so-called Child Welfare Councils. In the U.S.A., juvenile courts are competent to deal even with very young children, with the difference, however, that juvenile courts in many of the States are not, as in this country, modified criminal courts but chancery courts.

It is suggested that the age limit of criminal responsibility should be raised to fourteen years and that children below this age should, in case of delinquency, either be treated by the present juvenile courts on the same lines as these courts deal with juveniles in need of care or protection, or better still, that administrative bodies should be established for the purpose, perhaps as sub-committees of the children's committees set up under s. 39 of the Children Act, 1948. This would make it easier to abolish some of the rigid formalities and the stigma connected with the present juvenile court procedure and to gain fuller co-operation of teachers and the public.

## INSANITY AND CRIMINAL RESPONSIBILITY

Responsibility in law for criminal acts is a subject of some difficulty, but there can be little doubt that too many persons who, from a common-sense point of view, are not really responsible for their actions have been hanged or imprisoned.

### The M'Naghten Rules

The medieval view of criminal responsibility was that an act of any kind originated with the individual. In the case of the insane, responsibility for the crime was generally assumed and the offender was treated in the same way as the ordinary individual. At the trial of Arnold in 1724, the accused, who was under the delusion that the then Earl of Onslow was persecuting him by sending invading armies of devils into his bedroom every night, was said to have shot at and wounded the noble earl. Insanity was pleaded in his defence, but was dismissed as irrelevant by the judge, who told the jury that "a prisoner in order to be acquitted on the ground of insanity, must be a man that is totally deprived of his understanding and memory and doth not know what he is doing any more than an infant, than a brute or a wild beast". The same direction was given to the jury by the Lord Chief Justice at the trial of Bellingham in 1812.

In 1843, Daniel M'Naghten, under the insane delusion that he was the subject of persecution by Sir Robert Peel, shot and killed a Mr. Drummond in the belief that he was killing Sir Robert. The jury found him not guilty on the ground of insanity, and the case caused so much controversy that it gave rise to a debate in the House of Lords. Their Lordships put five hypothetical questions to the judges, all of whom, with one exception, agreed upon the answers. The principal answers were:

(1) That notwithstanding that the accused did the act complained of with a view, under the influence of an insane delusion, of redressing or avenging some supposed grievance or injury or of producing some public benefit, he is nevertheless punishable according to the nature of the crime committed if he knew at the time of committing such a crime that he was acting contrary to law.

(2) That the jury ought to be told in all cases that every man is presumed to be sane and to possess a sufficient degree of reason to be responsible for his crimes until the contrary is proved to their satisfaction; and that to establish a defence on the ground of insanity it must be clearly proved that at the time of committing the act the party accused was labouring under such a defect of reason from disease of the mind as not to know

the nature and quality of the act he was doing, or, if he did know it, that he did not know he was doing what was wrong.

(3) That if a person under an insane delusion as to existing facts commits an offence in consequence thereof, if he labours under such partial delusion only and is not in other respects insane, he must be considered in the same situation as to responsibility as if the facts with respect to which the delusion exists were real.

These rules have no legal authority, in so far as judges have no power to make new law by general declarations; but they have in fact been acted on by all the judges for over a hundred years and are still acted on.

## Medical Science

The 1922 Committee on Insanity and Crime recommended that "it should be recognised that a person charged criminally with an offence is not responsible for his act when the act is committed under an impulse which the prisoner was, by mental disease, in substance deprived of any power to resist". No action was taken on the recommendation.

In 1888 the then Lord Chief Justice had said: "The law in the matter of insanity is not incapable of being so interpreted as to do terrible injustice." In 1884 the Medical Officers of Hospitals and Asylums for the Insane resolved: "That so much of the legal test of the mental condition of an alleged criminal lunatic as renders him a responsible agent, because he knows the difference between right and wrong, is inconsistent with the fact, well known to every member of this meeting, that the power of distinguishing between right and wrong exists very frequently among those who are undoubtedly insane, and is often associated with dangerous and uncontrollable delusions." Nothing, however, was done. In giving evidence before the Capital Punishment Commission in 1866 several responsible persons gave evidence that they were satisfied that persons had been found insane who were never anything but sane, and that persons had been hanged who were in fact insane.

Mann's *Forensic Medicine and Toxicology* puts the medical view. "Acquaintance with the various forms of insanity is sufficient to show the inadequacy of the terms laid down to determine irresponsibility. . . . The medical view is that a man who is the victim of mental disease may know that a certain act is wrong and is punishable by law, but that an insane

impulse, whether rising from a delusion or not, may overcome
his self control and he may commit an act, not because he does
not know that he is thereby doing wrong, but because he cannot
prevent himself from doing it. . . . If a man who does murder is
arrested he is taken before the magistrates, and no matter how
insane he is, he is committed for trial to the assizes. This
defective treatment is productive of evil in a variety of ways. The
accused is not examined by an expert until a considerable time
after the commission of the act for which he was arrested; the
law demands proof of insanity at the time the act was committed, therefore, the nearer to it the examination of the state of
the prisoner's mind is made the more likely it is to remove
doubts."

*"Guilty but Insane"*

A further unnecessary complication has arisen. In 1882 a
lunatic fired a pistol at Queen Victoria and was found not
guilty on the ground of insanity. This verdict annoyed the
Queen. She maintained that whether or not the man was guilty
he had certainly fired a pistol at her, and she said that the
verdict in such cases ought to begin, not with the words "Not
Guilty" but with the word "Guilty". Her constitutional
advisers did not agree with her views but could not persuade
her to accept theirs. They therefore explained to the leaders of
the opposition party the position which had arisen, and in
1883, without controversy, the Trial of Lunatics Act was passed
providing that in future the verdict in such cases should be that
of "Guilty but Insane". Such a finding is, of course, quite
illogical, as all lawyers and laymen alike now agree; and it
carries no right of appeal.

*The Modern View*

In 1920, the legal correspondent of *The Times*, referring to the
M'Naghten Rules, expressed the hope that the Court of
Criminal Appeal would give "a legal decision which would
remove a blot from our criminal law and abolish a rule almost
universally condemned by experts. . . . The tests formulated in
M'Naghten's case were . . . really *obiter dicta*, though often
repeated. . . . Those tests, based on knowledge of the moral
character of conduct, are condemned by almost all doctors.
Those best qualified to speak are most decided in their objections to them; and the opposition is strengthened by experience.

. . . The late Dr. Maudsley declared the almost universal opinion of his profession when he described the legal rules on the subject of responsibility as 'unphilosophical in theory and discredited on all hands by practical experience of insanity'." In the same year *The Times* medical correspondent said: "During the past ten years the attitude of medical men to insanity has undergone a fundamental change of which the legal profession is as yet only dimly aware. It is for this reason that arguments take place between doctors and judges which leave both disputants unconvinced and the public mystified. The doctor is really speaking one language, the judge another." Nothing, however, was done. In 1911 a committee of the New York Bar Association, which examined the subject, condemned the English test which it rightly described as "formulated by judges ignorant of psychology." In 1923 a committee of the Medico-Psychological Association on criminal responsibility condemned the M'Naghten Rules.

It was in these circumstances that in 1924 Lord Darling introduced the Criminal Responsibility (Trials) Bill in the House of Lords, which would have added to the M'Naghten Rules a provision that: "If at the time the act was done or omission made which caused the death, the accused was suffering from such a state of mental disease as therefore to be wholly incapable of resisting the impulse to do the act or to make the omission," he should be found insane. The bill, however, was rejected. The Select Committee of 1930 recommended that the M'Naghten Rules should be revised to extend the area of absence of criminal responsibility in the case of the mentally defective and of those who labour under some distinct form of insanity. But it was not until 1957 that this was even attempted by the legislature. The Homicide Act of that year says that where a person kills or is a party to the killing of another, he must not be convicted of murder if he was "suffering from such abnormality of mind (whether arising from a condition of arrested or retarded development of mind or any inherent causes, or induced by disease or injury) as substantially impaired his mental responsibility for his acts and omissions in doing or being a party to the killing". In such a case the conviction must be for manslaughter. There is (so far) no comparable provision of the criminal law regarding any other offence than homicide; but the Mental Health Act, 1959, enables even a magistrate to commit an offender to a mental hospital, and there is, accordingly, less incentive than formerly to plead mental illness (e.g. kleptomania) in minor cases.

## What Ought to be Done

From the evidence available it is clear that the strictly legal view of mental responsibility for a crime has hardly shifted from its medieval conception, that the medical view is that the M'Naghten Rules are hopelessly out of date and responsible for many errors of justice, that there are inadequate arrangements for the relevant facts to be ascertained before trial, that the rule that it is always for the accused to prove insanity is not a good one, that little effort is made by the prison authorities themselves to test the accused's mental state even if, in the present state of the Prison Medical Service, they are competent to do so, and that once an accused is committed to Broadmoor he is rarely released.

The following reforms are therefore suggested:

(1) The illogical verdict of "Guilty but Insane" should be abolished and replaced by a verdict of "Not guilty on the ground of insanity". There should be a right of appeal against this verdict.

(2) The M'Naghten Rules should be revised and extended to include at least the amendments suggested by Lord Darling's Bill of 1924.

(3) The justices at the preliminary hearing should, at the request of either the prosecution or the defence or at their own discretion, have power to refer such cases to a special medical tribunal with power to make full enquiry into the family history and antecedents of the accused person, and the question of the accused's sanity and fitness to plead should be decided before and not at the trial. The result would be an authoritative medical history of and report upon the accused at an early stage of the case. There should be a panel of psychiatrists as permanent officers of the court, from whom one could be chosen to serve on the tribunal for the particular case. Investigation could be ordered by the court even though opposed by the accused. It should also be a rule that the prosecution must place in evidence before the jury the report of the medical tribunal. There is at present a rule of etiquette that it is the duty of prosecuting counsel to place all relevant facts before the jury; but to this rule there is the one odd exception, that he must not place evidence of insanity before the jury. When prosecuting

counsel has a medical report on the accused he passes it straight to counsel for the defence and leaves it to him to make what use of it he pleases. This exceptional rule, which was strikingly illustrated by the case of *R. v. Hanratty*,[1] should be abolished, for it should be regarded as a matter of public policy that when a criminal act has been committed under the influence of insanity the true facts should be reflected in the verdict of the jury.

(4) Enquiry should be made into the facilities for treatment available at institutions where those absolved from punishment on the ground of insanity are detained. If the last foregoing suggestion is adopted it is clear that many persons will be committed to these institutions for criminal acts of less serious character than at present, and consequently there should be a greater readiness to release them if their treatment is completed and it is safe to do so.

## DRUNKENNESS

The present law concerning crimes committed in a state of drunkenness appears to be in need of reform in two directions.

(1) In connection with the suggested revision of the M'Naghten Rules,[2] the legal position of persons who commit an offence in a state of drunkenness should be reconsidered. The present law, as laid down in *Beard's Case*,[3] and in particular the relation between that case and *Rex v. Meade*,[4] are, as the relevant discussion of the subject in the various textbooks shows, by no means clear.

(2) There is at present, and has been since the Inebriates Act, 1898, fell into disuse, no provision for any constructive treatment of the habitual drunkard. Convictions for offences of drunkenness, it is true, have fallen considerably since the turn of the century, and there has been an even more striking decline in prison sentences for this type of offence. Nevertheless, as shown in the annual reports of the Prison Commissioners, the rate of recidivism among this group of prisoners is still very

---

[1] *The Times*, 14 March 1962.
[2] See p. 234 *supra*.
[3] [1920] A.C. 479.
[4] [1909] 1 K.B. 895.

high and for habitual drunkards the present sytem of repeated small fines or short prison sentences is worse than useless.

Two alternatives present themselves. Either provision should be made, on the lines of Article 44 of Stephen's *Digest of Criminal Law*, for long-term detention with curative treatment which, owing to the great advances in the medical treatment of alcoholics made in the past fifty years, should be more effective now than it was under the Act of 1898. Alternatively—or perhaps in addition—magistrates should make far greater use of their powers to discharge offenders conditionally upon their taking treatment, and of the power to commit an offender to a mental hospital.

### HOMICIDE

*The Death Penalty for Murder*

The Labour movement has long stood for the abolition of the death penalty. In 1928, a manifesto in its favour was published, signed by Ernest Bevin, Margaret Bondfield, A. Creech Jones, George Lansbury, Susan Lawrence, Herbert Morrison, Ellen Wilkinson and other members of the Party. In 1934 a unanimous resolution of Conference supported the recommendation of the Select Committee of 1930 that the death penalty be at once abolished for an experimental period of five years. Upon the report stage of the Criminal Justice Bill this proposal, supported by the overwhelming majority of Labour members, was carried—only to be defeated by the subsequent actions of the House of Lords. A similar parliamentary convulsion in 1948 led to the appointment of a Royal Commission, under Sir Ernest Gowers, to recommend ways in which the death penalty could be reduced in scope—not abolished. There is ample evidence, both at home and abroad, to show that abolition of the death penalty does not in fact lead to an increase in murder. In our own country the death penalty has already been abolished for some 200 different offences without any resultant increase in the crimes for which it was abolished. Abroad it has been abolished in practically every civilised country in the world except the British Commonwealth (Queensland and New Zealand have in fact abolished it), Eire, France, Spain and some of the United States. The Gowers

Commission, which examined all the available evidence, reported that its abolition had not led to any increase in murder, and the enquiry also showed that its abolition had not led to an increase in murder by professional criminals or to the carrying of firearms by criminals in any country in the world.

In the past, the House of Lords, adopting the view of the judges that if the death penalty was abolished for this or that offence there would be grave increases in the numbers of those offences committed, has frequently either rejected or opposed abolition when carried by the House of Commons. History has shown that in such cases the view of the judges was invariably wrong, and that the increases in the offences in question, which they had prophesied would follow the abolition of the death penalty for them, did not in fact happen.

It is suggested that the time has come when, whatever the view of the House of Lords, the view so long held by the Labour movement and repeatedly carried on a free vote of the House of Commons should prevail.

## The Definition of Murder

In many parliamentary debates on the abolition of capital punishment, the need for a revision of the present law of murder has become apparent. As it now stands, under the Homicide Act, 1957, the doctrine of "constructive" or "implied" malice (between which there seems little difference) still survives, though the intention of the Act was to abolish it. Moreover, although the Gowers Commission considered such a course impracticable, the kinds of murder to be punished with death have been limited, the intention being mainly to deter the professional criminal from killing in the course of other crimes and to protect the lives of police and prison officers. The result is illogical and arbitrary: poisoners and stabbers and users of skull-crushing weapons are not "capital murderers" unless they happen to steal something at the time of the killing—which must be done in the course or furtherance of the theft and therefore, it is submitted (despite *R.* v. *Jones*[1]), *before* the theft takes place.

The death penalty could safely be abolished: but it should not be done at the cost of leaving the law of murder as it stands. The doctrine of strict liability, of total guilt where there was neither intention to kill nor foresight of consequences, should be expunged from the law.

[1] [1959] 43 Cr. App. R. 94.

*Euthanasia*

In close connection with the foregoing stands the question of euthanasia, i.e. the killing of another person at his request to save him from the agony of a painful and incurable disease. At present, this constitutes murder in strict law, as the consent or even the request of a person to kill him is legally null and void. In actual practice, euthanasia is occasionally carried out by doctors at their own risk for humanitarian reasons. It has been strongly urged in recent years that the medical profession should be relieved of this personal risk by the establishment of an official body of experts who would have to decide, at the request of the patient, whether there were adequate reasons for painlessly ending the life of the sufferer. Euthanasia would be lawful if carried out with permission of this body. If adequate safeguards, such as an appeal to a court of law, can be devised to exclude the danger of abuse by interested outsiders, there is much to recommend a statutory regulation of the problem on such lines. Otherwise, it might at least be provided, in connection with the reform of the law of murder, that homicide committed at the serious request of the victim to relieve him from further suffering must be treated not as murder but as manslaughter.

*Infanticide*

If a mother of a child under twelve months old kills the child, she is not found guilty of murder but may be found guilty of infanticide, provided that it can be shown that the balance of her mind was disturbed by the effects of the birth.

The law thus recognises that killing of the child may arise from the mental state of the mother. Not infrequently it is connected with an attempt at suicide by the mother. But far from making adequate arrangements for the health of the mother, the processes of the law make her state worse. As the law now stands, infanticide or an attempt to kill a child under twelve months cannot be dealt with summarily but only on indictment. Apart from the upheaval caused to the mother's family, this procedure results in serious strain to the mother at the very time when she should be undergoing medical treatment. She may be brought twice before the justices, first for remand and then for the taking of depositions. Finally, she is brought to trial after a period of (it may be) many weeks. During this time she will be confined to a prison hospital unless bail is granted. In hospital she is usually without psychiatric treatment when it is most needed. The trial itself imposes a yet further strain on her mental state, so that her cure is rendered more difficult.

A further objection to the present law is that it is illogical and runs counter to the principles of criminal responsibility. If a woman kills her child because the balance of her mind is disturbed, the verdict ought to be "Not guilty on the ground of insanity". Punishment should be out of the question. Yet under the present law a verdict of infanticide is capable of resulting in imprisonment for life.

The peculiar feature of infanticide from the medical point of view is that it is an act committed under the influence of an aberration of mind which is unlikely to recur, except in the circumstances of another childbirth. If the woman has recovered her mental balance at the time of the trial, there is no point in sending her to Broadmoor, for from the point of view of treatment there is no longer anything to cure, and from the point of view of preventive detention she is no longer dangerous, nor likely to be dangerous except in the circumstances of another childbirth and then only to her new baby. Thus a verdict of "Not guilty on the ground of insanity" should in this instance result in the woman being given freedom immediately she returns to normal. We think that this is the proper course to adopt, and that the Infanticide Act, 1922, as a mode of punishing acts done under the influence of insanity should disappear from the law.

This does not mean that an offence under the name of infanticide may not be permitted to survive. Many may feel that the killing of a baby by its mother, even though not as a result of insanity, should not be treated as a crime so heinous as ordinary murder. On the whole we feel that infanticide (defined without reference to insanity) should be a separate offence punishable less severely than murder, say with a maximum of five years' imprisonment. In effect infanticide would then be a kind of murder in the second degree. It would be a defence to the charge of infanticide to show that the killing was the result of insanity, whether arising from the birth or not. Infanticide as an offence would still be confined to the mother of the victim.

If this new kind of offence were embodied in the law, with a punishment considerably reduced from that of murder, the maximum punishments for abortion and child destruction would have to be reconsidered. It seems that in any event the maximum punishments for these two offences are too severe.

When a woman charged with infanticide is first brought before justices, they should remand her to an observation ward or mental hospital for a medical report and treatment if necessary. Consideration might be given to allowing justices to try infanticide (as newly defined) summarily, where they feel that there are circumstances of mitigation or excuse.

### ABORTION AND HOMOSEXUALITY

*Abortion*

The Report of the Inter-Departmental Committee on Abortion[1] estimated that there were between 110,000 and 150,000 abortions every year in England and Wales, of which 40 per cent, or from 44,000 to 60,000 were criminal. Dr. Glass thought the number of illegal abortions might be as high as 100,000. The contrast with the number of convictions (128 in 1944) is startling.

By s. 58 of the Offences Against the Person Act, 1861, it is an offence punishable with imprisonment for life unlawfully to administer any poison or other noxious thing or unlawfully to use any instrument or other means whatsoever, with intent to procure the miscarriage of any woman, whether she be or be not with child. It is interesting to note that the first statute making abortion an offence was not passed until 1803.

The majority report of the Committee called attention to the need for enforcing the existing law more rigorously and made proposals for strengthening it. It contained little which would solve the problem of criminal abortion and needs no further consideration here. The minority report by Dorothy Thurtle was in a different key. It recognised that factors which drive women to take desperate measures to get rid of an unwanted child cannot be dealt with merely by a policy of suppression and a strengthening of the law. The causes of illegal abortion are manifold and include economic reasons, health reasons and social reasons such as extra-marital pregnancy. The first line of defence is contraception, but this may fail or not be used. Many women then consider that it is for them to judge if the pregnancy should continue, and, if desperate enough, a woman will get an abortion, law or no law. But being illegal, it is,

[1] Published in 1939.

unless the woman is wealthy, liable to take place under the dreadfully insanitary conditions which are well known. Moreover, it may be conducted by means of dangerous instruments, such as knitting needles.

This law, like so many others, is out of harmony with the opinion of a large section of the public in this country. It is suggested, therefore, that some attempt should be made to bring the law more into harmony with public opinion, and attention may be called to the laws of some of the western democracies. For instance in Sweden, under a law of 1946, pregnancy may be terminated under specified conditions by a medical practitioner if, on consideration of the economic circumstances of the woman and the general conditions, it may be assumed that the bearing and rearing of the child would appreciably overtax her bodily and mental powers.

Mrs. Thurtle in her report did not make any radical proposals for reform but suggested, first, that gynaecological clinics should be set up by all local authorities. These clinics should, among other functions, give birth-control instruction to any woman who desires it; and a wider knowledge of contraception would help to bring the abortion rate down. Mrs. Thurtle then expressed her agreement with the view that the law permitting abortion on the ground of likely injury to the woman's health should be clarified and extended. Her other proposals for reducing the abortion rate were: that abortion should be legalised (a) for women who have had four pregnancies, (b) in cases of rape, (c) in cases of unlawful sexual intercourse with girls under 16, (d) in cases of incest, and (e) in the case of persons of defective inheritance who would be likely to pass their defect on to their descendants. The most important of these suggestions is that dealing with women who have had four pregnancies. The maternal mortality and morbidity rates are higher in the case of women who have had a number of previous pregnancies.

These proposed reforms are mild and would not in any way satisfy the radical reformers, but they would contribute to a reduction in the illegal abortion rate and enable the law to be enforced more rigorously. There has hitherto been an almost universal conspiracy of silence about abortion, broken only occasionally by such reports as those of the Inter-Departmental Committee and an earlier B.M.A. Committee; by courageous doctors such as Aleck Bourne, who in 1938 submitted himself

to prosecution (subsequently securing an acquittal) for inducing an abortion on medical grounds for a girl under
16 who had been raped; and by the world-wide public discussion that followed the discovery that the drug thalidomide,
medically prescribed for pregnant women, had in 1961/2
resulted in thousands of monstrous births, for which the
law of abortion was equally responsible. Illegal abortion is, as
we have said, widespread. Its quality varies greatly, from
medical practitioners who charge £100 or more, to women who
do it for a few shillings; and its effect on the woman's health
may be disastrous. Death is not infrequently the result. The
Report indicated that one-sixth of all women who die from
puerperal causes die directly as the result of having aborted
(including those which are spontaneous).

To remedy this state of affairs we suggest that the proposals
in the 1939 Report which we have discussed should be enacted.
The law would still not be nearly as liberal as that of Sweden.
The abortion rate would be reduced, and, concurrently,
sterner measures could with more support from public opinion
be taken against illegal abortion. We should add that legalised
abortion would, of course, take place only if performed by a
properly qualified medical practitioner and under proper
conditions to be laid down.

The minority report called attention to the Report of the
Departmental Committee on Sterilisation.[1] This report investigated the question of reducing inheritable mental defects
and mental disorder by sterilisation. The report concluded:
"Two main considerations impressed themselves on our minds
as our investigation progressed and guided us in framing our
proposals. In the first place we were impressed by the dead
weight of social inefficiency and individual misery which is
entailed by the existence in our midst of over a quarter of a
million mental defectives and of a far larger number of persons
who without being certifiably defective are mentally subnormal.
This mass of defectives and subnormals is being steadily
recruited and is probably growing. Certainly nothing is being
done to diminish it beyond the segregation of a portion of those
more obviously unfitted for community life. In the second place,
we were increasingly impressed by the injustice of refusing to
those who have good grounds for believing they may transmit
mental defect or disorder and who are in every way unfitted for

[1] (1934) Cmnd. 4485.

parenthood the only effective means of escaping from a burden which they have every reason to dread. Contraception is no remedy, since we are dealing with people the majority of whom cannot be expected to exercise the care without which contraceptive measures are bound to fail. Nor is voluntary abstinence any remedy. Facts must be faced. It is idle to expect that the section of the community least capable of self control will succeed in restraining one of the strongest impulses of mankind. The mere suggestion is so fantastic that it carries its own refutation. Without some measure of sterilisation these unhappy people will continue to bring into the world unwanted children, many of whom will be doomed from birth to misery and defect. We can see neither logic nor justice in denying these people what is in effect a therapeutic measure."

It then proposed that voluntary sterilisation should be legalised for mental defectives or persons who have suffered from mental disorder, sufferers from (or persons who are believed to be carriers of) a transmissible and grave physical disability, and persons likely to transmit mental disorder or defect. Stringent safeguards, similar to those prescribed by the Mental Health Act for admission to mental hospitals, were proposed, and additionally the consent of the Minister of Health would have to be obtained. There is said at present to be some uncertainty about the legality of sterilisation operations on ordinary responsible people. Whatever the law may be it is known that such operations are in fact carried out. This uncertainty, however, makes it desirable that the law should be clarified. It may be doubted if there is any case for restricting the sterilisation of normal adults but generally speaking we support the proposals of this Committee. The sterilisation of defectives and other persons not responsible should, of course, be subject to all the stringent safeguards proposed by the Committee, including the consent of the patient, and great care should be taken that in no circumstances is there any element of compulsion.

## Homosexuality

It is curious that lesbianism or homosexuality between women is no offence, while sexual relations between men or between men and animals can be punished with imprisonment for life (maximum sentence). This law appears to be based entirely on prejudice and bigotry, and no estimate is made of any actual injury to the community which may have been caused by the offence. If the crime is analysed it must be seen that, apart from elements of cruelty to children or animals or of nuisance if it is committed in a public place or place of public resort, little or no direct injury to the community is entailed. There may be some loss in the procreation of children but this does not justify treating the act as criminal, and it is submitted that the law should no longer concern itself with this relationship as such.

The reaction of some judges to this crime (there are, today, noteworthy exceptions) illustrates in a most remarkable degree the average lawyer's ignorance of current psychological knowledge. Many lawyers appear almost to take a pride in their ignorance of psychology, and the long and savage prison sentences for this offence, and remarks made by the Bench, often reveal considerable unconscious satisfaction in the punishment inflicted.

The act, as we have said, should not as such be punishable, but so far as it comes under the cognisance of society there should be facilities for the treatment of homosexuals who desire it. We understand, however, that not all homosexuality can be satisfactorily treated. To send someone to prison for the performance of this act is to punish him not for harming the community but for an act which is abnormal and which, in some cases, is probably uncontrollable. The moderate recommendations of the Wolfenden Committee,[1] removing private homosexual acts between adult males from the area of the criminal law (as in the case of females), should be put into effect without further delay. The delay hitherto has been inexplicable.

### CONTEMPT OF COURT

Contempt of court is considered here as criminal contempt, consisting in words or acts obstructing, or tending to obstruct, the administration of justice. The aspect of this part of contempt which needs to be considered is that comprised under the heading "speeches or writings tending to defeat the ends of justice".

The law is very widely defined and it is stated that scandalous attacks on judges are punished. Halsbury's *Laws of England*[2]

---

[1] (1957) Cmnd. 247.
[2] Third Edition, vol. 7, p. 7.

suggests that when a trial has taken place it is still doubtful if the judge may be given over to criticism, and that it is going too far to say that committals for contempt by scandalising the court itself are obsolete. It is of vital importance that sober and honest criticism of a court and a court's decision should be permitted, but in fact newspapers are afraid to criticise judges. Any words which might cast doubt on a judge's impartiality or his competence may be a contempt of court, as was seen in 1928, when Mr. Clifford Sharp, then editor of the *New Statesman*, was fined for saying that certain types of litigant could scarcely hope for justice in Mr. Justice Avory's court. It should therefore be laid down that criticism of this nature should not be contempt of court, and the offence of contempt of court should be more strictly defined.

In our opinion, contempt of court in the form of criticism of the judge should be a substantive offence, triable in the ordinary way, and not summarily punishable by the judge attacked. Similar defences should be allowed to those permitted in libel, which in essence it is. Thus the defendant should be permitted to prove the truth of his words, fair comment upon a matter of public interest, or qualified privilege. These defences would not apply to contempts consisting in the publication of comments upon a pending case before trial in such a way as to interfere with the administration of justice.

### PARTICULAR OFFENCES

*Public Mischief*

Any person who conspires with one or more others to commit an act tending to effect a public mischief is at common law guilty of a misdemeanour. Such act may be any act tending to the prejudice of the community. The court alone decides whether any particular act may tend to be a public mischief. Up to now this power has seldom been exercised so as to interfere with civil liberty, the most recent case being that of *Shaw* v. *D.P.P.*[1] in which the House of Lords held that the publication of a list of prostitutes' addresses (the "Ladies Directory") was a conspiracy to corrupt public morals and an act tending to the public mischief. It is, however, undesirable that the power to create new crimes should be vested in the courts of law, and their power to declare that particular acts

[1] [1961] All E.R. 330.

may tend to public mischief, and are therefore crimes, should be abolished. It should be left to Parliament to declare new crimes. Acts which have already been declared to be a public mischief should remain criminal. Closer definition should also be introduced into the law of conspiracy.

## Blasphemy

Offences such as blasphemy and blasphemous libel still disfigure the criminal law of this country. Blasphemy is a misdemeanour at common law, punishable by fine and imprisonment. The offence consists of scoffingly or irreverently ridiculing or impugning the doctrines of the Christian faith, the Holy Scriptures or Jesus Christ. If the blasphemous words are written, they constitute a blasphemous libel. There are also the statutory offences created by the Blasphemy Act, 1698. This Act provides that if any person who has been educated in or at any time made profession of the Christian religion asserts or maintains that there are more gods than one or denies the Christian religion to be true or the Bible to be of divine authority, he shall for a first offence be judged incapable of holding any office and on a second conviction be liable to three years' imprisonment. It is believed that, so drastic is this statute, there has never been a prosecution under it. There are also certain statutes of Edward VI's and Elizabeth's reigns which make it a criminal offence to utter any words or writing in derogation of the Book of Common Prayer or anything therein contained or of the sacraments. It is also a common law offence to utter or publish seditious words in derogation of the established religion.

It is noticeable that these offences only apply to Christianity, and it is not blasphemous to say anything, however offensive, of, for example, the Jewish or Mohammedan religions. In recent years there have not been many prosecutions for blasphemy and when they occur they are generally directed against uneducated persons who have attacked Christianity in a rather crude manner. It is to be remembered, however, that under these laws there were at one time many prosecutions of booksellers for selling the works of Thomas Paine and others, and there is no doubt that if the law relating to blasphemy were enforced in its full rigour a stop could be put to much criticism and free thought. Defenders of the law assert that it is only used when attacks against the Church are couched in such language that they might lead to a breach of the peace. If this is so the special laws are unnecessary and the ordinary law dealing with conduct likely to lead to a breach of the peace can be used to deal with scurrilous language used about Christianity.

### "*Obscene*" *Literature*

There is no censorship of books before publication in this country. But "obscene" books can be destroyed by court order, and those responsible for them punished. The present legal concept of "obscenity" is based on an *obiter dictum* by Lord Chief Justice Cockburn in 1868:

> "The test of obscenity is this, whether the tendency of the matter charged as obscenity is to deprave and corrupt those whose minds are open to such immoral influences and into whose hands a publication of this sort may fall."

Cockburn was trying an appeal under the Obscene Publications Act which had been enacted nine years earlier to strengthen the common law. It had only been passed on the assurance of his predecessor in office, Lord Chief Justice Campbell, that it was intended to apply exclusively to what was indictable under the law as it then was, namely, "works written for the single purpose of corrupting the morals of youth and of a nature calculated to shock the common feelings of decency in any well-regulated mind". If the law reverted to Lord Campbell's definition of "obscenity", omitting the word "single" (which restricts it unduly), serious writers and readers would have little to complain of.

The law at present is contained in the Obscene Publications Act, 1959, which was an attempt by Parliament to curb the censorious enthusiasm of the courts after a series of notorious prosecutions, involving world-famous and respectable British publishers, in 1954. This Act adopts Cockburn's definition, with modifications, but allows the defence to call evidence to show that the publication of the so-called obscenity was "for the public good" on the ground that it was in the interests of art, literature, science, or other object of general concern. In the case of *Shaw* v. *D.P.P.*[1] the House of Lords decided that an obscene publication can be prosecuted as a common law "conspiracy to corrupt public morals"; in which event the

[1] See p. 245, *supra*.

above-mentioned evidence as to literary or other merit becomes
once again inadmissible. The 1959 Act had been drafted with
the object of abolishing common law prosecutions for obscenity,
but it is apparent that it did not succeed. An amending
statute is necessary.

### *Vagrancy*

It would take too long to set out the anomalies of the various
Vagrancy Acts, from the middle of the fourteenth century to the
present day, that are still in force. Suffice it to quote a single
judicial remark about these Acts. "Is it not time," asked Lord
Justice Scott, "that our relevant statutes should be revised and
that punishment and arrest should no longer depend on words
which today have an uncertain sense and which nobody can
truly apply to modern conditions? To retain such laws seems
to me inconsistent with our national sense of personal liberty or
our respect for the rule of law. Clear and definite language is
essential in penal laws."[1]

Lord Justice Scott was referring in that case to the offence of
"being a suspected person frequenting or loitering in a street
or public place with intent to commit a felony", under s. 4 of
the Vagrancy Act, 1824. This is a much abused provision, and
one of tyrannical scope, which gives the lie to the British boast
that the citizen "cannot be held in custody on mere suspicion"
—he can be imprisoned for three months on the mere suspicion that he was in the street to steal. It has given rise to
many decisions on appeal, some of which are in obvious conflict
despite the sophistry with which textbook commentators force
them into reconciliation. It has also given rise to many injustices, and many convictions on evidence falling far short of
the standards required in other criminal cases. It is the provision
in this Act of 1824 which should be the first to be repealed in
any adequate revision of the criminal law.

### *Prostitution*

The problem of discouraging prostitution is not so much a
lawyer's problem as a social problem. The system in operation
until 1959 simply did not work; the same people passed through
Bow Street day after day, and the criminal law operated merely
as a system of taxation and an inducement to bribery. Much

---

[1] *Ledwith* v. *Roberts* [1937] 1 K.B. 232.

more effective action was needed against brothel-keepers and others who profit from exploitation of this sort.

In 1959 the law was so amended by the Street Offences Act as to make any woman a "common prostitute" who loiters in a street after a previous warning by a policeman, and then to subject her to penalties up to £10 on a first conviction, £25 on a second, and £25 *plus* 3 months' imprisonment for each subsequent one. All previous statutes, both general and local, dealing with the same subject were repealed; and as they nearly all provided for a forty shilling fine and no sentence of imprisonment, the change was so drastic and the consequences of conviction so far-reaching that most of the prostitutes disappeared from the streets. There is much uneasiness about the probability that the problem has been merely "swept under the carpet", and that the exploitation of prostitutes by ponces is more organized, more lucrative, and more difficult to detect. The few recent prosecutions for it, involving well-to-do "City" men very different from the traditional type of ponce, tend to confirm this fear: and it is also more difficult than before 1959 to find and rescue young girls entering upon a life of prostitution. These considerations show that the problem should be kept under constant review by Parliament: the gravamen of the offence has now passed to the "organisation men" without whom the trade could not survive as a paid profession.

## CRIMINAL PROCEDURE

### Police Procedure

The regular police forces in this country were established from 1829 to 1839. Anxiety was expressed in Parliament at the time as to the possibility that the establishment of such a force might put a weapon in the hands of the Executive equivalent to the "standing army" feared since Stuart times. We have heard talk of a Gestapo more recently.

The defects in our police system arise mainly from the fact that our police are under-paid, under-staffed and ineptly criticised. A policeman's pay is only about the average wage of labour, skilled and unskilled, in this country, and it is still rather below the earnings of what may be called his equivalent class. Even the old-fashioned professional criminal is now far better off than his predecessor of a generation ago. Formerly the receiver struck a hard bargain and the thief was lucky if he got 25 per cent of the value of what he offered. Now the number of receivers is legion, and better value is obtained. It is astonishing, considering the temptations to which they are exposed, that our police are, on the whole, honest and incorruptible. But there are exceptions, and unless changes are made these are likely to increase in number. When a man or woman receiving inadequate wages and dealing with considerable sums of money is brought before the court charged with an offence involving dishonesty we often hear the comment: "Well, what can you expect?"

It is generally admitted that the police forces are under-staffed even by pre-war standards. Considering the great increase in the duties that the police are expected to perform, their numbers are shockingly inadequate. They have to get results somehow and naturally enough they tend to become less scrupulous as to how they get them, and, as we have seen, the salary is not sufficient to attract many men of high intelligence. The deplorable result is that improper and illegal methods, condemned by a Royal Commission more than thirty years ago[1] are openly tolerated. One of these methods is what is called "detained for questioning".

"Detention for questioning" is imprisonment at the will of the police without definite limit. That it constitutes imprisonment is unquestionable. A Home Office Memorandum quoted in the 1929 Royal Commission's Report is as follows:

> "The word 'detention' is not a term of art, though it is used by some police forces with a special restricted significance not recognised by other forces. The technical term is imprisonment. Any form of restraint by a police officer—or indeed by anyone—is in law an imprisonment, and if the police officer has acted wrongfully an action for false imprisonment will lie. Whether the imprisonment or 'detention' is initiated by words or action constituting technically an arrest is for this purpose immaterial, nor is it material for the purpose of Rule (3) of the Judges' Rules. Any person who, in fact, is under restraint should be treated as in custody within the meaning of that rule."

The recommendations of the Royal Commission were unanimous. The following are quotations from them.

[1] See Report of the Royal Commission on Police Powers and Procedure (1929) Cmd. 3297.

"Any person who is in fact under restraint, and knows that he is under restraint, should be treated as being in custody for all purposes."

"Detention as a separate procedure is unnecessary and open to abuse, in that no definite limit is placed to the period during which persons may be 'detained'."

"A rigid instruction should be issued to the police that no questioning of a prisoner, or a 'person in custody', about any crime or offence with which he is, or may be, charged, should be permitted. This does not exclude questions to remove elementary and obvious ambiguities in voluntary statements, under No. (7) of the Judges' Rules, but the prohibition should cover all persons who, although not in custody, have been charged, and are out on bail while awaiting trial."[1] Beyond doubt it should also include defendants who are being prosecuted by summons, a point on which the police have always been left in doubt by the exclusive use, in the Judges' Rules, of the phrase "persons in custody".

Detention for questioning is becoming a general practice. Solicitors who practise in criminal matters are familiar with numerous instances in their own experience. Detention for questioning is almost certainly illegal and quite certainly objectionable.

On the other hand, the police should be given further powers for obtaining information. One way would be to enable a constable by summary process to bring before a magistrate any person whom he suspects of being able to give information. This person might then be questioned after being told that he need not answer any question which might incriminate him. No answers to questions at such examinations should be admissible in evidence in any proceedings against the person so examined.

It is sometimes found that the police have virtually ordered a witness to attend at a police station to make a statement. Practically every motorist is asked for a statement, and many are bluffed into thinking they are compelled to make one. It is sometimes difficult to persuade a man that he is not obliged to make a statement and we have evidence of complaints from men who had been repeatedly ordered to make statements and

[1] See Report, p. 118.

told to take no notice of what their solicitor had told them. The Report of the Royal Commission said:

> "We have received a volume of responsible evidence which it is impossible to ignore suggesting that a number of the voluntary statements now tendered in court are not 'voluntary' in the strict sense of the word."

As Mr. Justice Byrne once said:

> "The atmosphere of a police station seems to be singularly conducive to confession."

Would it be disrespectful to suggest that a memorandum should be issued by the judges explaining and re-emphasising the well-known "Judges' Rules"? If any of these rules are thought to be an unreasonable restriction upon the powers of the police to perform their functions an amendment should be made, and after that the rules should be enforced strictly.

The police are, on the whole, an excellent body of men. But the class of recruit they are getting is deteriorating, and will continue to do so until pay and conditions of service improve to an extent which, it is now clear, must be spectacular. The pay increases awarded by the Royal Commission of 1962—the Willink Commission—have made no impression on the problem. Watch Committees should be strengthened by the addition of men who know something about the job, and should cease to be the superannuation committees they often are. And magistrates should remember that there is no surer way to ruin the police than by supporting them against the weight of the evidence.

## Bail

Comparatively few people are familiar with the exact rights of the citizen in connection with bail or at what stages in criminal proceedings this question arises.

Over 98 per cent of criminal cases tried and disposed of in this country are dealt with before magistrates. We are here mainly concerned with the residuary cases which involve more serious offences, where the accused generally is arrested upon a warrant and, unless bail is granted, may remain in gaol for an undetermined length of time pending his eventual trial. It has to be remembered that, as a prisoner on remand, the accused person has to endure the most irksome restraints which our prison system makes possible. The Prison Commissers told the Streatfeild Committee (1958) that it is "a régime of depressing monotony". The question of bail first arises (in the case of a person arrested without a magistrate's warrant) while the accused is still at the police station. The police "must" grant bail if the case cannot be brought before a magistrate within 24 hours—unless the charge is "a serious one", a phrase which is undefined and which therefore leaves the police with a complete discretion whether to grant bail or not. Usually they grant it in every possible case, if for no better reason than that they have no accommodation for the prisoners they would otherwise acquire. They sometimes grant it *before* deciding whether to accept a charge, in order that further enquiries may be made (until this was made possible by the Criminal Justice Act of 1925, too many people were being detained in cells, uncharged, while the police enquiries went on, sometimes for days).

When the case comes before a magistrate, it may be that the prosecution need more time to prepare their case and a remand is granted, and it is within the magistrate's discretion whether the remand shall be one where the accused is allowed to be free on bail, or whether he shall remain in custody until the next hearing. A remand in custody cannot be for more than eight clear days; but this limit can easily be overcome by bringing the accused before the court every seven days, when a further remand can be granted, and so *ad infinitum*. The next stage at which the question of bail arises is when the prosecution has finally prepared its case and the magistrate has decided that there is a case to answer and that the prisoner must be sent to one of the higher criminal courts for trial. The accused may once again at this stage apply for bail pending the trial of the case, which may be quite soon, or not for several weeks or even months. In cases of treason the magistrate cannot grant bail, but the Secretary of State or a Divisional Court (a single High Court judge in vacation) can. In all other felonies and misdemeanours the magistrate has a judicial discretion to grant bail, but he does not generally do so in cases of murder or crimes of a very serious nature.

If the magistrate refuses bail at either of the two stages above referred to, there is a right of appeal to a High Court judge, which involves the service of a summons upon the prosecution and the magistrate, so that all parties are notified of the appeal.

This application for bail may be made at any time after the accused has been committed for trial, and before the actual trial. It is usually made to a judge in chambers, whether or not the courts are sitting.

On the face of it, bail is governed by well-settled and defined principles. It was laid down in an old case that the guiding question should be whether the accused will appear at his trial and not abscond. The granting of the bail, however, is in the discretion of police, judge, or magistrate; and they should consider the nature of the accusation, the nature of the evidence in support of it, the severity of the punishment which conviction would entail, and whether the sureties who are guaranteeing that the accused will appear at his trial are independent or whether they may be mere nominees of the accused. Most important of all is the rule that the character of the accused person as such is irrelevant and should not affect any question of bail. Character is relevant only indirectly, on the question whether the accused is likely to abscond or repeat the offence during the period of bail.

It will be seen that the law on the subject, if properly adhered to, is quite fair to the accused. There are two main reasons why he may justifiably desire bail rather than be remanded in custody. First, if he is innocent, it is an undeserved hardship for him to be sent to prison to await trial. The second point is, perhaps, more important. The effect of refusing bail is to make the preparation of the defence much more difficult. In a great number of cases it can be the turning point between success and failure. For example, defendants have the greatest difficulty in securing ordinary witnesses to attend the preliminary hearing or trial to give evidence. Although they are merely called to state the truth, they are reluctant to attend because they do not like becoming involved in any form of criminal proceedings. Experience has shown that innocent defendants have to travel considerable distances to persuade witnesses to attend their trial, with a view to giving evidence upon which their acquittal may depend.

The disadvantages of the present system governing bail have to be considered. Many defendants are not, in the initial stages of a prosecution, represented by solicitor or counsel. When the police raise any objections to bail, or the presiding magistrate comes to the conclusion that bail should not be granted, the defendant is not able to deal with the legal aspect of bail nor is he able to do justice to his case for bail. Magistrates are too ready to refuse bail when the police oppose it without assigning a reason; indeed, the police are sometimes indignant when asked to give a reason. The powers possessed by the police are so great that they are able to use the threat of opposing bail as a weapon for procuring information from a prisoner. Some police officers can be vindictive if defendants refuse to co-operate with them. Although the police do not as a body abuse their powers, there are too many individual instances of abuse.

To sum up, it would seem that seven immediate steps should be taken for the amendment of the law.

(1) There should be a speedier method of getting bail. It should be enough for the accused to make a simple application to the court, and the obligation should be on the court to obtain copies of the depositions necessary for deciding the matter.

(2) All undefended persons should have the benefit of legal assistance on the question of bail. The moment bail is refused, the presiding magistrate should ensure that there is a lawyer to represent the interests of the defendant and use his best efforts to secure bail for him.

(3) If the police intend to oppose bail in any proceedings, whether in the preliminary stages or otherwise, they should have ready an affidavit sworn by the officer in charge of the case, giving full reasons for refusal of bail and full particulars of the source of the information upon which he will seek to rely. It should not be a sufficient ground for opposing bail that the police have "not yet completed their enquiries" or that "the stolen property has not yet been traced". A copy of the affidavit should be given to the defendant or his counsel and the whole issue fought on its merits before the presiding magistrates. At the moment the police do not put their objections in writing but merely give the magistrates information from the witness box.

(4) The court, if it refuses bail, should always give its reasons for doing so and the evidence on which it has come to its conclusion. (It is assumed in this and other recommendations that the restrictions upon Press publicity suggested later are in operation.)

(5) As there will already be written evidence on the question of bail, there would seem to be no reason why the prosecution should be served with a summons before a defendant goes to the judge in chambers and applies for a grant of bail, having first

been refused by the magistrate. As the written evidence is already in existence, immediately the magistrate has made a decision refusing bail defending counsel or solicitor should be in a position to say that there will be an application to a High Court judge in chambers; and there is no reason why this application should not be made within a few hours. A delay of even twenty-four or forty-eight hours can be quite serious when the actual trial will follow during the course of the next few days. This quite often happens, and it is vitally important that a defendant who is dependent upon evidence to be supplied by independent witnesses scattered all over the country should be in a position to contact them.

(6) More judges should be available for the grant of bail. Instances have occurred where the vacation judge has not been available in London over Christmas, and in any case it may cause undue delay to take an appeal to London. Our proposal for regional criminal courts would help to solve this difficulty, and as an immediate solution, jurisdiction should be given to recorders and deputy recorders.

(7) If bail is refused sentence should automatically date from the day when the accused was first received into prison. At present this earlier period of detention is not always taken into account when the time is not long.

*Depositions*

The practice of giving orally the whole of the evidence on which the prosecution relies in courts of summary jurisdiction often entails waste of time and money. Without prejudicing defendants, much of this waste could be avoided.

It is suggested that the prosecution should be entitled to submit to the defendant and to the court, before the hearing, statements of any witnesses the prosecution proposes to call at the trial, which they regard as matters not likely to be disputed. The defendant should be informed by the court or by the prosecution in writing that he has a right to have any or all of the witnesses in question called at that court. If he does not exercise this right, the witnesses will be called at the trial only. The court should have the right to require the prosecution to call before it any witnesses on whose statements the prosecution relies in asking for a committal, even though the defendant has not asked for them to be called.

This proposal would be of particular value in such cases as

receiving stolen property, where the issue is guilty knowledge. At present, many hours may be occupied by witnesses, brought perhaps from distant parts of the country, to depose to matters not in dispute. In our opinion, what is required at the hearing before the magistrates is:

(1) that facts should be adduced which put them in a position to decide if there is a *prima facie* case;
(2) that the defendant should be in a position to submit that there is not a *prima facie* case against him;
(3) that the defendant should be fully informed of the case he will have to meet on his trial.

The adoption of some such reformed procedure as we have indicated would secure all these essentials and would assist the court, the witnesses and the parties engaged.

Much time is wasted in the taking of depositions. The magistrates' clerk may not be a good scribe; he is often an elderly person who cannot be expected to write quickly. The proposal made above for the use of written statements should be of some assistance, and wherever possible use should be made of silent typewriters operated by skilled persons.[1]

## Publicity Before Trial

The appearance of a Press report of the hearing before magistrates is apt to prejudice the subsequent trial before judge and jury. The case is in effect tried out in the Press, national and local, from the depositions, many of which are later held inadmissible. There is also, in many cases, a long accusatory speech for the prosecution, with no answering speech for the defence; and adverse remarks made by the police when opposing bail are reported, and may have a particularly damaging effect. The case is all the worse in that the evidence for the prosecution is commonly gone into at some length, while the defence is frequently reserved or not gone into. It is inevitable in these circumstances that reports of the preliminary proceedings should sometimes prejudice the jury. Counsel or judge may tell the jury to forget what they have read, but they cannot and they will not do so. Their minds have been affected

[1] For other proposals see the Report of the Byrne Committee on Depositions, (1949) Cmd. 7639.

and nothing can undo that fact. It is most important that this undesirable Press publicity should be restricted, and the unanimous recommendation of the Committee on Proceedings before Examining Justices,[1] that unless the accused has been discharged or until the trial has ended, any report of committal proceedings should be restricted to particulars of the name of the accused, the charge and the decision of the court, should be carried out.

### Giving Notice of the Charge

The practice of late indictment does great injustice to accused persons, which could be avoided if they were given reasonable notice beforehand of the contents of the proposed indictment. The accused should have a copy of the indictment or a proposed indictment at least seven days before the hearing. In some cases, insistence upon this rule may cause the hearing of the case to be delayed; consequently the accused should be entitled to waive his right to notice of the indictment, where he wishes to be tried at the earliest possible moment. Provision should be made to ensure that the accused has notice both of his right to a copy of the indictment and of his right to dispense with the suggested period of seven days' notice.

### Powers of the Appellate Courts

Criminal appeals lie either to the Court of Criminal Appeal (where the trial was on indictment) or to Quarter Sessions or the Divisional Court (where there was summary trial). The powers of these appellate courts should be reconsidered. For instance, the Court of Criminal Appeal has power to amend a conviction, as by substituting one conviction for another; but the Divisional Court does not possess this power. It is obviously desirable that where a person has been convicted on the wrong count in the charge, the appeal court should have power to put the matter technically right by substituting the right conviction rather than acquit the defendant altogether. This has often been pointed out by the Divisional Court itself. According to the learned editor of the Law Quarterly Review: "There have been a considerable number of cases in recent years in which the judges have called attention to desirable changes in the law, but as things are at present there can be little hope that their

---

[1] (1958) Cmnd. 479.

authoritative recommendations can be put into effect."[1] Under our proposals in Chapter I such recommendations would receive due consideration.

The Court of Criminal Appeal has pointed out time and again that it lacks the power to order a new trial, with the consequence that when a criminal has been acquitted on a technicality there is no power to try him again. It is carrying the "sporting theory of justice" too far to turn many serious offenders loose on the community merely because of a flaw in the proceedings taken against them. The power to order a new trial was proposed to be given by a Lords' amendment to the Criminal Justice Bill of 1947, and supported by the Lord Chancellor and the Lord Chief Justice, but was rejected in the House of Commons for (it is submitted) inadequate reasons.[2]

## PUNISHMENT

The thoughtful, law-abiding citizen who, whether as a juror, witness or relation or friend of an offender, comes into personal contact with our system of punishment for crime, seems to feel that there is something wrong with it. Punishments are still severe but crime does not seem to decrease. He wonders whether the judge, recorder or magistrate really knows enough about the individual he is sentencing, and whether his knowledge of penology (though he does not call it that) is as great as his knowledge of the law and of legal procedure. He tends to feel that we continue to administer a system of punishment hallowed by time, but probably not as effective as it could be in the light of increasing modern knowledge of the causes of crime and its prevention.

The passage of the Criminal Justice Act, 1948, marked a milestone in the road of penal reform, but much has necessarily depended upon the way in which the Act was worked. Since the Act, most of our problems are shifted from the sphere of law to the sphere of administration. In this section is it proposed to state the principles upon which we should proceed and to

---

[1] (1948) 64 Law Quarterly Review 171.

[2] See Prof. Goodhart's letter in *The Times*, 22 December, 1947, which, it is submitted, was not convincingly answered by Mr. Gerald Thesiger's reply on 24 December, 1947; see also Prof. Goodhart's further letter in *The Times*, 3 August, 1948; (1947) 111 Justice of the Peace Journal 621; (1948) 112 *ibid.* 322, 517, 518; (1948) 64 Law Quarterly Review 11; *R.* v. *Kingston* [1948], 32 C.A.R. 183; cp. *R.* v. *Neal* [1949] 2 K.B. 590.

indicate the next steps that in the view of competent authorities ought to be taken.

## The Objects of Punishment

It is necessary first to consider the objects of punishment.

Society has a self-evident right to protect itself against crime, both by taking steps to deter those who might be tempted to commit crime and by taking such steps as may be effective to reform the offender when he has committed it. Deterrence and reformation are therefore proper objects of punishment.

But it has been said that punishment should also be retributive—that is to say, it should express society's abhorrence at the offender's action and act as a public substitute for that private vengeance which society forbids to the victim and his friends. "An eye for an eye," it is said, is a sound principle. Now, retribution, whether the word describes vengeance or is a softer word meaning, as some modern theologians will say, a "re-tribute" or repayment by the offender of his debt to society, is in the first place strictly unnecessary. We are a law-abiding country as a whole, and there is no reason to think that a degree of punishment which is not necessary either for deterrent or for reformative purposes is necessary in order to prevent the victim and his friends from taking the law into their own hands, i.e. exacting their *own* tribute. Lynch law is not likely in England.

Moreover, retribution as an object of punishment in itself is increasingly regarded as both unnecessary and unjustifiable. The concept of retribution as an object of punishment implies a relationship between the severity of the punishment and the degree of guilt. But guilt attaches to the offender—not to the offence. Modern psychological knowledge of unconscious motivation shows that it is in reality quite impossible for any lawyer, and probably for anyone, to make an assessment of the quantity of guilt present in any individual case. Yet without a quantitative assessment of guilt there is nothing with which to equate the severity of punishment. Thus retributive punishment becomes little more than a measure of the revulsion felt for the offender or for the offence as expressed by the action of the State.

Moreover, if the proper objects of punishment, deterrence and reformation, must be made subject to, or qualified by, a third element, retribution, the latter will interfere with the real object of punishment, the protection of society, and such interference would seem a high price to pay for the emotional satisfaction of inflicting public vengeance.

It would therefore seem that the view, increasingly held for many years, that retribution as such should have no place in a national penal code, is right, and should be publicly recognised in any consideration of this subject.

The two legitimate objects of punishment would thus be deterrence and reformation.

*Past Attempts to Achieve these Objects*

It used to be generally thought that deterrence should be the principal object. It was thought, too, that what was primarily required was severity of punishment. If only punishment were sufficiently severe it would not only deter the offender (even if his suffering did not reform his character) but also sufficiently deter others who saw what had happened to him and would happen to them if they did not overcome any temptation to crime. A good sentence of the "cat" would not only ensure that the offender did not commit that crime again but also be an awful warning to others.

The nineteenth century had a simple explanation of human behaviour. Men had before them the choice of good and evil, and they made their choice freely, becoming good or bad in varying degrees. It was generally believed that fear of punishment would affect the choice of action. So the penal system was made harsh and severe with the primary purpose of terrorising the bad into controlling their wickedness. And the object of reformation was not wholly forgotten, for, entangled with the concept of deterrent punishment, was the belief in reformation through repentance wrought by suffering. The two birds would be killed with one stone.

So came the solitary, silent and inhuman prisons of the nineteenth century, devised with the best intentions and believed to be admirably suited to achieving the objects of punishment.

We are concerned not with any underlying doctrinal conflict but with the actual result in terms of human life and the freedom of the community from crime. So judged, the result was disastrous. As the Gladstone Committee reported in 1895, the effect was to turn the casual offender into the habitual criminal and to make recidivism—the growth of the habitual criminal—almost inevitable.

*The Causes of Our Previous Failures to Reduce Crime*

There are still people, including some judges, who, in spite of the findings of the Gladstone Committee, the Departmental Committee on Corporal Punishment (1938), and all the other available evidence on this subject, still retain an almost child-like belief that all that is necessary to reduce crime is to make punishments bigger, worse and longer. It may therefore be worth while considering at this point why this view did not achieve in practice what its advocates believed it would achieve, either in terms of deterrence or of reformation.

In the first place, it is of course impossible to measure the effectiveness of punishment in procuring general or individual obedience to the law. It seems, however, to be reasonably certain that, as regards the great majority of persons, punishment plays only a very minor part among the many and complex forces which prevent grave breaches of the accepted moral and social code. But it is probable that it is a determining factor in the prevention of trivial offences which incur little moral reprobation. If, for example, every form of punishment was abolished for murder, rape and arson, only a very small number of persons would thereby become more disposed to commit these crimes. It is, for instance, doubtful if incest was more frequent before it was made a crime in 1908. On the other hand, if motoring offences could be committed with impunity, the relevant laws and bye-laws would probably soon become a dead letter. *It would therefore seem (and this is the point) that the deterrent influence of punishment is in inverse ratio to the gravity of the offence.*

Moreover, in an ordered community obedience to authority has, by tradition, become so deep-seated as to appear almost instinctive, and in so far as this kind of obedience requires the buttress of sanctions, the disgrace, or even the mere inconvenience, of appearing in court seems for most people to suffice. Nor would the actual conditions of prison life appear to play any substantial part in the calculations of most first offenders.

The fact is that experience has shown that the supposed effectiveness of severe punishment as a deterrent has not been borne out in practice. All those who have made a study of this subject are now agreed that the incidence of crime in any given place at any given time depends partly upon the social and economic circumstances, partly upon the conviction rate, and partly upon the steps taken to deal with recidivism—to prevent the first offender from becoming the habitual criminal.

Social and economic circumstances cannot be altered by our penal laws. If it be true, as we believe it is, that certainty of conviction rather than barbarity of punishment is the best deterrent, it remains to consider how far severity of punishment is effective to prevent recidivism.

### The Conflict Between Deterrence and Reformation

The recommendation of the Gladstone Committee, recognising the failure of severity of punishment with its accent on deterrence rather than reformation, was that deterrence and reformation should be the primary and concurrent aims of the penal system. Unhappily the two have since been shown to be largely incompatible.

The experience of the nineteenth century made it clear that severity of punishment not only has a strictly limited effect as a deterrent, but also tends to defeat itself as an agent of reformation. The view generally accepted by psychiatrists, that a common predisposing factor in crime is a deep-seated and often unconscious grudge or resentment against society, is of great interest in explaining the failure of a penal system of negative repression—the deterrent effect of severity being outweighed by its fortification of this resentment.

This incompatibility between penal treatment as a deterrent to the offender and penal treatment as a reforming influence had been foreseen even by some of the witnesses before the Gladstone Committee. Thus Sir Godfrey Lushington (a Home Office administrator) said:

"I regard as unfavourable to reformation the status of a prisoner throughout his whole career: the crushing of self-respect, the starving of all moral instinct he may possess, the absence of all opportunity to do and receive a kindness, the continual association with none but criminals, and that only as a separate item among other items also separate; the forced labour and the denial of liberty. I believe the true mode of reforming a man or restoring him to society is exactly in the opposite direction of all these. But of course this is a mere idea; it is quite impracticable in a prison. In fact the unfavourable features I have mentioned are inseparable from prison life."

This inherent incompatibility between deterrence and

reformation lies at the root of all modern penal problems. It has become more and more apparent that our efforts to make punishment both deterrent and reformative cannot succeed. Those forms of punishment which, if any, are likely to be deterrent are more likely to exacerbate than to reform the offender. We do not seem able to make up our minds which of these two should be the primary object of punishment. The interests of society primarily require the reduction of recidivism to the minimum possible, and for that purpose, while deterrence is of little use, the really determining factor is the degree to which our penal system promotes, or at least does not lessen, the prospects of the offender's reform.

## Reformation

While, as has been pointed out above, prison conditions play little part as an actual deterrent, they have effects of great importance in deciding the future attitude and actions of the man or woman who actually experiences imprisonment, and therefore in determining the character and extent of recidivism.

The clear implication is that the prison system should be designed primarily to reduce recidivism. It is therefore necessary to consider first who those persons are who are in danger of becoming recidivists, and secondly the broad principles likely to govern a successful handling of this raw material.

The age group showing the highest number of offences per 100,000 of the population centres round puberty, roughly thirteen to sixteen, and thereafter there is a steady and progressive decline as the age group increases. The probability of recidivism, on the other hand, is greatest in adolescence, roughly sixteen to twenty-one, and thereafter decreases.

Juvenile delinquency may be regarded in the main as a nuisance rather than as a danger. Its real importance is limited to that very small proportion of the juvenile delinquents who are likely to become the habitual criminals of the future. Sixteen to twenty-one is the critical age. For here the element of mischief which plays so large a part in juvenile delinquency recedes, and serious criminality and the problem of recidivism begin to emerge. The importance of age is brought into sharp relief if we compare this group with e.g. the group of forty and over. In the first place, offences per 100,000 are four times more numerous in the younger group. In the second place, of those with previous offences who are brought into prison for the first time, seven out of ten of the younger group return, as against only one out of ten of the older group.

This then is the raw material of habitual criminality. How shall we handle it?

Every action of a court in relation to a proved offence, whether it be admonition or imprisonment, is in essence a psychological experiment: for it is an attempt to influence character or conduct. Unfortunately, it is largely a voyage on uncharted seas. The revolution in the psychological concept of motivation, and the realisation of the part played by the unconscious mind, have so far done little more than to throw into sharp relief our profound ignorance of these complex matters and to bring a truer realisation of the difficulties involved. The development of the child guidance clinic and of mental treatment on probation or under sentence will inevitably play an increasing part in the positive treatment of delinquency.

Meanwhile, in spite of the "cat" attitude still prevalent in some quarters, including sometimes the judicial bench, the Prison Commissioners' actions show an increasing realisation of the true factors involved. The conditions and atmosphere of the "open" prisons, the pre-release hostel schemes, and the granting of pre-release leave, are fundamentally different from those still operative (and, for reasons of building design, to some extent necessarily operative) in our Victorian prisons inherited from the past. This may well be the result of the Commissioners' experience of the Borstal system which, from its inception, has repudiated both retribution and deterrence and has concentrated on reformation.

It is very questionable whether the physical hardships of Borstal are less than those of prison. Both involve loss of freedom, segregation and discipline. The reformative process itself is bound to be uncomfortable. It makes demands on the offender not for passive obedience but for activity of body and mind, and for responsible government of his life within the community as a preparation for responsibility in the greater world to which he will be discharged. The lazy prisoner prefers the irresponsible existence of the old prison where the highest aim was "to give no trouble".

Nevertheless, because the conditions essential to reform are positive and not merely repressive, and because a relationship of friendliness is fundamental to the process of reform, these sanctions do not appear to exacerbate that resentment which lies so close to the roots of recidivism.

It may be noted that this change in the policy of the prison commissioners is paralleled by a similar but publicly avowed policy in Sweden. The Swedish Penal Code Commissioners, in the Penal Code which became law in 1947, say:

> "The loss of liberty need not be accentuated by repressive steps taken as a deterrent. . . . Neither can it be assumed that the deterrent effect of a sentence of imprisonment increases or decreases according to the degree of severity in prison conditions. . . . The function of the prison officer in modern penal treatment is to serve society by an effort to put the prisoner on his feet, and not to become a representative for the revengeful sentiments of the least enlightened members of society."

There is one form of punishment which English law does not encourage but which, we think, courts should have wider powers to impose. Most crimes today are crimes against property, but the forms of punishment pay little regard to the position of the injured person, to whom the loss may be serious. A fine, payable to the community, does nothing to restore his or her position. Yet the "natural" punishment is that the offender should be obliged to work and to contribute a proportion of his earnings until he has paid back to the victim all or such part of the value of the property in question as the court may order, and we consider that courts should be given increased powers to make such orders in suitable cases. Recent reports of working parties set up by the Home Office, the Conservative Party, and "Justice" (the British Branch of the International Commission of Jurists) have shown several ways in which this object could be achieved but particularly how an offence of violence could be punished in this way, though there is a general realisation that the only effective compensation must come from public funds.

### The Objects We Should Have in View

It follows from what has been said that mere retribution—punishment for punishment's sake—should form no part of our penal system; that, while all punishment may well have some useful deterrent value, the primary object of punishment should be reformation; that the courts should have power to make restitution orders of the kind referred to above; that the principal penal problem today is how to prevent recidivism, and particularly how to prevent the adolescent from becoming an habitual criminal; that while our knowledge of human motivation is still small, experience has shown that modern penal establishments on modern lines contain prospects of success not to be found within the old prison walls, of which we still have many; that both freedom and facilities should be afforded to the Prison Department of the Home Office to carry out whatever experiments are needed; that greater attention should be paid to the conviction rate because of its deterrent effect; and that greater care should be taken over sentences, particularly first and second sentences of imprisonment.

*What Should Be Done?*

In order to attain these objects the following practical steps should be taken:

(1) The police force should be enlarged and strengthened so as to increase the likelihood that offenders will be brought to justice, and thus to increase the real deterrence of the penal system.

(2) In cases of offences against property, courts should be given increased powers to make restitution orders of the kind referred to above, and victims of personal violence should be compensated, to the extent that their assailants are unable to do so, by the State.

(3) As there may be some deterrent value in the sentencing of offenders in open court, no change should be made in that practice.

(4) There is, however, force in the citizen's feeling that our judges, recorders and magistrates, when they sentence offenders, have too little knowledge of what really goes on in the different kinds of penal establishments, too little knowledge of the real circumstances of the offender and of the factors which really caused him to do what he did, and too little knowledge of the nature of the process they are setting in motion, which only begins when the prisoner leaves the dock. It is therefore strongly urged that, whenever an offender is sentenced to

imprisonment for the first or second time, he should be remanded in custody in a special remand centre until (after a full enquiry into his circumstances and history) his case has been reviewed by a sentencing board. This should include one lawyer, two doctors (one of whom should be a general practitioner and one a psychiatrist but neither of whom should be a prison medical officer), one representative of the Home Office, one lay member and, if practicable, the trial judge, recorder or chairman. The board (at least one member of which should be a woman) would have absolute powers to confirm the sentence or to substitute any lesser penalty which the court could have imposed, the sole criterion being which course is the most likely to result in that offender's not committing any further offence. Independently of this, judges and magistrates themselves need courses of criminological training.

(5) The Home Office should be given such staff and financial scope as will enable it to institute and develop varying forms of penal establishments suitable for the many varying kinds of offenders.

(6) Each penal establishment ought to have a duly qualified psychiatrist. Much crime cannot be cured by doctors, but they have a place to fill in any modern penal system. It is not creditable to our penal system that, although our courts continue to tell offenders that "any treatment you require you will get in prison", the total complement of qualified psychiatrists in the British Prison Service is still far too small to satisfy even modest requirements.

(7) One of the primary objects of our penal establishments should be to enable the offender to work and to train him in such work as will enable him to earn his livelihood honestly on his release. He should have a reasonable working day, instead of a day of about five hours work and most of the remainder spent in a cell with nothing whatever to do. He should be able to contribute to his family's support by the work which he does in prison, and in the interests of the criminal's reform industrialists and trade unions alike should withdraw their opposition to the sale of goods made in prisons, and to the use of prison labour in industry.

(8) The remuneration and conditions of service of prison
officers should be improved to such an extent as may be
necessary to attract to the service, not more gaolers, but
men and women able to play their full part in a social
service of great importance to the community.

# X

# REVENUE LAW

*Simplifying the Law*

Revenue law is very much "lawyers' law", and the mystery surrounding it has deepened to such an extent that it has become almost impossible for the average citizen to find his way through the growing maze of statute and case law supplemented, for reasons best known to the Inland Revenue, by extra-statutory concessions. Those unable to afford professional advice and assistance have to rely on the good will of Revenue officials. Many of these officials are extremely helpful, but the fact remains that they are, after all, civil servants who in the nature of things must have the interests of the Revenue primarily at heart.

The first thing that is needed, therefore, is a simplification of the law or, at any rate, some improvement which will make the law more accessible and intelligible. The Income Tax Act, 1952, which consolidated the Income Tax Act, 1918, and over thirty subsequent Finance Acts, was a step in the right direction, and for the preparatory work leading to this important consolidation due credit should be given to the Labour Government. Since then, however, there has been a large amount of new legislation, some of it incorporating changes recommended by the Royal Commission on Taxation.[1] It has been left to the ingenuity of publishers to show where these changes fit into existing legislation, but anyone familiar with the standard works on income tax—estate duty being treated separately in almost equally elaborate textbooks—will know how difficult it is, even for that select band of revenue lawyers, to find the law on any given problem. It should be made a statutory requirement that the income tax and estate duty provisions of each new Finance Act must be incorporated, say within three to six months of their entry into force, in a consolidating Act which will then be up to date in every particular. We do not believe that this would place any great additional burden on parliamentary draftsmen. It is a comparatively simple task.

[1] Reports of the Royal Commission on the Taxation of Profits and Income: Cmd. 8761 (1953); 9105 (1954); and 9474 (1955) (Final Report).

In this context it may also be pointed out that the relegation of important statutory provisions to elaborate schedules is undesirable. This practice is not, of course, confined to revenue legislation, but it is more irksome there than in more easily intelligible branches of the law. Furthermore there is no reason why extra-statutory concessions, which usually are known only to the initiated, should not be made part of the statute law. The taxpayer is entitled to rely on the letter of the law, and he should be equally entitled to rely on what the Inland Revenue seems to regard as a kind of lesser law.

## The Schedules and Cases

The abolition of Schedule A tax should go some way towards a more modern system of assessment, but the value of retaining no fewer than a total of four Schedules (after the disappearance of Schedule A) and ten Cases is still highly qestionable. Schedule B, to take an example, has virtually lost its justification, and so has the residuary Case VI of Schedule D. Each of the existing Schedules has its own rules of assessment, and we get such anomalies as the assessment of some types of income by reference to the year of charge and others by reference to some period other than the year of charge. The problem is further complicated for those who are liable to surtax which, after all, is income tax masquerading under a different name. It is a trite observation that income tax is a tax on income, and the rule should therefore be that all income, regardless of source, should be administered as one income. The principle of "one taxpayer —one assessment" has much to commend it. This reform should not be difficult to achieve since there is a good and valid precedent in assessments to profits tax, where all income connected with the trade or business is brought into one computation and all allowable expenditure, as well as wear and tear allowances on capital assets, deducted.

If this system were to be adopted for individual taxpayers, the anomalies arising from the different expenses rules applicable to Schedule D and Schedule E receipts would disappear. Under the former, disbursements and expenses may be deducted in computing profits if they are "wholly and exclusively laid out or expended for the purposes of the trade, profession or vocation". Under Schedule E, on the other hand, expenses may be deducted only if they are "wholly, exclusively *and necessarily*" laid out in the performance of a person's duties. In *Morgan* v.

*Tate & Lyle Ltd.*[1] it was held that expenses could be deducted in respect of a propaganda campaign designed to show that the nationalisation of the sugar refining industry would be harmful to "workers, consumers and stockholders alike". It will be remembered that this propaganda campaign (the central figure of which was "Mr. Cube") was launched as a result of fears that the next Labour Government might nationalise the sugar processing and refining industries. The case of Mr. Cube shows how widely the expenses rule of Schedule D can be interpreted, although—leaving aside this particular case—it is debatable whether the rule of Schedule D is too wide or that of Schedule E too narrow. In *Lomax* v. *Newtown*,[2] at any rate, it was said that the words "wholly, exclusively and necessarily" are stringent and exacting and deceptive in the sense that "when examined they are found to come to nearly nothing at all".[3]

The position is further complicated where a taxpayer is assessed partly under Schedule D and partly under Schedule E. In *Mitchel* v. *Ross*,[4] which was such a case, Lord Evershed said "that Parliament might well consider the justification and sense, at the present day, of the considerable distinction between the two Schedules in the matter of deductions and allowances".[5] In fact, this distinction has long been regarded as a wholly unjustified widening of the gulf between self-employed and employed taxpayers. The latter are, in any event, far less advantageously placed than the former, by having tax deducted at source.

### The Period of Assessment

Schedule D taxpayers, though treated more leniently in the matter of expenses, also have their justified grievances. The basis period by reference to which they are assessed to tax is a source of considerable annoyance to them. The general rule is that the basis of assessment is the income of the year preceding that of assessment. Yet this does not mean, as might be expected, that the income of last year is assessed this year. It really means that the measure of this year's income is—artificially—the income received last year; nevertheless it is this year's income,

[1] [1954] 35 T.C. 367.
[2] [1953] 34 T.C. 558.
[3] Per Vaisey, J., at p. 562.
[4] [1960] 2 All E.R. 218, C.A.
[5] At p. 223.

and this year's income only, which is being assessed. This is known as the "preceding year rule". This general rule does not apply to the opening and closing years of a business or other source of income. The "opening years" provisions in particular are a source of considerable hardship and mystification because taxpayers find it difficult to understand why they should be assessed to two years' tax within the year following the opening up of a new source of income.

In the case of trades and professions there is a further departure from the rule where there is a change in the date to which the accounts are made up. In these cases there is no account for a period of twelve months ending in the preceding year, and it is for the Commissioners to decide the period of twelve months which is to determine the year of assessment.[1] With all these complications it seldom happens that during the life of a business its total assessments coincide with its total profits. The adoption of a current year basis, so that this year's tax is consistently levied on this year's income, would remove a host of anomalies in the assessment of income tax and render obsolete much of the legislation which has been enacted to limit the extent to which the provisions relating to the basis period might favour the taxpayer.

## Tax on Capital and Capital Gains Tax

A tax on capital as such has never been seriously considered. The view is generally taken that high taxes on income and high rates of estate duty will see to it that inordinate accumulations of capital do not occur. This view is wholly unrealistic and not shared by a large number of countries which have known a graduated tax on capital assets for many years. The only alternative which has been considered from time to time is a form of capital gains tax. One has now been introduced by the Finance Act, 1962, as Case VII of Schedule D. It is a short-term gains tax which in many countries would be called no more than a tax on short-term speculative profits. All it does is to treat as income liable to tax certain gains which, it used to be said, were outside the scope of tax law (although it could well be argued that most of the gains now taxed under Case VII could have been assessed previously under Case I or Case VI). The period between acquisition and disposal of assets which is sufficient to give rise to a charge to tax—six months, except in the case of

[1] Income Tax Act, 1952, s. 127(2).

land, where it is three years—is so short that liability to tax can be avoided by anyone prepared to wait until the vulnerable period has expired.

It has been suggested that it would be a comparatively simple matter to lengthen the vulnerable period by amending legislation; but unless the whole concept of this tax were to be changed at the same time, this would mean that the period during which losses can be set off against gains would have to be similarly lengthened. In fact, as the Royal Commission has pointed out, the problem of giving relief for losses presents the greatest obstacle to the introduction of a true capital gains tax.[1] As far as the newly introduced capital gains tax is concerned, it will be observed that s. 10 of the Finance Act, 1962, carefully hedges the loss relief available to a taxpayer with elaborate conditions.

The problem still remains that, capital gains tax or no capital gains tax, there are many people who enjoy an "income" which is not subject to tax because technically it is an accretion to capital. Possibly the best way out of the dilemma would be to abandon the search for some effective yet equitable means of obtaining revenue from capital gains, and instead to restrict, as far as possible, the opportunities which still exist for taking, in the guise of capital, profits which in reality are income. In addition, an annual tax on the higher ranges of personal wealth should be given serious consideration. Its object would be not only to exact taxation according to ability to pay but also to do something to counteract the impression among those who possess no capital wealth that social justice is not being done.

*Taxation and Economic Planning*

The history of the last few years has amply demonstrated the urgent need for a planned economy. Revenue law, in order to ensure the success of planning, must be integrated with the programme of the planning authority. The basic motive which seems to have animated Chancellors in the past has been the "tax-gathering" motive, without sufficient consideration being given to the benefit that would arise in other directions if less tax were collected from any particular source. This is not to say that lip service has not been paid to this idea from time to time. Tax incentives, such as tax remission on exports, special investment allowances for certain industries, and tax benefits

[1] See Final Report, para. 91.

for approved workers' training schemes, not necessarily confined to the taxpayer's own junior employees or apprentices, (so that the skill of the country's working population as a whole can be increased, without penalising the person willing to undertake this vital additional responsibility) might well figure prominently in the thoughts of future Chancellors.

## Taxation of Companies

The measures referred to in the preceding paragraph would, of course, also involve consideration of the law affecting the taxation of companies. Reference to this is made in the Company Law section of Chapter VII.[1]

## Appeals against Assessments

The present machinery of appeals against tax assessments appears to work very well, and where the taxpayer is prepared to argue his own case before either General or Special Commissioners the cost can be negligible. Very often, however, specialist assistance is necessary in preparing and arguing the appellant's case. It seems wrong that the taxpayer should in such cases be required to suffer the double disadvantage of having to foot the bill and of having to do so out of taxed income. It is suggested that the cost of such professional assistance should be an allowable deduction.

The matter could be taken a stage further in the type of case where an appellant is deprived of the fruits of victory before the Commissioners because the Revenue takes the case to the courts. The taxpayer may be financially unable to risk costs being awarded against him were he to lose, or it may be simply that there is insufficient tax at stake to justify the costs, even of a successful appeal. In either event he will probably avoid the expense by consenting to the case being decided in favour of the Revenue and withdrawn from the list (although in certain cases the Revenue may offer to bear his costs so that the point at issue can be made the subject of a judicial ruling). Where the Revenue appeals against a decision of the Commissioners, the taxpayer should be given a statutory right to have his costs paid, win or lose.

## Tax Evasion and Tax Avoidance

Evasion of tax has come to mean the non-payment of tax

[1] See pp. 195–6, *supra*.

which is legally due, and avoidance of tax the arrangement of one's affairs so that no liability is legally exigible. The second is within the law, the first is not. These conventional meanings may not fully accord with dictionary definitions, but to avoid confusion the terms "evasion" and "avoidance" will be used here in the sense just described.

The problem of evasion is scarcely one which concerns the *reform* of the law. If it is already illegal, its prevention is a matter of enforcing the existing law. In any event, since the Finance Act, 1960, it cannot be said that the Inland Revenue has inadequate powers to deal with tax evasion when it comes to light; the problem is mainly the administrative one of discovering the facts. The 1960 Act brought the chargeable penalties into relationship with the tax evaded, abolishing the penalty of £20 plus three times the whole tax chargeable on the defaulter's income for each year involved (which was established to be the law under the Income Tax Act, 1952, by the House of Lords in the case of *C.I.R.* v. *Hinchy*[1]). The Act also extended the period within which proceedings for penalties could be instituted, and in addition the Revenue has acquired greatly augmented powers of recovering the tax due for back years outside the normal six-year time limit. Whereas formerly the recovery of such "out of date" tax depended on showing fraud or wilful default, the Revenue, since the Finance Act, 1960, need show only "neglect on the part of the taxpayer".

Legal "avoidance" presents a different problem, and the constant campaign waged by the legislature to close loopholes inevitably reduces the prospect of a true simplification of revenue law. Some of the most complicated legislation of recent years has been concerned with anti-avoidance, especially the Finance (No. 2) Act, 1955, against "dividend stripping"[2] and those provisions of the Finance Act, 1960, which are designed to prevent the disposal of land and property as "capital" (by selling the shares of a company owning such assets). The Finance Act, 1960, also contains the "blanket" anti-avoidance provisions of s. 28; these, in the most abstruse terms, confer powers to counteract any transaction in securities undertaken in order to obtain a "tax benefit".

---

[1] [1960] 38 T.C. 625.

[2] Broadly speaking, this is a device whereby a company, having acquired the shares of another company, and having incurred trading losses, seeks tax relief following receipt of dividends in respect of the shares acquired. For details, see s. 4 of the Act.

There are, however, still many devices available whereby income can be received in the form of capital, and the execution of covenants and settlements can still effect substantial reductions in the settlor's tax liability. It is not easy to single out any one of these devices for special attention, particularly since Parliament is not slow to alter the law whenever any particular device results in too great a loss of revenue or too easy an avoidance of tax. Opinions may differ as to the extent to which covenants and settlements should be further restricted where they effect a real transfer of income to someone else; but it seems difficult to justify the continued existence of devices such as that of the discretionary settlement, which not only reduces the yield of surtax where no beneficiary has an immediate interest in the income but also results in a loss of estate duty. Estate duty is in fact particularly vulnerable to avoidance devices by means of gifts and settlements, and it would be worth considering its replacement by some form of gift tax.

Another form of avoidance (or should it be termed evasion?) which is frequently spotlighted in the Press is that of the "expense account" executive. Flats, yachts, educational benefits, and shooting and fishing facilities have all been mentioned. There can be little doubt that cases of extravagant living out of non-taxed income are far from uncommon, yet one is left with the feeling that, here again, the problem is not one of the law but of its administration. After all, there can be no lack of stringency in a law which can bring into assessment a club subscription paid on behalf of a bank manager (*Brown* v. *Bullock*[1]) or the rates, lighting and heating bills relating to the residence of a works manager (*Butter* v. *Bennett*[2]).

*Summary of Proposals for Reform*

The most urgent reforms needed in the field of revenue law may be summarised as follows:

(1) The law should be simplified and divested of its impenetrable mysteries which at present make it a reserve of the specialist.

(2) The numerous Schedules and Cases should be abolished and the principle of "one taxpayer—one assessment" adopted.

---

[1] [1961] 3 All E.R. 129, C.A.
[2] [1961] 3 All E.R. 1041.

(3) The taxpayer should be assessed on his true income, i.e. on a current year basis.

(4) The expenses allowed in the case of employed persons should, as recommended by the Royal Commission, be "all expenses reasonably incurred for the appropriate performance of the duties of the office or employment".

(5) There should be a true capital gains tax, and consideration should be given to an annual tax on the higher ranges of accumulated wealth.

(6) The anti-avoidance provisions of the law, particularly as regards covenants and trusts, should be strengthened and applied more strictly than at present.

# LEGAL EDUCATION

TRAINING FOR PRACTICE as a solicitor or barrister is in the hands of the Law Society and the four Inns of Court; the latter exercise their functions partly direct and partly through the Council of Legal Education—a body jointly appointed by them. The Inns and the Council on the one side and the Law Society on the other control the right of entrance to the two branches of the legal profession. They do that by laying down certain minimum educational qualifications for entry into training; by providing training facilities and holding examinations; and by prescribing certain other conditions a candidate must fulfil in order to qualify for practice.

In the case of solicitors, certain essential features of the training (minimum educational qualifications; length of service under articles of clerkship; type of tuition provided by the Law Society) have recently undergone radical changes, and all of these have been changes for the better. There have been no radical changes (except one: the requirement of 12 months' pupilage in chambers before, or at the beginning of, practice) on the barristers' side; but there have been several improvements, some of them of considerable value. However, on neither side have the changes introduced since the end of World War II altered certain salient features of the system which are unique in the sense that no advanced country, comparable with Great Britain in size, wealth and social organisation, has them. It is a controversial question whether these unique features are attractive and desirable; but no attempt can be made to answer that question without first presenting a summary account of the system itself.

## Solicitors

Under the new regulations which came into force on 1st January, 1963, enrolment as a student is conditional upon the prior attainment of a fairly high educational standard. The candidate must have passed university examinations sufficient for the award of a degree (not necessarily in law); or he must have passed the G.C.E. examination in not less than five subjects with a minimum of two passes at advanced level or in not less than four subjects with a minimum of three passes at advanced level.[1] Every student must see service as an articled clerk in a solicitor's office, but the commencement and duration of this service vary according to academic status and the passing of either Part I or Part II of the Law Society's new Qualifying Examination. The non-graduate student can choose between entering into five years' articles or first passing Part I of the Qualifying Examination[2] (after taking a course at the new College of Law[3]) and then entering into articles for four years. Graduates in a subject other than law need not serve for more than two and a half years and are even allowed to be absent during the last half-year to prepare for Part II of the Qualifying Examination[4]; but both of these concessions are conditional upon Part I being passed before entry into articles. Finally, graduates in law need never serve more than two and a half years and are eligible for exemption from Part I in all those subjects in which they have passed examinations at a university; moreover, a law graduate who is wholly exempt from Part I may, with the Law Society's consent, take his Part II examination before entering upon articles and, if successful in that examination, need enter into and serve two years of articles only. This period of two years is the minimum period that any future solicitor must have spent acutally working in a solititor's office. In contrast to the system which existed prior to 1st January, 1963, this minimum period will be unbroken[5], with

---

[1] Candidates aged 28 and over will be allowed the alternative of taking the Law Society's own Preliminary Examination or will be excused any examination on proof of five years commissioned service in H.M. Forces or as an officer in the Colonial Civil Service.

[2] There are six subjects for Part I : Outlines of Constitutional and Administrative Law, Outlines of the English Legal System, Contract, Torts, Criminal Law, and Land Law.

[3] The new College of Law was recently formed by amalgamating The Law Society's School of Law and Messrs. Gibson & Weldon. Its principal function is to provide a recognised course leading to Part I of the Qualifying Examination; but courses in preparation for Part II and for the external LL.B. (London) degree are also available. The Law Society does not at present recognise any other course leading to Part I. The system of "approved law schools" (i.e.provincial universities providing courses for articled clerks, by special arrangement with the local Law Schools) has disappeared.

[4] Part II of the examination comprises seven papers. Six are compulsory: Conveyancing, Accounts, Revenue Law, Equity and Succession, Commercial Law, and Company Law and Partnership. The seventh paper is (at the candidate's option) either Family Law, Local Government Law or Magisterial Law.

[5] Save for a maximum of one month each year for holiday and a maximum of three months for illness over the two-year period.

no absence for study or examination. There is a further departure from precedent in that (apart from non-graduates who are required to attend a recognised course in preparation for Part I of the Qualifying Examination) compulsory theoretical instruction is abolished; and (yet another novelty) once a candidate has passed any three subjects of either Part at one examination, he may take any one or more of the remaining subjects of that Part at any subsequent examination. But there has been no departure from the old system on the vitally important point that once the candidate has qualified for admission as a solicitor (by completing the required service under articles *and* passing Part II of the examination) he is entitled to start practice at once and on his own without first undergoing some further training as an assistant solicitor.

*Barristers*

Entry into the barristers' branch of the profession still follows the traditional pattern. The student must first of all become a member of one of the four Inns of Court. The preliminary educational qualifications are now to all intents and purposes identical with those required by the Law Society; but the inducements offered to law graduates are less generous. Admittedly, the law graduate is eligible on a subject-for-subject basis for exemption from the whole or any section of Part I of the Bar Examination[1]; but without special leave from the Council of Legal Education he cannot present himself for Part II[2] unless he has kept six terms, i.e. has attended a number of dinners at his Inn over a period of not less than 18 months. No student (graduate or non-graduate) can be called to the Bar without attendance at a prescribed number of dinners over a period of, normally, not less than three years; but he need not attend any of the courses held under the auspices of the Council. There is now a considerable variety of such courses. They include lectures and tutorials, designed mainly for non-graduates and covering the whole field of Parts I and II of the

---

[1] Part I comprises the following: Roman Law; Constitutional Law and Legal History; Contract and Tort; Real Property or (subject to approval by the Director of the Council of Legal Education) Roman-Dutch Law or two half-papers in respectively Hindu, Mohammedan and African Law; and Criminal Law.

[2] Part II comprises the following: Common Law; Equity; Procedure (Civil and Criminal); Evidence and Company Law (one half-paper in each); and at the candidate's option, any two of the following: Conveyancing; Divorce; Conflicts; Public International Law.

examination; special tutorial classes for graduates; weekly question papers marked and commented upon by a panel of tutors; and (a new feature) an introductory course intended for those who will shortly begin pupilage or recently have done so with a view to practising at the Bar in England and Wales. The object of this course, which is essentially practical and of short duration (approximately ten days), is to provide aid in the acquisition and use of many of the professional skills of the Bar.[1] In addition, pupilage is now compulsory in the sense that before being called to the Bar the student must undertake not to practise as a barrister in England or Wales unless he has completed, or has commenced and intends to complete, a period of not less than twelve months' pupilage in the chambers of one or more practising members of the Bar.

## The Case for Reform

The salient features of the picture emerging from these regulations and facilities may be summed up as follows:

(1) A person may become a solicitor or barrister or, indeed, a member of the judiciary without any university training in law; in fact, without any university training at all.

(2) A candidate may be called to the Bar without ever having engaged, even outside a university, in any full-time study of or training in the law.

(3) Although the minimum standards of preliminary education are now substantially equal in both branches, solicitors (still called "the lower branch" of the legal profession) receive longer and more thorough practical training (and are required to pass examinations which cover wider ground) than barristers; and yet, the higher judiciary is still being recruited exclusively from the Bar.[2]

These features of the British system are unique if compared with the training required in other countries of comparable wealth and social organisation, and they are not desirable features.

[1] In addition, since 1951, post-final practical courses have been held three times a year (in each case over a period of three months) for persons who have passed the Bar examination and intend to practise overseas.

[2] A person can still become a barrister (though not a solicitor) without passing any examination in subjects as vital as Revenue Law, Commercial Law or Conveyancing. This anomaly is not mitigated by the fact that neither branch of the profession requires its new recruits to have read, let alone to have been examined in, either Private or Public International Law.

As regards academic training, the case for it rests on two propositions. First, English law, which is largely uncodified and operates with highly sophisticated methods of discovering and interpreting precedents, is one of the most complicated legal systems that have ever existed anywhere; to comprehend its substance and technicalities at its present stage of development (and the development of the law has been immense during the past half century, in both volume and depth) requires a rigorous intellectual discipline such as only a high-level academic training can engender. Secondly, it is highly desirable that those who practise and administer the law in a welfare State of the late twentieth century should be aware of the function of law in society and appreciate the interaction between law and social and economic progress. The training facilities now provided for intending solicitors and barristers are not concerned with either the social function of the law or with law as one of the social sciences.

The solicitors' branch of the profession, by its revised regulations, has placed such a high premium on a law degree that it is to be assumed that from now on an annually increasing proportion of new entrants will have passed through a university law school. That is as it should be; and it would be anomalous if the Bar did not move in the same direction. Indeed, to the present writers the advantages of an academic training in law appear to be so compelling that they would prefer to see it made a condition of entry into either branch of the legal profession.[1] In the case of intending solicitors it would be easy to adapt the Law Society's new regulations to this somewhat radical reform. Law graduates who take Part II of the Qualifying Examination before entering into articles would serve for two years; law graduates preferring to take Part II at the end of their articles would serve six months longer. In the case of Bar students, in order to preserve a tradition which it would be hard (and possibly wrong) to break, it would be necessary to work out a new combination between dining terms, academic training and

[1] Consideration could be given to making an exception, in the case of the solicitors' branch, for the benefit of the "ten-year man", i.e. a persion who, since attaining the age of 18 years and before entering into articles, has completed not less than ten years' service as a solicitor's clerk. In the barristers' branch there might be a case for maintaining the present system, and dispensing with a law degree, for the benefit of persons who, when seeking admission as students of one of the Inns of Court, give an undertaking that they will not practise at the Bar in England and Wales.

admission to the Final Examination. The normal pattern would be for the undergraduate to keep his dining terms concurrently with his university course and take his Bar Final Examination at any time after taking his law degree.[1] A somewhat different pattern would have to be devised for the law graduate who, at the time of commencing his academic course, had not envisaged a career at the Bar and kept no concurrent dining terms. In his case the solution might well be to allow him to proceed, at any time after taking his law degree, to the Bar Final Examination, but require him to keep extended dining terms throughout his period of pupilage.[2]

In suggesting these patterns of qualification we have assumed that the law faculties of the British universities would be willing and able so to modify their examination requirements as to enable the Council of Legal Education to exempt law graduates from the whole of Part I of the Bar Examination.[3] As regards the Final Examination we would suggest that both its coverage and its standard should be assimilated to Part II of the new Qualifying Examination for solicitors.[4] There are several reasons for this suggestion. First, Part II of the Qualifying Examination has a wider coverage, better attuned to the requirements of practice; the inclusion of Revenue Law and Commercial Law as compulsory subjects and of Magisterial Law and Local Government Law as optional subjects are significant cases in point. Secondly (and this is an even more important consideration), it is eminently desirable to facilitate the transfer of practitioners from one branch of the legal profession to the other. At present a barrister of five years' standing may seek admission as a solicitor without serving

---

[1] For a candidate who has passed his final examinations with reasonable success at a university, the Bar Final Examination will present little or no difficulty; in the United States it has come to be regarded almost as a formality.

[2] By "extended dining terms" we mean nine dinners each term instead of the present maximum of six. Twelve months' pupilage would allow the candidate to keep four extended terms and thus attend the same minimum number of dinners (36) which under the present regulations is compulsory for Bar students who concurrently take an academic course.

[3] This assumption does not apply to Hindu, Mohammedan, Roman-Dutch and African Law. All of these are optional subjects for Part I of the Bar Examination, and it would be open for those wishing to opt for any of these subjects in lieu of the Law of Real Property to read for this section of the Part I examination either privately or by attending the courses provided by the Council of Legal Education.

[4] Consideration should, however, be given to omitting Accounts from the list of subjects to be covered by the Bar Final Examination thus revised, and to substituting either Criminology or Comparative Law.

articles but not without taking Part II of the Qualifying Examination; conversely, a solicitor of five years' standing cannot be called to the Bar without first taking the Bar Final Examination. These requirements, which operate as a strong disincentive to transfers from one branch to the other, could be easily abandoned if only the present differences between the two sets of final examinations were eliminated.

Equalising, along these or similar lines, the academic training and the final examination required for entry into either branch of the legal profession would still leave one element of in-equality: the minimum duration of articles is two years, that of pupilage in a barrister's chambers only one year. It would be logical and desirable, but alas impracticable, to extend the term of compulsory pupilage by another year. If only because of severe limitations of space, it might become very difficult to find seats in chambers for intending pupils if the compulsory term of pupilage were extended. It follows that either the legal profession as a whole must acquiesce in a situation which would allow an intending barrister to qualify a year earlier than an intending solicitor; or to bridge the time-gap by requiring intending barristers to take a post-graduate course of at least one year's duration at a university law school. In any event, however, it would appear desirable for the Law Society and the Inns of Court to take stricter powers of supervision than those which they are exercising at present over the variety and quality of work in which clerks and pupils receive practical training; and, in particular, they should ensure that all articled clerks and pupils gain some experience in advocacy.

The present writers are well aware that the existing shortage of university places (from which law faculties suffer nearly as acutely as science departments) may make it difficult to intro-duce before 1970 (at the earliest) the major reform advocated in the present chapter, i.e. the taking of a law degree before entry into either branch of the legal profession. There is, however, no cogent reason why, during the transitional period, progress should not be made with the second important reform: the assimilation of the two sets of final examinations.

Another reform which could be carried out during the period of transition would be the abolition of the anomalous rule whereby Bar students who have passed their final examination are prevented from being called to the Bar until they have kept all the prescribed dining terms; the obvious remedy would be to allow such candidates to be called to the Bar immediately after passing their final examinations and require them to attend the missing number of dinners during their compulsory term of pupilage.

## Academic Training

Finally, a few observations on the academic teaching of law. The courses at present provided in British universities have a sufficiently wide coverage and high standard to warrant the recommendation that a law degree should be treated as a condition precedent to entry into the legal profession; and yet few of those practitioners who have had a university training (and even fewer of those who teach law at a university) would disagree with the proposition that there is no room for complacency and much room for improvement. Although, unlike the law schools of the Law Society and the Inns of Court, the universities do provide facilities for the study of those social sciences which are relevant to the understanding and practice of the law, it is not mandatory for law students to avail themselves of these courses. In this respect the system is too liberal and its results are less satisfactory than those which are achieved by comparable law schools on the Continent of Europe. Possibly, this deficiency of the English system could not be removed without extending the course leading to a first degree from the present three years to four years (which is, in fact, the minimum duration of a comparable course in most Continental universities). If this were done, the shortage of university places, to which reference has already been made, would continue for an even longer period than that which is at present in contemplation. That, from the point of view of the legal profession, would be even more undesirable than the present lack of compulsory training in those disciplines which are adjacent to the law.

Akin to the problem which was touched upon in the preceding paragraph is the continuing tendency of law teaching to look to the past rather than the present, and to extol rules and practices which served well in times long gone by instead of encouraging the young generation to adopt a critical approach to that which is obsolete and unsatisfactory. There is far too much consideration of the historical development of rules and institutions, and far too little time devoted to the analysis of the law in action. A great deal of foreign experience could be put to excellent use in this country; but apart from a few pioneering universities, Comparative Law still remains a discipline and technique which is largely ignored. Even more disquieting is the disinclination of the majority of our law schools to give due attention to those branches of the law which are indispensable to the growing number of lawyers whom the large organisations of industry and commerce and Government departments (including the nationalised industries) are increasingly anxious to absorb. Too few of our law faculties are engaged in the systematic teaching of the law relating to business (a much wider discipline than Commercial Law) let alone of Revenue Law; and by and large even the teaching of that ubiquitous and ever growing subject, Administrative Law, is being treated with less enthusiasm than it deserves. Possibly, and even probably, there is no efficient way of teaching Business Law and Administrative Law short of enlisting the help of practitioners on a part-time basis. This has been recognised, and acted upon by the greater part of Continental universities; but in this country there has been, since the end of the war, a growing tendency against associating the practitioner with academic teaching, at any rate as far as senior posts are concerned. There is a strong case for the re-consideration of this tendency not only with reference to teaching but also with a view to associating practising lawyers with academic projects of research. The re-thinking of the proper co-operation of practising and academic lawyers in both legal education and the practice of the law is an urgent and challenging task.

# INDEX

Compiled by G. NORMAN KNIGHT, M.A., Barrister-at-Law, Chairman of the
Society of Indexers

Page numbers in **bold type** indicate main references; "*(bis)*" after a page
number denotes two separate references to the item on that page.

Abortion, 239–40, **240–3**
Abse, Leo, his Matrimonial Causes
Bill (1962), 122*n.*, 138*n.*, 140*n.*
Academic training in law, **283–4**, 285,
**286–7**
Accidents:
employees' liability for, 221–2; in-
dustrial, 71, **72**, **73–4**; prevention of,
**222–4**; road, **71–3**; State insurance
for, 177
ACTS OF PARLIAMENT (*see also* Statute),
32, 33
Affiliation Proceedings Act (1957),
122*n.*
Aliens Act (1905), 55
Anchors and Chain Cables Act
(1899), 166
Blasphemy Act (1698), 246
British Nationality Act (1948), 51*n.*
Cheques Act (1957), 166
Children Act (1948), 229
Children and Young Persons Act
(1933), 229
Commonwealth Immigrants Act
(1962), **53**, 54, 55, 56
Companies Act (1928), 2
Companies Act (1947), 2
Companies Act (1948), 2, 69, 187,
190, 192, 193
Companies (Consolidation) Act
(1929), 2, 152
Consolidation of Enactments (Pro-
cedure) Act (1949), 12
Conspiracy and Protection of Prop-
erty Act (1875), 205
Criminal Justice Act (1925), 253
Criminal Justice Act (1948), 17*n.*,
259 (*bis*)
Education Act (1944), 225
Employers and Workmen Act (1875),
225
Evidence Act (1938), 21
Expiring Laws Continuance Acts
(annual), 13
Factories Acts (1833–1948), 221,
**222–3**, 225
Factors Act (1889), 156
Fertilizers and Feeding Stuffs Act
(1926), 166
Finance Act (1962), 186, 273, 274

ACTS OF PARLIAMENT (*cont.*)
Finance Acts, 181, 183, 185 (*bis*),
276 (*bis*)
Fire Prevention (Metropolis) Act
(1744), 112
Food and Drugs Acts (1938–50), 166
Foreign Compensation Commission
Act (1950), 8*n.*
Furnished Houses (Rent Control)
Act (1946), 96, 107
Guardianship of Infants Act (1925)
Hire Purchase Act (1938), 59, 153,
159, 163, 164, 166
Hire Purchase Act (1954), 163
Homicide Act (1957), 233, 237
Housing Act (1936), 48
Housing Act (1957), 101, **109**
Housing Act (1961), **110**
Income Tax Act (1918), 270
Income Tax Act (1952), 181, 185,
270, 273*n.*, 276
Industrial Court Act (1919), 199
Inebriates Act (1898), 235, 236
Infanticide Act (1938), 239
Inheritance (Family Provision) Act
(1938), 145, 146, 147
Intestates Estates Act (1952), 146
Judicature Act (1873), 15, 16
Land Charges Act (1925), 93, **97–8**
Land Registration Act (1925), 79,
80, 95
Landlord and Tenant Act (1927), 110
Landlord and Tenant Act (1954),
108 (*bis*), 116
Law of Property Act (1925), 83, 90,
91, 93, 96, **97–8**, 114
Law Reform (Enforcement of Con-
tracts) Act (1954), 63
Law Reform (Frustrated Contracts)
Act (1943), 156
Law Reform (Married Women and
Tortfeasors) Act (1935), 129*n.*,
134*n.*
Leases Act (1845), **115**
Legal Aid and Advice Act (1949), 4,
18
Legitimacy Act (1958), 125*n.*
Limitation Acts (1623 and 1939), 81
Limited Partnership Act (1907), 178,
198

ACTS OF PARLIAMENT (*cont.*)

London Building Acts (Amendment) Act (1939), 92

Magistrates' Courts Act (1952), 21

Maintenance Agreements Act (1957), 122*n.*

Maintenance Orders Act (1958), 122*n.*, 218, 219

Marriage (Enabling) Act (1960), 122*n.*

Married Women (Restraint upon Anticipation) Act (1949), 129*n.*

Married Women's Property Acts (1870 and 1882), 129, 130*n.*

Matrimonial Causes Acts (1857–1958), 125*n.*, 126*n.*, 127*n.*, 130*n.*, 136*n.*, 147 and *n.*

Matrimonial Proceedings (Children) Act (1958), 122*n.*, 147

Matrimonial Proceedings (Magistrates' Courts) Act (1960), 122*n.*, 136, 139*n.*, 144

Mental Health Act (1959), 233, 243

National Insurance Acts (1946–53), 226

New Towns Act (1946), 50*n.*

Obscene Publications Acts (1859 and 1957), 247

Occupier's Liability Act (1957), 5, 77, 102

Offences Against the Person Act (1861), 240

Offices and Shops Act (1963), 225

Official Secrets Acts (1911–39), 44–5

Partnership Act (1890), 197 (*bis*)

Payment of Wages Act (1960), 216

Prescription Act (1832), 92

Rent Acts, **105–8**

Restrictive Trade Practices Act (1956), 8, 58, 69

Rights of Light Act (1959), 92

Road Traffic Act (1930), 171, 173

Road Traffic Act (1960), 72, 173*n.*

Sale of Goods Act (1893), 68, 156 (*bis*), 157, 159, 161, 166

Settled Land Act (1925), 85

Shops Act (1950), 225

Shops Clubs Act (1902), 218

Slaughter of Animals Act (1895), 227

Small Tenants Recovery Act (1838), 114

Statute of Frauds (1677), **63–4**

Statute of Frauds Amendment Act (1828), 63

Street Offences Act (1959), 249

Terms and Conditions of Employment Act (1959), 210, 211, 218, 220, 225

Town and Country Planning Act (1944), 50*n.*

Town and Country Planning Act (1962), 40*n.*, 41*n.*

ACTS OF PARLIAMENT (*cont.*)

Trade Disputes Act (1906), **206–7, 209**

Trade Union Act (1871), 210*n.*

Trade Union Act (1913), 213

Transport Act (1962), 59

Trial of Lunatics Act (1882), 232

Tribunals and Enquiries Act (1958), 4, 36, 51

Truck Acts (1831–96), 216, 217, 218

Vagrancy Act (1824), **248**

Variation of Trusts Act (1958), 5*n.*

Wages Attachment Abolition Act (1870), 219

*Ad hoc* Committees, **3–4**, 6, 10, 13, 14

Administrative law, **34–56**, 287

Administrative tribunals, *see* Tribunals

"Administrators' law", 9

Adultery:
damages for, 141; self-crimination for, 21

Affiliation proceedings, 146

Age of:
contracting capacity, **68–9**; criminal responsibility, **229**

Agreements (*see also* Contracts):
collective, *see* Collective agreements; types which should be enforceable without consideration, **61–2**

Alienation of land, 85

Aliens, **52–6**

American Law Institute, 22

American Restatement of Commercial Law, 153, 170

Animals, damage caused by, **77–8**

Annulment of marriage, 125, 126

Appellate Courts, **16–8**
reforms proposed for powers of, **258–9**

Appellate tribunals, 37

Apprenticeship, **225–6**

Arbitration:
compulsory, for enforcing collective agreements, 202, **215–16**; "grievance", *see* Grievance arbitration

Arbitration clauses, insurance policy, **177**

Arrest without warrant, **228**, 253

Articled clerks, 280, 285

Articles of Association, 180, 182–3

Artificial insemination as ground for divorce, 140

Association of Provincial Stock Exchanges, 186

Attachment of earnings orders, 149, 219

Australia, hire purchase in, 164, 165

Avory, Sir Horace, J., 245

Bagehot, Walter, his "liberal fallacy", 27

Bail, **252–6**; proposed amendments to law, **255–6**

Bailments, **168**

Balance sheets, company, 184

Banking, **166–8**

Banks and Discount Houses, accounting by, **188**

Barristers:
admission as solicitors, 284; solicitors' admission as, 285; special fees of, 19; training of, 279, **281–3, 284–7**

Bastardy cases, blood tests in, 22

Beck, Adolf, case of, 17

Belgium:
coal-miners' rehabilitation in, 226; job security in, **201–2**

Bentham, Jeremy, on Ministry of Justice, 7

Bevin, Ernest, 236

Bills of Exchange, 166, **167** (bis)

Blasphemy, 227, **246–7**

Board of Trade, 2, 3, 32; Companies Department of, 2, 184, 188, 193, 195

Bondfield, Margaret, 236

Borstal system, the, 265

Bourne, Dr. Alec, 241–2

Breach of contract:
employees', 203, 204, **206,** 208, **221–2;** remedies for, **67–8**

Breach of covenant by tenant, 113, 114

Breach of the peace, blasphemy and, 247

British Dominions:
codification in, 11; Ministries of Justice in, 7

British Medical Association Committee on abortion, 241

British Transport Commission, Passenger Charges Scheme of, 59, 171

Broadmoor Mental Hospital, 234, 239

Bryan, Carmen, proposal to deport, 56

Building societies, 105

Burton, Baroness, on Molony Report, 154n.

Business tenancies, **108–9**

Buyer, protection of, see Consumer

Byrne, J., on prisoners' confessions, 252

Cabinet, the, 28, 31

Campbell, 1st Baron, L.C., on obscenity, 247

Canadian Bar Review, 72n.

Capacity of contracting parties, **68–9**

Capital gains tax (1962), 186, **273**

Capital punishment, **236–7**

Capital tax, a, 128, 273

Carriers, **168–70**

Carstairs, Prof. C. M., on marriage breakdown, 140n.

CASES CITED:
Allen v. Allen [1961], 131, 135n.
Anglo Overseas Agencies Ltd. v. Green & Another [1960], 184n.
Armitage v. Attorney-General [1906], 127n.
Associated Provincial Picture Theatres Ltd. v. Wednesbury Corporation [1948], 49n., 51

CASES CITED (cont.)
Barcock v. Brighton Corporation [1949], 224n.
Bell v. Lever Bros. Ltd. [1932], 67
Beresford v. The Royal Insurance Co. [1938], 174
Birch v. Wigan Corporation [1953], 48n.
Bird v. British Celanese Ltd. [1945], 218n.
Boissevain v. Weil [1950], 70
Braithwaite v. Elliott [1947], 106
British Transport Commission v. Gourley [1956], **76**
Brown v. Bullock [1961], 277
Butter v. Bennett [1961], 277
Buxton v. Minister of Housing & Local Government [1960], 41n.
Campbell Discount Co. Ltd. v. Bridge [1961], 164n.
Candler v. Crane, Christmas & Co. [1951], 75
Chandler v. D.P.P. [1962], 45n.
City Equitable Fire Insurance Co., Re [1925], 151
Cobb v. Cobb [1955], 135n.
Commissioners of Inland Revenue v. Hinchy [1960], 276
Conway v. Wade [1909], 207
Cook v. Cook [1962], 130n.
Couldery v. Bartrum [1881], 60
Cross v. British Oak Insurance Co. [1938], 175
Czarnikow v. Roth, Schmidt & Co. [1922], 64n.
D.P.P. v. Smith [1961], 16
Donoghue v. Stevenson [1932], 77, 160
Duke of Chateau Thierry, Ex parte [1917], 54n.
Ellis v. Johnstone [1963], 78
Forsey and Hollebone's Contracts, Re [1927], 96
Fribance v. Fribance [1957], 135n.
Frost v. Minister of Health [1935], 49n.
Fry, Ex parte [1954], 49n.
Gibson v. Lawson [1891], 209
Green v. Russell [1959], 62
H. v. H. [1953], 125n.
Hawkins v. Price [1947], 63
Hindley v. Hindley [1957], 130n.
Hine v. Hine [1962], 135
Hoddinott v. Hoddinott [1949], 131n., 135n.
Ingram v. Little [1960], 67
Joel v. Law Union [1908], 172n.
Jon Beauforte (London) Ltd., Re [1953], 69n.
Ledwith v. Roberts [1937], 248n.
Lister v. Romford Ice Cold Storage Co. [1957], **221–2**
Liversidge v. Anderson [1942], 54
Lomax v. Newtown [1953], 272
Lowcock v. Brotherton [1952], 106

CASES CITED (cont.)
Lynch v. Thorne [1956], 100
Merchants' Insurance Co. v. Hunt [1940], 173n.
Metropolitan Police v. Croydon Corporation [1957], 76
Mitchell v. Ross [1960], 272
Morgan v. Tate & Lyle Ltd. [1954], 271-2
Nakkuda Ali v. Jayaratne [1951], 49n.
No. 88 High Road, Kilburn, Re [1959], 108
Orman v. Saville Sportswear Ltd. [1960], 219n.
Otto v. Bolton [1936], 100
Overstone Ltd. v. Shipway [1962], 164
Parke v. The Daily News [1962], 194
Parojcic v. Parojcic [1959], 125n.
Pickup v. U.D. Dental Board [1928], 227n.
Pinnel's Case (1602), 60
Polemis and Furness, Withy & Co., Re [1921], 74
Prescott v. Birmingham Corporation [1955], 50, 51
Printing & Numerical Registering Co. v. Sampson (1875), 57n.
R. v. Arnold (1724), 230
R. v. Beard [1920], 235
R. v. Beck [1904], 17
R. v. Bellingham (1812), 230
R. v. Electricity Commissioners [1924], 49n.
R. v. Hanratty [1962], 235
R. v. Hendon R.D.C. [1933], 49n.
R. v. Jones [1959], 237
R. v. Kingston [1948], 259n.
R. v. L.C.C. [1931], 49n.
R. v. M'Naghten (1843), 230
R. v. Manchester Legal Aid Committee [1952], 49n.
R. v. Meade [1909], 235
R. v. Metropolitan Police Commissioner [1953], 49n.
R. v. Neal [1949], 259n.
R. v. Postmaster-General [1928], 49n.
R. v. Secretary of State for Home Affairs [1962], 52n.
Rimmer v. Rimmer [1953], 135n.
Rookes v. Barnard [1962], 208
Scottish Co-operative Wholesale Society Ltd. v. Meyer [1958], 183n.
Shaw v. D.P.P. [1961], 16, 245, 247
Silver v. Silver [1955], 126n.
Smith v. East Elloe Rural District Council [1956], 49, 50
Smith v. Selwyn [1914], 78
Sparrow v. Fairey Aviation Co. Ltd. [1962], 223n.
Valier v. Valier [1925], 126n.
Venicoff, Ex parte [1920], 54
Wagon Mound, The [1961], 74

CASES CITED (cont.)
Windmill Investments (London) Ltd. v. Milano Restaurant Ltd. [1962], 113
Zurich Insurance Co. v. Morrison [1942], 172n.
Caveat emptor, 100
Central land charges registration, 93-5, 96
Certiorari, order of, 51
Chancery Division, 124, 148
assignment of probate work to, 15
"Charge by way of legal mortgage", 97
"Charges" in respect of house, 111
Cheques, 166-8
Chief Metropolitan Magistrate, deportation advice from, 55
Children:
age of criminal responsibility, 229; broken marriages and, 138; custody of, 142-3; domicile of, 141-2; employment of, 225; "Family Charter" and, 123; killing of, by mother, see Infanticide; maintenance of, 129, 132, 136, 144-6; parental power over, 143-4; "recognized", 145, 147
Circuit system, 19
Civil servants, 25, 26, 30, 38, 44
Crown's right to dismiss, 200
Cockburn, Sir Alexander, L.C.J., on obscenity, 247
Codification of the law, 8, 10-12, 106; English examples of, 11; law reform to precede, 12
Collective agreements, 202, 203, 210-12; enforceability of, 211, 215-16; wages payment, 217, 218, 219-20
College of Law, 280
Commercial Court, 15, 20-1
Commercial law, 150-98, 282n., 287
American Restatement of, 153, 170
Commissioners of Income Tax, 275
costs of Revenue's appeals from their decisions, 275
Committal proceedings, Press reports of, 257-8
COMMITTEES (see also Ad hoc and Permanent and Standing), 3-6, 27-32
Abortion, Inter-Departmental Committee on (1939), 240-1
Administrative Tribunals and Enquiries, Committee on (1955-7), 26, 36, 37, 38, 41
Byrne Committee on Depositions (1949), 257n.
Capital Issues Committee, 186
Capital Punishment, Select Committee on (1930), 236
Central Housing Advisory Committee, 109
Cohen Committee on Company law (1945), 2

COMMITTEES (*cont.*)
Corporal Punishment, Departmental Committee on (1938, Cmd. 5684), 262
County Court Procedure, Austin Jones Committee on (1947–9), 19
Criminal Law Revision Committee (created 1959), 4, 10
Davies (Edmund) Committee on Personal Injuries (1962), 77
Denning Committee on Procedure in Matrimonial Causes (1946–7), 19
Estimates, Select Committee on, 28
Evershed Committee on Supreme Court Practice and Procedure (1947–53), 15, 19 (*bis*), 20, 22
Gladstone Committee on Prisons (1895, Cmd. 7702), 261, 262, 263 (*bis*)
Greene Committee on Company law (1927), 2
Hanworth Committee on Business of the Courts (1932–3), 15, 20
Insanity and Crime, Committee on (1922), 231
Jenkins Committee (1962), 2, 150, 178, 183, 184, **187–90**, 191, 192
"Justice" Committee on Matrimonial Proceedings in Magistrates' Courts (1962), 19, 22
Karmel Committee on the Truck Acts (1962), 217
Law of Civil Liability for Damage Done by Animals (1953), 78
Law Reform Committee (created 1952), *see* Law Reform Committee
Law Relating to Personal Injuries (1962), 77
Law Revision Committee (1934–9), 4, **61–3**
*Lister's Case*, Inter-departmental Committee on (1957), 222
Local Land Charges, Committee on (1952), 95
Machinery of Government, Lord Haldane's Committee on the (1918), 7
Ministers' Powers, Committee on (1929–32), 26
Molony Committee on Consumer Protection (1959–62), 150, **154–5**, **156–62**, 164, 166
Nationalized Industries, Select Committee on, 28
Private International Law Committee, 4, 10
Proceedings before Examining Justices (1958), 258
Radcliffe Committee on Security Procedures in the Public Services, (1961), 44
Roxburgh Committee on Land Charges (1956), **94–5**, 96–7

COMMITTEES (*cont.*)
Statutory Instruments, Select Committee on, 30, 34
Sterilization, Departmental Committee on (1934), 242
Streatfeild Committee on Business of the Criminal Courts (1958), 253
Tucker Committee on Procedure before Examining Justices (1957–1958), 19, 20
Wolfenden Committee on Homosexual Offences and Prostitution (1957), 244
Common law:
blasphemy under, 246; consideration under, 60; safe system of work in, 223; obscenity under, **247–8**; privity of contract under, 62; sale of goods under, 153
Commonwealth immigrants, **52–6**
"Community of gains" or of "surplus", spouses', **134–5**
Companies, **177–96**
access to books of, 193; annual returns of, 184; certificate to start trading, **190–1**; conflict with Commons' Committees, 32; distribution of profits by, 196; employees' representation on boards of, 195 (*bis*); limited, *see* Limited liability; minimum paid-up capital before trading, 191; private, *see* Private companies; public, *see* Public companies; subsidiary and interlocking, 191
Company law, **150–96**
consolidation of, **2–3**; reforms proposed for, **190–6**
Comparative law, 287
Comparative Legislation, Society of, *Journal*, 72n.
Compensation for loss of employment, **200–2**, 203
Compensation for "unjustified harm", **78**
Compulsory purchase, **38**
Compulsory Purchase by Local Authorities (Inquiries Procedure) Rules (1962), **38**
Conditions of contract, 65, 68
Conservative Party, 266
Consideration (contract), **59–62**
Consolidation of statute law, **2–3**, 13, 22, 106, 113
income tax, **270**
Conspiracy, tort of, and strikes, 206, 208
Constitutional law, **24–56**
"Constructive" or "implied" malice, 237
Consumer protection, 58–9, 134, 156–7, **160–1**, **166**
Contempt of court, **42–4**, 46, **244–5**

Continental law:
age of criminal responsibility, 229; forged endorsements under, 167–8; job security under, 200–2; *nemo dat* rule absent from, 156; quasi contract in, 70; "recognized" children under, 145; specific performance in, 68

Contract, law of, application to commercial law, 151

Contract of employment, 200–4
breach of, 203, 204, 206, 208, 221–2; civil servants', 199–200; collective agreement and, 211; employer's indemnity implied in, 221–2; "freedom of", 217; infant's, 69; terms of, 211

Contracts, 57–70
bailment, 168; breach of, *see* Breach of contract; capacity of parties to, 68–9; conditions in, by reference, 59; "freedom" of, 168, 170, 217; Government, 210; illegality of certain, 69–70; inaccurate and misleading statements in, 64–6; insurance, *see* Insurance; intention to be legally bound by, 64; "sanctity" of, 57–8, 120, 170; standard forms for, *see* Standard-form contracts

Contributory negligence, 221, 224

Controlled tenancies, 105–8
transmission of, on death, 106

Conversion, tort of, 78

Conveyancing, 98, 99, 282n.
cost of, 103–5; land registration and, 80; stamp duty, 105n.; time factor in, 102–3

Conviction rate as crime deterrent, 262–3, 267

Coroners' Courts, 18–9

Corporations, contracts by, 69

Corruption by public authority, 49, 51

Costs, legal aid for, 23

Council of Legal Education, 279, 281, 284

Council on Tribunals, the, 36–7
immigration and, 55; Report of, 40n.

County Courts, 18
leasehold enfranchisement price to be determined by, 117, 119; remedies available to landlord in, 114; undefended cases transferred to, 15

Court of Appeal, 16

Court of Criminal Appeal, 16–8, 232
power to amend conviction, 258; proposed power to order new trial, 259

Courtaulds Ltd., hidden reserves of, 188–9

Courts, the:
administrative tribunals or, 35; criticism of, 245; new crimes created by, 245–6; new law made in, 160; organization of, 15–9; political power exerted by, 47; procedure of,

19–20; public authorities' decisions controlled by, 47–52

Covenants, tax avoidance through, 277, 278

Covenants affecting land, 88–91, 111–12

Covenants against assigning tenancy, 111

Covenants in leases, 120, 121
standard, 115

Covenants in restraint of trade, 225

Covenants to repair, 110

Crane, on land registration, 92n.

Creditors, composition with, 60

Crick, B.: *Reform of the Commons*, 27n.

Crimes:
classification of, 227–9; extradition, 52, 53, 54; power of creating new, 245–6

Criminal appeals, 16–18
legal aid and advice for, 18, 23

Criminal law, 3, 227–69
evidence in, 21; strikes and, 204–6

Criminal procedure, 249–59

Criminal responsibility:
age of, 229; insanity and, 229–34

Criminal Responsibility (Trials) Bill (1924), 233, 234

Crown, the:
refusal to disclose documents during litigation, 45; right to dismiss its servants, 200

"D" (Defence) Notices, 44–5

Damages:
adultery, 141; breach of contract, 68; innocent misrepresentation, 65–6; negligence, 73–7

Dangerous goods, 157, 166

Darling, 1st Baron, his Criminal Responsibility (Trials) Bill (1924), 233, 234

Death:
notional date of, 21; presumption of, 21; transmission of controlled tenancies on, 106

Death penalty for murder, 236–7

Defamation, *see* Libel

Defence, Ministry of, 44

Delegated legislation, 10, 25, 32–4

Denning, Lord, M.R., on negligence, 75

Dependent children, 130, 138
definition of, 144, 147–8

Deportation orders, 52, 53, 55–6

Depositions, 256–7

"Detention for questioning", 250–1

Deterrence as object of punishment, 260, 261, 265
conflict with reformation, 263–4

Detinue, tort of, 78

Developers, property, 89, 90, 91, 101

Devlin, Lord, on "all or nothing" rule, 156

Dicey, Professor A. V., 36
Directors, company, 180, **191-2**
  duties of, 189; "earned income" of,
  196; liability for fraud, 180, 181, 184,
  192; maintenance of, in office, 186;
  "reckless trading" by, **192**
Discretionary trusts, 84-5
Dismissal of employees, 202
  "abusive" (France), 201; civil service, **200**
Distress, right of, 114
"Dividend stripping", 276
Divisional Court:
  criminal appeal jurisdiction of, 17;
  proposed power to amend conviction,
  258
Divorce, **136-41**, 149
  custody of children on, **142-3**;
  grounds for, **136-41**; matrimonial
  property and, 130; recognition of
  foreign, 127
Divorce Court, 15, 124
Domicile, **127-8**
  children's, **141-2**
Domicile Bills (1958 and 1959), 4, 142n.
Drug addiction as ground for divorce,
  140
Drunkenness:
  crimes committed in state of, **235-6**;
  habitual, and divorce, **139-40**

Earned income, 128, 196
Easements and profits, **92**
Education, Ministry of, 30
Eire, death penalty abolished in, 236
Electrical Trade Union, litigation, 212
Employees:
  collective agreements for, see Collective; companies', 190, **194-5**; dismissal of, see Dismissal; employers
  indemnified by, **221-2**; insurance
  problems of, **220-1**; rehabilitation of
  injured, **226**; safety of, **222-4**; spare
  time of, **224-5**; wages of, see Wages;
  "workmen" or? **199-200, 207, 216-7**
Employers:
  collective agreements to be binding
  on, 215; compulsory insurance of,
  222; fair terms by, 210; indemnity
  against breach of contract, **221-2**
Employers' associations, 210, 212
Employment:
  compensation for loss of, **200-2**, 203;
  contract of, see Contract of employment; termination of, **200-4**;
  terms and conditions of, **210-12**
"Enterprise of National Interest",
  **195-6**
Equity, 11, 57, 58
Estate agent's commission, **103-4**
Estate duty, 84, 182, 183, 185
  avoidance of, 277
Euthanasia, **238**

Evershed, Lord:
  on House of Lords' jurisdiction, 16;
  on Schedules D & E, 272
Evidence, law of, **20-2**
Examinations:
  Bar, 281, 282, 284, 285; solicitors'
  qualifying, 279-81, 282, 283-4, 285
Execution orders, 114
Executive and Legislature, 32-3, 35
"Expense accounts", 277
Expert evidence, 22
Extradition, 52, 53, 54

Factories:
  accidents in, **72, 73, 223**; H.M.
  Inspector of, 73
Factory inspectors, 224, 225
Factory legislation, 3, 221, **222-3**, 225
"Family Charter", a, **122-3**, 126, 134n.
"Family Division" of High Court, 15,
  **123-4**, 127, 148
  children and, 142, 145
Family law, **122-49**
Family relations, paucity of information
  as to, **148-9**
Felony:
  arrest for, without warrant, 228;
  bail in cases of, 253; misdemeanour
  and, **227-9**; tort which is also a, 78
Fire insurance:
  arbitration clauses in, 177; tenant's
  repairs and, 112
First and second offenders, remand
  centre for, 268
Flats and maisonettes, 88, 89, 119
Football pool coupons, 64
Foreign Compensation Commission,
  51n.
Franks, Sir Oliver, 36
Fraud, companies', 178-9, **180**, 191
Freedom of speech, 24, **42-7**
Freeholders, lease enfranchisement and,
  115, 118, 119
French law:
  codification of, 11; death penalty
  abolished in, 236; job security under,
  **201**, 202; matrimonial property
  under, 134n.
Fry, Margery, on compensation for
  crimes of violence, 176n.
Furnished dwellings, **107-8**
  repairs of, **109**

General Council of the Bar, 6
General damages, **75-6**
General strikes, 205
Geneva Convention (1931), 167
German law:
  codification of, 11; collective agreements (wages) under, 218; job
  security under, **201** (bis), 202;
  spouses' community in, 134
"Giant's Strength, A", 215

"Gift tax" to replace estate duty, 277
Goddard, Lord, C.J., 49*n.*
Goff, Robert: "Law of Restitution", 70*n.*
Good faith:
contracts, 66, 171, 173; directors', 191
Goodhart, Prof., on Court of Criminal Appeal, 259*n.*
Goods:
hire purchase, repossession of, **163–4**; merchantibility of, 159, **161–2**; right to reject, **162**
Government departments, **2–3**, 29, 30; Commons' Committees and, 31; "Law Commissioners" to be consulted by, 9; ministerial control of, 28; statutory tribunals and, 34–5
Governments, **25–6**, **26–32**
function of, **25**, 33
Great Britain almost alone lacks Ministry of Justice, 7
Green, J.: "Automobile Accident Insurance . . .", 72*n.*
Greene, Lord, M. R., on insurance "traps", 172*n.*
"Grievance arbitration", **202–3**, **214–6**
Ground rent, 119, 120, 121
"Guarantees", manufacturers', 77, 154, **161**
"Guilty" and "innocent" spouses, **137**
"Guilty but insane", **232**
appeal from verdict, 17, 232; replacement of, suggested, 234

Habitual drunkenness, as ground for divorce, **139–40**
Hague Rules (1921), 169
Haldane, 1st Viscount, L. C., 7
*Halsbury's Laws of England,* on contempt of court, 244–5
*Hansard,* 56*n.*, 154*n.*
Hanson, A. H., and H. V. Wiseman: "The Use of Committees by the House of Commons", 27*n.*
*Harvard Law Review,* 78*n.*
Health, Ministry of, 2, 3
consent of, to sterilization, 243
Hearsay rule of evidence, **21**
High Court, rearrangement of (suggested), 124
High Court Judges:
bail appeal to, 253, **256**; County Court Judges acting as, 15; deportation recommendations from (proposed), 56
Hire purchase, **152–3**, **162–5**
money limit for protection, **163**
Home Office, 3, 20, 148, 157, 266
Memorandum on "detention", **250**; Prison Dept. of, 267, 268
Homicide, **236–40**
Homosexuality, **243–4**

House of Commons, 24, 26
control by, through Committees, **27–32**; Fair Wages Resolution of (1946), 210
House of Lords:
appellate jurisdiction of, to be abolished, 16; capital punishment and, **237**
Houses:
defective, **100–2**; local authority-built, **107**
Housing and Local Government, Ministry of, 2, 3, 32
Husband and wife, *see* Marriage *and* Matrimonial

Illegitimacy, **145**, 147
Immigration boards, 55
Immigration officers, powers of, 52 and *n.*, 53
Imperial Chemical Industries Ltd., take-over bid by, 189
Implied malice, 237
Incest, 241, 262
Income tax, 84
companies', 181, 182; consolidation of law on, **270**; loss of future earnings, **75–6**; married couple's, 128; period of assessment, **272–3**, 278; Schedules and Cases, **271–2**, 277
Indemnity, employer's, against employee's breach of contract, **221–2**
Indictment, notice to accused, **258**
Industrial Court, the, 206, 210, 225
collective agreement awards by, 211, 215
Industrial law, **199–226**
Infanticide, **238–40**
Infants (under 21), contracts by, **68–9**
Inheritance, **146–8**
Injuries, personal, **77**
Inland Revenue (*see also* Revenue), 181, 182, 276
costs of appeals from Commissioners' rulings, **275**; extra-statutory concessions by, 270, **271**
Inns of Court, 281
dining terms at, 281, 284; educational role of, 279, 281, 285, 286
Inns of Court Conservative and Unionist Association, 6
Inquests, coroners', abolition of, 19
Inquiries, local, **38–42**
Insanity (*see also* "Guilty but insane"):
criminal responsibility and, **229–34**; divorce for, 138; infanticide and, 238, 239
Inspectorate for terms and conditions of employment, 212
Inspectorates relating to child labour, 225
Insurance, **171–7**
bailee's negligence, **170**; compulsory

employer, 222; employee's problems, **220-1**; injuries to passengers, 73; landlord's, **112**; "universal scheme of", **71-2**

International Commission of Jurists, 6, 266

Interpretation of statutes, 6, 13, 51

Intestacy, succession on, **146-7**

Intimidation in trade disputes, **208-9**

Investment, control of, **195-6**

Irish immigrants, 53

Jessel, Sir George, M.R., on contracts, 57, 60 (*bis*)

Job security, **201-4**
 shop stewards', 214

Joint tenants, sales by survivors of, **98-9**

Jones, A. Creech, 236

Jowett, Fred, on Parliamentary reform, 27 (*bis*)

Jowitt, 1st Viscount, L.C., 7

Judicial Committee, *see* Privy Council

Judicial review, **47-52**

Judges, criticism of, 245

Judges' Rules, the, 250, 251, 252

Judiciary:
 Executive and, 35; independence of, 7, 24

Justice:
 administration of, **15-23**; natural, 48, 51

"Justice, a Ministry of":
 composition and functions of, **8-10**; need for, **7-8**

"Justice" (British section of International Commission of Jurists), 6, 16, 266
 report on Contempt of Court (1959), 42, 43

Juvenile courts, **229**

Juvenile delinquency, **264-5**

Kahn-Freund, O.: "Matrimonial Property . . .", 134*n*.

King, Cecil H., on Press freedom, **42**, 44, **45-6**

Klein, Dr. Viola, on women at work, 133*n*.

Labour, Ministry of, 2, 3, 205, 210, 225

Labour Government, first post-war, 12

Labour Lawyers, Society of, ix, x, 6

"Labour tribunal" for wages, 217

Land charges, **93-7**
 notice of, **96-7**

Land Charges Department, **93-5**
 Register of, 95

Land law, **79-121**
 reforms proposed, **82-3**, **94-105**

Land registration, **79-84**, 104
 compulsory, 83, 94, 105; easements, 92; extension of, **83-4**; three principles of, 80

Land Registry, the, 79, 80, 83

Landlord and tenant, law of, 3, **105-21**

Landlord's right of re-entry, 114

Lands Tribunal, **90**

Lansbury, George, 236

Laski, H. J., on Commons' Committees, 28

"Law Commissioners", **8-10**, 13-14
 consultations with, 9, 10, 14; emoluments of, 8-9; responsibilities of, 9-10

*Law Quarterly Review* (1948), 258

Law Reform Bills, annual, 13

Law Reform Committee, **4-6**, 10
 "family Charter" to be reviewed by, 123; "innocent misrepresentation" recommendations, **65-6**; perpetuities proposals, **86-7**

Law Society, the:
 Compensation Fund of, 104; Council of, 6; educational role of, 279 (*bis*), 280*n*., 283, 285, 286; *Gazette*, 92*n*.

Lawrence, Susan, 236

Leasehold Bill (1962), **117-19**

Leasehold enfranchisement, **115-21**

Leases, **105-21**
 agricultural, 110; covenants in, 88; land registration of, 81-3; long, *see* Long leases; new, date of their commencement, **108-9**; occupation after termination of, 114; right to grant, and quiet enjoyment, **111-12**; solicitor's costs regarding, 105; streamlining of, **115**

Legal aid and advice, **22-3**
 bail applications, 255; criminal appeals, 17-18, 23

Legal education, **279-87**
 reform of, **282-7**

Lesbianism, 243

Lessors and lessees, 36, 94, 110, **111-12**, 115

Libel, law of, **45-7**

Liberal Lawyers, Association of, 6

Life insurance, suicide and, 18, 174

Life tenants, 85

Limited liability companies, 177-8, 190; contracts by, 69

Limitation of actions, **77**

Limitations of alienation, 85, 86, 87

Local authorities:
 discretionary powers of, 50; houses built by, control of, **107**; land registration and, 83-4; property decisions by, 38

Local government employees, 199

Local inquiries, **38-42**

Local land charges registration, **95-7**

Local planning authorities, 39, **40**

London Stock Exchange:
 rules of, **186-7**; Share and Loan Committee of, 185, **187**, 194

Long leases, 89, 97, **115-16**
 prohibition of (proposed), 119, 121

Lord Chancellor, 3, 4, 5
  administrative action by, 4; concur-
  rence in joint committee's legislation,
  12; Law Reform Committee of, *see*
  Law Reform . . .
Lord Chancellor's Office, 20
  drafting of revised legislation should be
  done in, 10; strengthening of, 7–8, 13
Lord Chief Justice, Court of Criminal
  Appeal and, 17
Lords Justices for Court of Criminal
  Appeal, 17
Loss of earnings, damages for, **75–6**
Lushington, Sir Godfrey, on penal
  treatment, **263**

Machinery of law reform, **1–14**
M'Naghten Rules (insanity), 139, **230–
  231, 232–4**
  suggested revision of, 234, 235
Magistrate, questioning of suspect
  before, 251
Magistrates' Courts, 252
  bail granted by, **253**, bail refused by,
  253, 255; legal aid in, 23; newspaper
  reports of committal proceedings,
  **257–8**; police evidence and, 252;
  power to commit to mental hospital,
  233–4, 236; proceedings against small
  tenants in, **114–15**; reformed procedure proposed, **257**
Maintenance:
  children's, 129, 132, 136, **144–6**;
  failure to maintain as ground of
  divorce, 139; husband's, 136, 139;
  wife's, **128–9, 132–3**, 136
Maintenance orders, 126
Malmström, Ake, on matrimonial
  property law, 134*n*.
*Mandamus*, order of, 51
Manning, Serjeant, on *servitium amisit*,
  144*n*.
Mann's *Forensic Medicine and Toxicology*,
  on insanity, **231–2**
Manslaughter, 238
"Manual labourers", 199, 216
Manufacturers, responsibility of, **160–1**
Marriage, 123, **124–36**
  breakdown of, 123, **137–8, 140–1**, 149;
  legal aspects of, **126–36**; requirements
  prior to, **125–6**
Marriage guidance, 138–9
Master of the Rolls, the, 17
Matrimonial Causes and Reconcilia-
  tion Bill (1962), 138*n*., 140*n*.
Matrimonial property, **128–36**
  reforms recommended, **130–6**
Maudsley, Dr., on M'Naghten Rules,
  233
Medico-Psychological Association, on
  M'Naghten Rules, 233
Memorandum of Association, **183–4,**
  194

abolition of, proposed, **190**
Merchantability of goods, 159, **161–2**
"Mercy killing", *see* Euthanasia
Mergers, company, 187, 196
Merrivale, Lord, on void marriages,
  126*n*.
Meston, Lord, his Domicile Bills (1958
  and 1959), 4, 142*n*.
Ministers:
  Commons' Committees and, 31;
  delegated legislation and, 32, 33;
  responsibility of, 26, 39; "satisfaction"
  of, 50–1, 52
Ministries, *see* Education, Health,
  Labour, etc.
Mirror principle of land registration,
  80, 81
Misdemeanours, felonies and, **227–9**
Misrepresentation, 159
  innocent, 65, 66; insurance, 171, 174
Mistake (contracts), **66–7**, 70
  fundamental, effect of, 67
*Modern Law Review*, 4*n*., 53*n*., 70*n*.,
  134*n*., 165*n*.
Montesquieu, Baron Charles de, 32
Morrison of Lambeth, 1st Baron, 236
Mortgages, 93, **97–8**
  priority of, 97–8
Mortgagor and mortgagee, 111–12
Motor Insurers' Bureau, 177
Motorists asked for statements, 251
Moulton, Fletcher, L.J., on insurance
  practices, 172*n*.
Murder:
  bail in cases of, 253; "capital", 237;
  death penalty for, **236–7**; definition of,
  **237**

National Assistance Board, 146
National Insurance, 220, 226
National insurance tribunals, 34, 35, 55
Nationalised industries, investigation
  of, 28
Natural justice, rules of, 48, 51
Negligence, 70, **71–8**, 99
  carrier's liability for, 169; character
  or credit references, 63, 168; con-
  tracting out of liability for, 59, **77;**
  contributory, 221, 224; employees'
  liability for, **221–2**; strict liability for,
  72
"Negligence clauses", 151, **169–70**
Negotiable instruments, **166–8**
*Negotiorium gestio*, 70
*Nemo dat quod non habet*, 67, 153, **155–6;**
  161, 167
New York Bar Association, on M'-
  Naghten Rules, 233
New Zealand, death penalty abolished
  in, 236
*News Chronicle*, closing down of, 187,
  **194**
Notice of appeal (criminal), 18

Notice of indictment, **258**
Notice of termination of employment, **200, 201–2**
Notices to quit, **112–13**
Nullity declaration and decree, 126, 130

"Obscene" literature, **247–8**
Official secrets, 42, **44–5**
Ontario, insurance liability in, 173, 175
Onus, negligence action, 71
"Open" prisons, 265
Opposition, the, and Commons' Committees, 31
Options:
    consideration and, 61; land acquisition, **87**
ORDERS IN COUNCIL, 32
    Aliens Order (1953), 52
    compulsory registration of title, 83
    Conditions of Employment and National Arbitration Order (1940), 206
"Outgoings" in respect of house, **111**
Overriding interests, **80–1**, 82, 92

Paine, Thomas, 246
Parents:
    custody of children and, 142–3; power of, **143–4**
Parliament, 2, 12, **26–32**
Parliamentary draftsmen, 10
Partnership, 183, 184, **196–8**
    articles of, 197, 198; "limited", 178, 188; taxation of, 181
Party system, the, 31
Party walls and structures, **91–2**
Patents and inventions, employees', **224**
Pay, see Wages
Penal reform, 259
    objects of, **266–7**; steps to be taken, **267–9**
Perjury, 228
Permanent Committees, **4–6**
Perpetuities, **85–7**, 89
    class gifts and, **87**
Personal injuries, law relating to, **77**
"Persons aggrieved" (town and country planning), 41
Picketing, peaceful, **209**
Planning, see Town and country
Police, the, **249–52**
    affidavit of reasons for opposing bail, **255**; increase and strengthening of force, 267; "underpaid, understaffed and under-criticised", 249–250, 252
Policies (insurance), standardisation of, **176**
Policy:
    administrative tribunals and, 39, 42; Commons' Committees and, 30–1

Political strikes, **205**
Pollock, Sir Frederick, on consideration, 60
Positive covenants, 88, 89
Pregnancy, termination of, see Abortion
Prerogative orders, 51, 52
Prescription, 81, **92**
Press, freedom of the, 24, **42–7**
Press publicity before trial, 255, **257–8**
Presumptions:
    child-bearing age, 86; death, 21
Prison Commissioners, 253, 265
    strengthening of, **268**
Prison conditions, **265**
Prison Medical Service, the, 234, 268
Prison officers' pay, 269
Privacy, right of, 78
Private companies, **178, 179–84**
    abolition of distinction from public companies, 190, 192; disadvantages of, **183–4**
Private House Owners (Protection) Bill (1962), 102
Privity of contract, **62–3**
Privy Council, Judicial Committee of, 124
    Commonwealth judges to sit on, 16; on collective agreements, 211
Probate, land, 85
Probate, Divorce and Admiralty Division, **15**, 124
Procedure:
    courts', **19–20**; criminal, **249–59**; criminal and civil, in negligence, **73**; police, **249–52**
Profits tax, 181, 182, 186, 196, 271
Promises, gratuitous, 59, 61
Property:
    matrimonial, **128–36**; succession to, **146–8**
Proposal forms, insurance, **172–3**, 175; filled in by agents of insurers, 173
Prostitution, **248–9**
Protection of Depositors Bill (1962), 178
Psychiatrist for each penal establishment, **268**
Public authorities:
    bad faith by, 49, 51; Courts' control of their decisions, **47–52**
Public companies, 179, 183, **184–7**;
    accounting by, 188; distinction from private companies, abolition of, 190; private companies as subsidiaries of, **180**
Public health, 79
*Public Law*, 40n., 44n.
Public mischief, **245–6**
"Public policy", 151, 153
Punishment, **259–69**
    objects of, **260–7**; reforms proposed, **267–9**
Pupilage in chambers, **282**
Purchaser, *bona fide*, **155–6**

Quasi contract, **70**
Quebec, hire purchase in, 165
Queen, the, her legislative function, 32–3
Queen's Bench Division:
"Admiralty and Commercial Court" part of, 15; dates for witness actions, 20; judges of, 17
Queensland, death penalty abolished in, 236
Quiet enjoyment, **111–12**

Real property, **79–84**
Recidivism:
criminals', 261, 262, **264**, 266, 267; drunkards', 235
Redundancy, 216
References as to character or credit, **63**; bankers', **168**
*Reform of the Law, The*, ix, x, 59, 63, 155, 176
Reformation as object of punishment, 262, **264–6**
conflict with deterrence, **263–4**
Reforms, immediately necessary, **13–14**
Registrar of Friendly Societies, and trade unions, **213–4**
Registration:
companies, 69, 178; land, **79–84**; land charges, **93–7**
Regulations, new law by, 32, 34
Remand in custody, 252, 253, 268
Remoteness of damage, **73–4**
Remoteness of vesting, 85
Rent:
abatement of, for premises no longer existing, **112**; actions for double, **114**; non-payment of, 113, 114
Rent control, **106–7**
Rent tribunals, **36**, **107–8**
Repairing covenants, 88, 89
Repairs, **109–11**
Representations, 63, 65–6, 168
Rescission of contract, 65, 66 (*bis*)
Reserves, company, 189, 193
Restitution by offenders, **266**, 267
Restrictive covenants, 88, **89–91**, 93, 94
Retail trade, 153, 158, 159
Retribution as object of punishment, **260–1**, 265, 266
Revenue law (*see also* Taxation; Income Tax; Inland Revenue; Profits Tax; Estate Duty), **270–8**, 282*n.*, 287; proposals for reforming, **277–8**; simplification needed, **270–1**
Right of Privacy Bill (1961), 78
Rights over another's land, **92**
Rowntree, Griselda, and Norman H. Carrier: *The Report on Divorce in England and Wales, 1858–1957*, 148
ROYAL COMMISSIONS, 3, 4, 10, 13

ROYAL COMMISSIONS (*cont.*)
Capital Punishment Commission (1866), 231
Gorrell Commission on Divorce and Matrimonial Causes (1909–12), 140*n.*
Gowers Commission on Death Penalty (1948), 236–7
Housing of the Working Classes (1884), 116
Marriage and Divorce (1956), 122, 134*n.*, 135*n.*, **137–8**, 149
Peel Commission on Despatch of Business at Common Law (1934–1936), 15, 21
Police Powers and Procedure (1929), **250–1**, 252
Taxation of Profits and Income (1953–5), 128, 270*n.*, 274, 278
Willink Commission on Police Pay (1962), 252
Rules of Court, 3, 21, 197
revision of (1962), 20, 123*n.*
Ruoff, T. B. F.: *The Torrens System*, 80*n.*

"Safe system of work", 221, **223–4**
Sale of goods, **153–65**
payment by instalments, **152**
Sale of new properties, **99–102**
Salter, Lord, on Commons' Committees, 28
Sankey, 1st Viscount, L.C., 4, 7
Saskatchewan, road accident insurance, 72
Schedules D and E (income tax), **271–2**
"expenses" under, **271–2**, 277
Scott, Sir Leslie, L.J., on Vagrancy Acts, 248
Scottish law:
"abuse of rights" in, 78; consideration under, 61; coroners' inquests non-existent in, 19; discretion in disclosing Crown documents, 45; hire purchase in, 163–4
Scrutton, L.J., on unenforceable contracts, 64
Secondary evidence of documents, 21
Second-hand goods, sale of, 159
Security, National, 44–5
immigrants and, 54, 54, 55
Self-service stores, 159
Sentences:
commencing date of (bail refused), 256; increase of, on appeal, 17
Separation, judicial, **136–41**, 149
custody of children on, **142–3**
Separation agreements, 149
Separation orders, **136–41**, **149**
Service tenancies, **106**
Settlements of land, **84–5**
Shareholders, 187, **188**, 189, **192–4**
minority, 182, 183, 193

Shares:
   transfer of, 182, 183, **193-4**; voteless
   equity, **188**
Sharp, Clifford, contempt case of, 245
Shearman, J., on misdemeanours, 227
Shop stewards, recognition of, **214**
Skeffington, Arthur, M.P., his Bill on
   contracts (1954), 63
Smith, Adam, his doctrines, 151
Social science, law as a, 283, 286
Solicitors:
   barristers' admission as, 284; call to
   the Bar of, 285; conveyancing fees of,
   **104-5**; surviving joint tenant and, 99;
   time taken for conveyance, **102-3**;
   training of, 279, **279-81**
Spain, death penalty abolished in, 236
Speaker, the, concurrence in joint com-
   mittee's legislation, 12
Special damages, 75
Specific performance, **68**
Stable, J., on insurance, 173n.
Stamp duty on conveyances, 105
Standard-form contracts, **58-9**, 152
   liability excluded for misrepresenta-
   tion in, 66
Standing Committees, 29, 30
Statement, police orders to make, **251-2**
Statute law, **10-11**
   consolidation of, **2-3**, 13; delegated,
   see Delegated legislation; extra-
   statutory concessions (I.T.) should
   be made part of, 271; interpretation
   of, 6, 13, 51
Statute of Frauds (1677), **63-4**
Statutory instruments, 30, 34
Stephen, Sir James: *Digest of Criminal
   Law*, 236
Sterilisation, legalization of voluntary,
   **243**
Stock Exchange quotations, **185**, 186
   suspension of, **187, 194**
Street, Professor: *Law of Torts*, 74
Strict settlement, **84-5**
Strikes, 195, 203, 204
   criminal law and, **204-6**; general, 205;
   political, **205**
*Sub judice*, 43
Sub-tenancies, **108-9**
Succession to property, **146-8**
Suicide:
   Coroner's Court verdict, 18; life
   assurance and, 18, 174; mother's,
   connected with infanticide, 238
Surtax, 181, 185, 186, 196, 271
"Suspected person" (Vagrancy Act),
   248
Swedish law:
   penal code in, **266**; termination of
   pregnancy under, 241, 242
Swiss law, codification of, 11

"Take-over bids", 186, 187, 189, 192,
   194, 196
Tax assessment:
   appeals against, **275**; period of, **272-
   273**, 278
Tax avoidance, 128, **275-7**, 278
Tax evasion, **275-6**
Tax incentives, **274-5**
Taxation, **271-8**
   companies', **181-2**, **185-6**, 275; control of investment and, **195-6**;
   economic planning and, **274-5**; married couple's, **128**
Tenancies:
   business, **108-9**; controlled, **106**;
   covenants against assigning, **111**;
   service, **106**
Tenants in common, 98
Thalidomide births, 242
Thesiger, Gerald, on Court of Criminal
   Appeal, 259n.
Third parties:
   contracts should be enforceable by, if
   benefited, 62-3; insurance and, 173,
   **174-5**; local inquiry, 40, 41; road
   accident insurance, 72
Thornberry, C.: "Law, Opinion and
   the Immigrant", 53n., 55, 56n.
Thurtle, Dorothy, on abortion, **240-1**
Tied cottages, **107**, 109
*Times, The*, 259n.
   on law of insanity (1920), **232-3**
Title to land, registration, 79-80, 94
Torts, **70-8**
   compensation for, not punishment of,
   71; law of, and strikes, **206-10**; trade
   unions', **209**
Town and country planning, 3, **38-41**,
   79
   restrictive covenants and, 90
Town and Country Planning Appeals
   (Inquiries Procedure) Rules (1962),
   38, **39-41**
Trade disputes, **204-10**
   statutory definition of, 207, 210
Trade name, goods sold under, 158
Trade unions:
   actions in tort against, 209; collective bargaining and, 210, 212; elections and expulsions by, **212-13**;
   officials of, 208; protection of, 210;
   rules of, **213-14**; wage payments and,
   218, 220
Transport, **168-71**
Transport, Ministry of, 30, 32
Transport Tribunal, the, 59
Treason, bail in cases of, 253
Tribunals (administrative), 25, **34-7**
   Council on, **36-7**; Courts' relationship to, **51**; immigration and, 55;
   legal aid and, 23, **37**; legal representation at, 37
Trustees, joint tenants as, **98-9**

Trusts for sale, 84-5

*Ultra vires*, 41, 47-8, 69, 184
Unemployed, retraining of, 226
Unions, *see* Trade unions
United States of America:
    bailee's negligence rules, 170 (*bis*);
    consumer protection in, 166; death
    penalty in, 236; grievance arbitra-
    tion in, 202, 215; juvenile courts in,
    229; Ministry of Justice in, 7;
    "negligence clauses" discouraged in,
    151; quasi contract in, 70; Restate-
    ment of Commercial Law, 153, 170;
    right of privacy protected, 78; shop
    stewards in, 214; warranties of
    merchantibility in, 161
University course for legal qualifica-
    tion, 282-4, 286-7

Vagrancy, 248
Vaisey, J., on Schedule E, 272n.
"Vice-Chancellor", a, 8, 13
Victoria, Queen, and insanity verdict,
    232
Violence, compensation for victim of,
    266, 267
Void and voidable marriages, 125-6

Wade, E. C. S.: "The Machinery of
    Law Reform", 4n., 5n.
Wages, 210, 216-20
    attachment of, 149, 219; payment

during interrupted work, 220; pay-
    ment during sickness, 219-20
Wages Acts Inspectorate, 212
Wages Councils, 217
Wages Regulation Orders, 220
Wales, South, leases in, 115
Walker, Lord, on marriage breakdown,
    137n.
Wardship of court, 143, 144
Warehousing, 168-70
Warrant, arrest without, 228, 253
Warranties (express and implied), 65,
    100, 101, 112, 161; insurance law,
    175
Warren and Brandeis, on right of
    privacy, 78n.
Warsaw Rules, 169
Watch Committees, 252
Wilkinson, Ellen, 236
    her Hire Purchase Bill, 163
Williams, Dr. Glanville, ix, x
Witnesses:
    character attacks on, 21; death of,
    before trial, 22; reluctance to appear,
    254; unnecessary attendance of, 257
"Workmen" or employees? 199-200,
    207, 216-7
Wright, D. C.: "The Law of Torts",
    72n.
Wright, Lord, on consideration, 61

Young, G. M., on Commons' Com-
    mittees, 28